Palgrave Studies in African and Development Economics

This series provides a wide-ranging analysis of African economics, development economics, and global transformation. Combing theoretical and empirical evidence, it offers thoughtful and policy relevant insight to the economic challenges and opportunities seen within the developing world. It engages with emerging and topical debates, including issues relating to sustainable development, food security, and the green transition, to make sure countries in Africa and the developing world are included in these important discussions.

Weiwei Chen

Chinese Manufacturing Firms in Ethiopia

Firm Diversity and the Political Economy of Investment

palgrave
macmillan

Weiwei Chen
The Open University
Milton Keynes, UK

ISSN 3004-9601 ISSN 3004-961X (electronic)
Palgrave Studies in African and Development Economics
ISBN 978-3-032-24321-8 ISBN 978-3-032-24322-5 (eBook)
https://doi.org/10.1007/978-3-032-24322-5

This Palgrave Macmillan imprint is published by the registered company Springer Nature Switzerland AG.
The registered company address is: Gewerbestrasse 11, 6330 Cham, Switzerland

Preface

Over the past two decades, China's overseas foreign direct investment (OFDI) in Africa has expanded rapidly, reaching well beyond resource extraction and large-scale infrastructure. Its significance lies not simply in volume, but in its rapid rise over the past decade, the different modalities it takes, its shifting geographical and sectoral distribution, and its profound socio-economic implications for host countries. Ethiopia has become a notable destination within this shift, particularly for Chinese manufacturing in textiles, garments, and construction materials.

This book grew out of a puzzle that repeatedly surfaced during my fieldwork in Ethiopia: why do firms that enter under the same host-country policy framework experience such different trajectories? Some expand, stabilise, and establish export-oriented production, while others struggle to survive, move into short-term trading, or withdraw altogether. My attempts to address this gap in Ethiopian public debate have shown how widely circulated "investment myths" can flatten complex realities, misread firm behaviour, and obscure what Chinese investment means for host-country socio-economic development. This book takes that puzzle seriously by tracing what happens after entry: the decisions firms make and the ways policy is implemented, negotiated, and enforced in practice.

As a Chinese researcher trained in Development Studies and based at a Western research institute, my position has shaped both my access and my perspective. Over the past decade, I returned to Ethiopia across multiple periods to follow firms, managers, workers, officials, and intermediaries as conditions changed. The analysis draws on longitudinal fieldwork conducted between 2015 and 2025 and more than 200 interviews in Ethiopia and China. It also draws on observation and repeated engagement with firms and institutions over time. The names of firms and individuals are pseudonymised in this book to protect anonymity.

The book maps the range of Chinese manufacturing firms active in Ethiopia and treats investment as an evolving process rather than a single moment of entry. It examines why firms come, but focuses especially on what happens afterwards: securing land and industrial space, meeting export requirements, navigating workplace relations, managing environmental compliance, and dealing with everyday frictions in operations. To connect firm diversity to outcomes, the book introduces a typology of Market-Embedded Firms and GPN-Integrated Firms, which helps clarify why firms investing in the same sector, targeting the same market, and operating under similar policies can respond in markedly different ways.

The book is organised around two periods: pre-2020 and post-2020. The pre-2020 chapters examine a phase of accelerated industrialisation driven by Ethiopia's export-oriented industrial policies and the rapid growth of industrial parks, tracing the negotiations that shape entry and early consolidation. The post-2020 chapters examine a more volatile period marked by overlapping disruptions, including the COVID-19 pandemic, the suspension of AGOA, tightening foreign exchange conditions, and domestic political instability, and show how firms and state agencies adjusted under pressure. The post-2020 chapter, therefore, examines how both Chinese manufacturing firms and Ethiopian institutions adapted under pressure, and what "resilience" looked like in practice amid domestic and global disruptions.

I hope this book will be useful to readers interested in China–Africa relations, industrial policy, and African development, as well as to those seeking a grounded account of how investment works in practice. Rather than offering a binary judgement on "Chinese investment," it clarifies how firm diversity, sectoral conditions, host-country political economy, and timing shape development outcomes, and it directs attention to the practical questions that matter for building more inclusive and sustainable industrial futures.

Milton Keynes, UK Weiwei Chen

Acknowledgements

To my dearest daughter, Lakshmi Chen Vadgama: you are such a treasure to me. You have made me stronger and more resilient in everything I am passionate about, including my research on Chinese investment in Ethiopia. In June 2025, I left you for the first time since you were born to return to Ethiopia for three weeks of fieldwork after the COVID-19 pandemic. You may not yet know where Ethiopia is, but you already understand that it is the country I keep talking about—the place that profoundly shaped my academic journey and continues to drive my work.

My deepest gratitude also goes to my husband, Professor Nikhil Vadgama, and to my parents-in-law, Mr Ashok Vadgama and Mrs Parul Vadgama. I would not have been able to complete this project without their patience, love, and generosity.

I am profoundly grateful to my PhD supervisor, colleague, and lifelong friend, Professor Carlos Oya, whose continuous guidance, insightful advice, and constant encouragement enabled me to bring this book to fruition. I am also honoured to have been part of the ESRC-funded IDCEA project (2015–2020), which shaped my doctoral research and continues to inform the follow-up work on Chinese investment in Ethiopia that underpins this book. My sincere thanks also go to Professor Christopher Cramer, Professor Dic Lo, Professor Rachael M. Gisselquist, and Professor Giles Mohan for their continuous support and mentorship during my doctoral and postdoctoral periods, which strengthened the work at a critical stage.

I am indebted to government agencies such as the Office of the Prime Minister, the Ministry of Industry, and the Industrial Parks Development Corporation. I am particularly grateful to colleagues at the Ethiopian Investment Commission for their cooperation. I also thank institutions and individuals at GIZ Ethiopia for their assistance and guidance at key moments in the research.

This book was, in part, made possible by the generosity of the many Chinese firms, Chinese investment associations, and all respondents who gave up their time to meet me and granted access for observation, interviews, and surveys. I am particularly grateful to interviewees who not only shared their experiences but also helped me navigate everyday life in Ethiopia, enabling me to conduct participant observation both in Ethiopia and in China. I also received a great deal of encouragement and practical guidance from the Chinese diaspora in Ethiopia—entrepreneurs, managers, technicians, and many others—and I am grateful for the long-term friendships that grew from this work. I hope these acknowledgements can serve as a small token of thanks for their kindness and openness.

Finally, I would like to thank Professor Arkebe Oqubay, Palgrave Macmillan's commissioning editor Wyndham Hacket Pain, the editorial team, and the anonymous reviewers for their constructive input, professionalism, and detailed comments. Lastly, I would like to thank all who contributed directly and indirectly to this book but whose names I could not mention. I also acknowledge the use of an AI language model to assist with language editing and clarity during the final preparation of the manuscript. All interpretations, arguments, and any remaining errors are solely my own responsibility.

Competing Interests

The author declares that she has no competing interests. Part of the early fieldwork in Ethiopia was supported by the Economic and Social Research Council (ESRC), grant ES/M004228/1, at SOAS, University of London; beyond this, the author has no financial or non-financial interests that could be perceived to influence the research, analysis, or interpretation presented in this manuscript.

Ethics Approval

Ethics approval for the research underpinning this book was obtained from the relevant institutional review board(s) at the author's institution. All research procedures were conducted in line with the principles of the Declaration of Helsinki. Participants provided informed consent.

The majority of firms and interviewees referred to in this book have been pseudonymised to protect anonymity and confidentiality. This applies to firm names, individual respondents, and site-specific identifiers, unless explicit permission was granted for attribution. A limited number of institutional actors—most notably well-known industrial parks and formally constituted business associations—are identified by name where anonymisation is not feasible or would undermine analytical clarity. In all cases, identifying personal information has been removed.

The author retains access to the original, non-anonymised data solely for purposes of verification and academic integrity. These materials are not shared and are available only for validity checks where strictly necessary, in accordance with ethical approval and informed consent agreements.

Competing Interests The author has no competing interests to declare that are relevant to the content of this manuscript.

Contents

About the Author

Weiwei Chen is currently the Investment Advisor (non-remunerated) of the Ethiopian Investment Commission (2026-onwards) and a Visiting Research Associate at the Open University (UK). She was a postdoctoral research associate at The Open University, where she led UK-based research for the European Research Council–funded REDEFINE project (2020–2025) on Chinese infrastructure investment in Europe. Her research examines China's globalisation in both the Global South and the Global North, with a focus on Chinese foreign direct investment, state–business relations, and the socio-institutional dynamics shaping firms' internationalisation. Dr Chen received her PhD in Development Studies from SOAS, University of London (2021). She previously worked on two ESRC-funded research projects on Chinese firms' employment dynamics and labour practices in Ethiopia and Angola (2015–2019; 2020–2021), was a PhD fellow at UNU-WIDER, and consulted for the International Trade Centre in Ethiopia. She has delivered guest lectures on the political economy of Chinese investment in Africa at the Wharton School (University of Pennsylvania) and St Mary's University. Her research has been published in academic articles including *the Journal of International Development, Journal of International Relations and Development, Journal of Economic Geography* and *Global Sustainability*, and her commentary has appeared in *The Conversation Africa* and other public platforms. She is also co-editing the Special Issue "Global China: Breaking New Ground – Innovative Methodologies for Researching Global China" for the *Journal of Contemporary Chinese Affairs* (2025). She regularly engages policy and diplomatic audiences in Africa and Europe through policy briefings and invited talks.

Abbreviations

AGOA	African Growth and Opportunity Act
BoP	Balance of Payment
BRI	Belt and Road Initiative
CAD	Comparative Advantage Defying
CAF	Comparative Advantage Following
CADFund	China–Africa Development Fund
CARI	China–Africa Research Initiative
CCCE	China Chamber of Commerce in Ethiopia
CCPIT	China Council for the Promotion of International Trade
CCPPNR	Promotion of the Peaceful National Reunification
CM	Construction Materials
CME	Coordinated Market Economies
COMESA	Common Market for Eastern and Southern Africa
DBGs	Diversified Business Groups
DS	Developmental State
EBA	Everything But Arms
EM_MNES	Emerging market multinational enterprises
EPC	Engineering, Procurement, and Construction
EIC	Ethiopian Investment Commission
EIP	Eastern Industrial Park
EIPMC	Eastern Industrial Park Management Committee
EIZCG	Eastern Industrial Zone Committee of Guidance
EIZIA	Eastern Industrial Zone Investors Association
EV	Electric Vehicle
FDI	Foreign Direct Investment
FoEs	Foreign-owned Enterprises
FOCAC	Forum on China–Africa Cooperation

FSAs	Firm-Specific Advantages
FX	Foreign exchange
FYP	Five-Year Plan
GoE	Government of Ethiopia
GPNs	Global Production Networks
GPN-IFs	Global Production Network-Integrated Firms
GTP	Growth and Transformation Plan
GVCs	Global Value Chains
HGER	Homegrown Economic Reform
HIP	Hawassa Industrial Park
HR	Human Resources
IDCEA	Industrial Development, Construction and Employment in Africa
ILO	International Labour Organisation
IMF	International Monetary Fund
IP/IPs	Industrial Park/Parks
IPDC	Industrial Parks Development Corporation
IPP	Industrial Parks Proclamation
ISI	Import Substitution Industrialisation
ITC	International Trade Centre
JV/JVs	Joint Ventures
KD	Knock-Down
LC / LCs	Letter of Credit / Letters of Credit
LM	Light Manufacturing
MEFs	Market-Embedded Firms
MOFA	Ministry of Foreign Affairs of the People's Republic of China
MOFCOM	Ministry of Commerce of the People's Republic of China
MoI	Ministry of Industry (Ethiopia)
MIIT	Ministry of Industry and Information Technology
NCE	Neo-classical Economics
NBE	National Bank of Ethiopia
NDRC	National Development and Reform Commission (China)
ODM	Original Design Manufacturer
OECD	Organisation for Economic Co-operation and Development
OFDI	Outward Foreign Direct Investment
OEM	Original Equipment Manufacturer
OPC	Ordinary Portland Cement
OSS	One-Stop Service
PLCs	Private Limited Companies
PMO	Office of the Prime Minister
PPD	Public–Private Dialogue
PoEs	Private-owned Enterprises

QA	Quality Assurance
R&D	Research and Development
RCM / RCMs	Reciprocal Control Mechanism / Mechanisms
SBRs	State–Business Relations
SEZs	Special Economic Zones
SNNP	Southern Nations, Nationalities, and Peoples' Region
SMEs	Small and Medium-Sized Enterprises
SOEs	State-Owned Enterprises
TIDI	Textile Industry Development Institute
TNCs	Transnational Corporations
UNCTAD	United Nations Conference on Trade and Development
UNIDO	United Nations Industrial Development Organization
USTR	Office of the United States Trade Representative
VC	Variegated Capitalism
VoC	Varieties of Capitalism

List of Figures

List of Tables

CHAPTER 1

Introduction: Rethinking Chinese Investment in Africa

Introduction

In late June 2018, during a meeting between the Eastern Industrial Park (EIP) Management Committee and an investigator from the Ethiopian Investment Commission (EIC), the discussion moved quickly away from general "investment climate" talk and into the everyday frictions of service delivery. The senior manager described the park as "out of the system": even a small issue raised by an investor could take "at least 1–2 months" to move through local government. He sighed, then became visibly upset as he spoke: investors, he said, "knew about the bureaucracy. But it is too much…" Local officials, he added, often came "not to support or help us to solve problems but for the sake of donation." At the time, the park's one-stop service presence was still partial. Offices for the EIC and customs were in place, but most other services remained outside the park, so constraints were relocated rather than resolved. (Fieldnote, PO1, 29 June 2018, Ethiopia; all personal identifiers removed and pseudonymised. See Appendix C)

Seven years later, in another private industrial park, work began at 7:40 am in a large-scale light manufacturing factory. After the midday break (11:40 am–1:30 pm), the production line resumed at 1:30 pm. The discussion did not focus on wages as such, but on delivery discipline: fixed shipment schedules, and how easily production is thrown off by logistics and clearance. Managers returned repeatedly to transport and customs -- buyers' complaints about long lead times and slow clearance; uncertainty along the Djibouti corridor; and

W. Chen, *Chinese Manufacturing Firms in Ethiopia*, Palgrave Studies in African and Development Economics,
https://doi.org/10.1007/978-3-032-24322-5_1

the difficulty of planning when timelines cannot be guaranteed ("orders are placed strictly against delivery schedules, so guaranteed timelines are crucial"). At one point, the Production Manager asked me, "Dr Chen, do you know exactly how much tariff we now have to pay after the withdrawal of AGOA (African Growth and Opportunity Act)?" -- a striking question, given that US orders had already stopped. The conversation then moved to two immediate operational pressures: the reliability of the Addis Ababa-Djibouti corridor (including disruption around the Dire Dawa part at the time of my visit), and the absence of an EIC one-stop service station inside the park. Even routine compliance -- certification for electricians, forklift operators, and welders -- was described as a possible point at which production could be interrupted when auditors or inspectors arrived. (Fieldnote, PO17, 13 June 2025, Ethiopia; firm/site identifiers pseudonymised. See Appendix B and C)

These two observations establish the book's analytical point of departure. The politics of "China in Africa" cannot be understood solely through official policy statements, large-scale investment announcements, or diplomatic rhetoric. It is constituted in the everyday encounters through which production is organised and kept running—or breaks down. Utilities, logistics, customs clearance, the training and maintenance of the labour force, and access to foreign exchange are not background conditions to investment; they are the institutional interfaces through which state authority is exercised and contested and through which firms' accumulation trajectories are shaped. Whether investment translates into sustained production, employment, and export earnings depends on how these routine interactions are handled, negotiated, and consolidated over time.

Debates about China's role in Africa are frequently conducted through simplified public narratives. In one dominant framing, Chinese finance, construction, and investment are presented as a pragmatic alternative to Western aid and conditionality, emphasising rapid project delivery, fewer explicit policy conditions, and the rhetoric of "mutual benefit" and "win-win cooperation" (State Council of the PRC, 2006; FOCAC, 2018). In another, China is framed as a new imperial power, locking African states into debt dependence or resource-backed bargains and displacing domestic producers through uneven competition (Alden, 2007; Taylor, 2006; Carmody, 2011). Both framings capture fragments of reality, but they also encourage analysis that is overly aggregated and too often detached from everyday production processes and the routine bargaining between firms and state agencies through which investment is negotiated, implemented, and made productive (Brautigam, 2009; Power et al., 2012; Mohan & Lampert, 2013; Lee, 2017).

This polarisation is amplified because "China in Africa" has become a proxy battlefield in wider geopolitical competition. Categories such as "debt trap," "neo-colonialism," and "South-South cooperation" circulate more rapidly than the empirical detail needed to assess what is actually happening on the ground (Hurley et al., 2018; Brautigam, 2018). Such labels rarely specify which Chinese actors are involved, which contracts and regulatory arrangements are in play, or how host-country political economic contexts shape what is negotiated, implemented, and enforced.

This book takes a different entry point. Rather than starting from aggregate investment volumes, high-profile investment announcements, or state-to-state agreements, it centres analysis on production and the conditions under which manufacturing investment is organised, sustained, or disrupted. Manufacturing provides a particularly revealing lens because it focuses on the organisation of production in practice: factories depend on reliable utilities, predictable customs clearance, workable logistics, disciplined workforce organisation, and—under conditions of FX scarcity—routine access to imported inputs and spare parts. These requirements bring firms into continuous, active engagement with state actors at various levels. As a result, manufacturing investment makes visible how the state is exercised in everyday terms, how regulatory rules are interpreted and enforced, and how firms negotiate constraints over time. Whether Chinese investment translates into sustained production, employment, and export earnings depends less on formal policy design than on how these everyday interactions are delivered, bargained over, and consolidated.

A starting point concerns scale and measurement. In aggregate, Chinese outward foreign direct investment (OFDI)[1] to Africa remains a modest share of China's global OFDI—around 1.48% (CARI 2024 cited in Chen, 2025)—despite the prominence of "strategic partnership" rhetoric. This includes, for example, Forum on China-Africa Cooperation (FOCAC) declarations that frame China-Africa relations as a "comprehensive strategic and cooperative partnership" and routinely announce large-scale, multi-year funding commitments (FOCAC, 2018). At the same time, the

[1] FDI refers to "an investment involving a long-term relationship and reflecting a lasting interest and control by a resident entity in one economy (the foreign direct investor or parent enterprise) in an enterprise resident in an economy other than that of the foreign direct investor (the FDI enterprise, affiliate, or foreign affiliate)" (UNCTAD, 2012, p. 3).

investment figures most widely circulated are methodologically weak. Publicised announcements are often conflated with realised capital formation, while firm-level operations and balance-sheet exposure are often overlooked. This is partly because investment is frequently channelled through offshore jurisdictions—doubling estimated OFDI (stock) when offshore centres are included (Chen, 2025, pp. 1–2)—and partly because ownership structures are layered, and smaller firms and translocal[2] are poorly captured in official statistics. For this book, the analytical priority is therefore not to amplify aggregate investment figures, but to examine how investment is put together in practice—by firm type, sector, and host-country political economy context—in order to connect broad claims about China-Africa capital flows to the granular realities of how firms operate, negotiate, and embed locally. Even where overall flows are limited, sectoral concentration and spatial clustering—and the forms of state engagement they trigger—can shape outcomes in specific countries and sectors (Chen, 2025).

A key problem behind many "China in Africa" myths is what Lee (2017) calls methodological nationalism—an assumption that the national origin of a firm or agency determines outcomes (Chen, 2022). "China" collapses policy and commercial banks, state-owned enterprises (SOEs) at different levels, private conglomerates, family-owned manufacturers, and diaspora-linked entrepreneurs into a single actor. "Africa" collapses diverse political and institutional capacities into a single imagined space of uniform "weak governance." The result is an analytical dead end: it becomes difficult to explain why similar Chinese firms behave differently across African settings, or why similar policy tools generate different outcomes within the same country.

At the same time, moving from a national lens to production processes also reshapes how "agency" and "impact" are analysed. A multi-scalar approach is required to connect micro-level firm strategies and operations, meso-level sectoral regimes, and macro-level policy and institutional contexts. Rather than treating power as something that radiates from a single centre—whether the Chinese state, Western donors, or African governments—a more productive move is to treat influence as an empirical outcome, produced through relationships and institutional mechanisms.

[2] "Translocals" are firms that are started, owned, or managed by foreign nationals, often drawing on advisory networks abroad, but are registered only in the host country (Rounds & Zhang 2017, p. 6, cited in Oya & Wanda, 2021, p. 18), cited in Chen (2025, p. 2).

Relationality, in this sense, is not a slogan but an analytical claim about how bargaining, resistance, accommodation, and adaptation unfold through the everyday interactions that connect firms, state agencies, workers, and buyers (Allen, 2003, 2004; Mohan & Lampert, 2013).

Industrial policy has also returned globally—and unevenly—in the wake of supply-chain disruption and geopolitical rivalry, and its justification is increasingly framed in the language of security and resilience as much as development (Ahumada & Chang, 2025). Yet this shift does not dissolve asymmetries in the global economic order: late industrialisers remain exposed to volatile trade preferences, concentrated buyer power, and renewed forms of conditionality that narrow policy space (Rodrik, 2018; Lee, 2017). Drawing on a decade of fieldwork-based research in Ethiopia, this book shows that industrial policy does not operate as a coherent national blueprint, but through a set of institutional settings—industrial parks, export discipline, FX allocation, and aftercare arrangements—that are continually shaped and reshaped through state–business relations (SBRs).[3] In this sense, the Ethiopian case provides a micro-level complement to macro-level critiques of the global economic order: asymmetric rules matter not only because they constrain states formally, but because they condition the everyday practices through which firms adapt, learn, or fail to consolidate manufacturing investment under uncertainty and crisis.

The core argument developed across the book is that outcomes hinge on the interaction between firm diversity and the effective arrangements through which institutions operate in practice. Formal institutions—such as strategies, policies, and regulations—matter, but they do not determine outcomes on their own. What firms encounter instead are specific, often negotiated arrangements that combine formal rules with informal practices, discretionary enforcement, and ad hoc problem-solving. Firms respond, adapt, and change in relation to how these arrangements are delivered and enforced in everyday interactions with state agencies. In turn, these arrangements shape the conditions under which firms operate,

[3] SBRs refer to "relations between the public and private sectors. The forms vary significantly, ranging from formal, regular coordination arrangements to informal, ad hoc interactions. They may cover the whole economy or target specific sectors, types of firms, or policy processes. In some situations, they involve highly organised relationships; in others they are loose relationships between the state and business" (Te Velde, 2013, p. 9). See Chap. 2, Section "State–Business Relations: Developmental States, Political Settlements and Deals" for further discussion.

steering them into different trajectories: enabling some to consolidate and build capabilities for expansion and reinvestment while pushing others towards stagnation, downsizing, or exit.

Statement of the Problem and Research Questions

Statement of the Problem

This book addresses three specific problems in the existing research on Chinese manufacturing investment in Ethiopia: (1) limited comparative analysis across different types of firms; (2) insufficient multi-scalar analysis linking micro firm-level strategies and behaviour to meso-level sectoral regimes and politics of production organisation, and macro-level of government policies and institutional context; and (3) short time horizons combined with partial and problematic data.

Conventional perceptions of Chinese investment in Africa are often simplistic and sometimes biased. Chinese SOEs have traditionally been seen as playing a large role throughout the continent (Lee, 2017). Lee critically points out that "popular discourse and consciousness do not distinguish between state and private Chinese investors, who were all lumped together as 'Chinese companies'" (2017, p. 93). The methodological nationalism inherent in these narratives not only conceals the diversity of Chinese capital in Africa but also combines African countries into a single, fragile, and homogeneous entity assumed to be incapable of managing Chinese investment. In practice, Chinese investment in Africa is complex, fluid, and diverse, and it is therefore difficult to classify investors by nationality or to treat public/private ownership as a sufficient organising criterion.

In reality, neither the Chinese state nor Chinese businesses are homogeneous (Gu et al., 2016). Power et al. (2012) emphasise that China-Africa relations are no longer directed unilaterally by the Chinese side. Chinese players vary by motive, scale, sectoral position, and timing. Lee (2017, p. 6) stresses that how Chinese firms behave abroad depends on local improvisation and their capacity to bargain with host states, especially in least-developed economies. This book pays particular attention to Chinese private firms because their motives, constraints, and practices differ most sharply from those of SOEs and a few large private "national champions." They are typically smaller and less capitalised; they lack guaranteed access to policy-bank or state-led finance; they rely more on *guanxi*,[4] diaspora brokerage, and business networks to discover opportunities and to navigate licensing, land and utilities, customs and tax administration; and they face tighter working-capital and FX constraints. These features generate distinct motives, risk exposures, production regimes, and bargaining mechanisms, which in turn help to explain heterogeneous outcomes across firms operating in the same place and time. In my fieldwork, these differences were observable even across firms sharing the same industrial park and sub-sector, with "similar" investors following sharply divergent trajectories once confronted with Ethiopia's daily engagements with state actors and buyers' compliance and delivery requirements. In practice, the first advantages these latecomer firms could mobilise were organisational: keeping documentation in order, using interpreters to manage shop-floor supervision, and securing dependable shipping and clearance. These helped them meet buyers' delivery schedules even when they entered without strong brands or proprietary technology.

Africa—a continent of 54 states—cannot be treated analytically as a single fragile entity exploited by China (Lee, 2017; Chan, 2008). China's engagement in Africa has often been mobilised in Western political debate as a rhetorical device, with some politicians casting China's growing influence as inherently suspect. The then Secretary of State Hillary Clinton, for instance, cautioned African audiences to beware of "new colonialism" (Clinton, 2011). In this framing, criticism of China's role in Africa can serve domestic political positioning, often with limited engagement with empirical evidence. As one author has noted, "in Washington, Republicans and Democrats generally look at China as a new imperial power in Africa: bad news for Africans" (Brautigam cited in Washington Post, 2018).

Another former Secretary of State, Rex Tillerson, argued that they (China):

> do not bring significant job creation locally; they don't bring significant training programs that enable African citizens to participate more fully in the future; and oftentimes, the financing models are structured in a way that the country, when it gets into trouble financially, loses control of its own infrastructure or its own resources through default. (Tillerson, 2018)

[4] In Chinese contexts, *guanxi* is widely understood as a form of social capital that can facilitate the development of business relationships with individuals as well as with state actors. Such social capital is not confined to national boundaries: Chinese investors in Africa frequently mobilise *guanxi* in their business operations (Ado, 2020, p. 85).

Similar claims have also appeared in UK political discourse. The then Prime Minister Boris Johnson described China's engagement with Africa as "extraordinarily one-sided," suggesting it had produced a "vast imported workshop" (Foreign Policy, 2020).

Such accusations neglect the heterogeneity of African states—their varied historical ties with China, policy capacities, and political economic conditions—and overlook the uneven evolution of state capability (Cheru & Oqubay, 2019; Gisselquist, 2017). The literature on African agency stresses that governments are not passive recipients of foreign capital: they exercise agency—unevenly and often contentiously—within specific domestic political economies to select, shape, and discipline investment (Mohan & Lampert, 2013; Scoones et al., 2016; Behuria, 2019). Ethiopia exemplifies this agency: it combined and sequenced export-driven industrial park policy, park-level one-stop service (OSS) station, and preferential market access to bring in particular investors in light manufacturing (LM),[5] while routing construction materials investment through strategic import substitution objectives and procurement schedules.

Recent interventions on a "new international economic order" highlight the uneven re-legitimation of industrial policy across the global economy and the persistence of asymmetric rules governing trade, investment, and technology (Ahumada & Chang, 2025). This renewed industrial policy turn can also be read as a contemporary double movement, as the expansion of market-led globalisation has been met by counter-movements to re-embed markets and reclaim policy autonomy.[6] Building on this, policy space is conceptualised here not as a fixed national attribute but as relationally produced through interactions among firms, state agencies, and regulatory environments that extend beyond the host country. In Ethiopia, industrial policy was operationalised through spatially embedded policy tools whose effects were mediated by firm-level capabilities and ongoing state–business bargaining. From a global production networks (GPNs) perspective, these policy tools also select, direct, and condition heterogeneous varieties of capital, helping to account for differentiated trajectories between market-embedded firms (MEFs) and global production network-integrated firms (GPN-IFs) and for patterns of coupling,

[5] In this book, the light manufacturing industry refers to textiles and garments, as well as leather and leather products.

[6] See Polanyi (1944/2001) for the original formulation of the concept of the "double movement."

decoupling, and reconfiguration under crisis and shifting geopolitical constraints (Coe & Yeung, 2015; Yeung, 2016; Lee, 2017; Chen, 2025).

Although the importance of Chinese private OFDI in Africa has been widely recognised (Shen, 2015; Sun, 2017; Brautigam et al., 2013; Chen, 2025), rigorous, extensive, and ground-based comparative research on this topic remains insufficient. Three problems come to light when looking at existing studies on Chinese manufacturing investment in Ethiopia.

First, many studies lack systematic comparison across different types of Chinese firms. While firm diversity is often acknowledged, it is rarely analysed in ways that explain why outcomes diverge so sharply in practice. Second, existing work often lacks a multi-scalar analysis that connects firm-level strategies and organisational behaviour to sectoral regimes, global and domestic production networks, and government policies and institutional contexts. Scale is frequently treated as linear or additive, rather than as something that moves across and connects analytical levels. As a result, host-country institutions are too often reduced to a static "investment climate," instead of being examined as operating arrangements in practice—namely, the routine procedures, enforcement patterns, and bargaining mechanisms through which firms encounter, negotiate, and manage day-to-day operational constraints.

The third problem concerns both data and temporality. Reliable data are scarce, and what is available is often partial and methodologically problematic (see Chap. 3). Manufacturing investment cycles are long, and investment trajectories typically unfold in various stages: a pre-investment phase (identifying opportunities, conducting due diligence and feasibility studies, making investment decisions, and structuring finance), followed by an investment and operations phase (installation, consolidation, reinvestment, upgrading, and—at times—exit). These processes often extend over a decade or more. Short time horizons, therefore, miss the period in which shocks, tightening macroeconomic constraints, and shifts in enforcement and service delivery sort firms into divergent trajectories.

This book addresses these problems by comparing different types of Chinese manufacturers that are prominent in Ethiopia—particularly in the LM industry and the construction materials (CM)[7] industry—to examine their distinct investment logics, core drivers, investment trajectories, and evolving relations with the host-country government. The analysis begins

[7] In this book, the construction materials industry refers to cement, steel, gypsum boards, aluminium, and plastics.

at the firm level, focusing on managerial strategies and organisational practices. It then applies a multi-scalar framework that links investor behaviour to sector specificities (in terms of specific markets and products), positioning within global and/or domestic production networks, and the national and sub-national policy and institutional context. Drawing on international business and management, political economy, economic geography, and economic sociology, the book offers an interdisciplinary analysis of the nature and dynamics of Chinese manufacturing investment in Ethiopia.

Research Questions and Methodology

A mixed research methods approach is employed in this study, drawing mainly on qualitative research—particularly ethnographic studies—complemented by limited quantitative analysis. In exploring the nature and dynamics of Chinese OFDI in Ethiopia's manufacturing sector, the book asks the following research questions:

- Why are Chinese firms investing in Ethiopia's manufacturing sector?
- How have Chinese private firms consolidated their investments in Ethiopia, and to what extent have their investment trajectories varied—and why?
- What are the dynamic relations between Chinese private businesses and the Ethiopian state?

Each question is accompanied by a set of subsidiary questions designed to operationalise the research design. These three questions are interlinked: the drivers and motivations of firms contribute to a variety of accumulation logics and strategies, which are in turn shaped by—and result in—different institutional bargaining mechanisms connecting state and capital.

A key motivation for framing the book this way is that the most policy relevant questions in Ethiopia are now less about why firms arrived and more about how they have consolidated, adapted, or exited since 2020. Ethiopia's business environment shifted sharply after 2020, shaped by pandemic disruptions, intensified FX scarcity, domestic political instability, changes in preferential market access, and escalating geopolitical tensions. The book treats these shocks as analytically revealing because they expose what is robust in firm capabilities and what depends on institutional implementation. Resilience and adaptation are thus conceptualised here not as inherent firm attributes, but as relational outcomes produced through the interaction of firm capabilities, policy tools, and ongoing state–business bargaining under conditions of stress.

To answer these research questions, the book adopts a mixed research methods approach that is predominantly qualitative—centred on comparative ethnographic study—and complemented by limited and exploratory quantitative analysis (mainly descriptive). Quantitative evidence alone is insufficient in this field for two reasons. First, available data on Chinese private investment in Ethiopia are often partial and problematic. Second, even where data exist, they cannot adequately capture the conflicts, contradictions, and collaborations through which investment is negotiated and made productive on the ground—dynamics that are frequently obscured behind simple observable indicators. Historical political economy approaches offer valuable tools for identifying longer-run patterns (Behuria, 2019), but they need to be grounded in how contemporary investment processes unfold in practice.

The study treats Chinese private FDI in Ethiopia as a two-way, ongoing, and interactive process. Following Lee's argument that capital is processual, relational, and embedded (2017, p. 648), it uses comparative ethnography to build a grounded account of how firms operate, adapt, and bargain in specific institutional settings. In this sense, the research follows the extended case method tradition (Burawoy, 1985), linking macro-level broader political economic conditions and policy constraints to micro-level firm processes and state–business encounters over time and situating present interactions within the historical and institutional context in which they are produced.

Empirically, the book draws on longitudinal, multi-sited research on Chinese manufacturing investment conducted in multiple waves between 2015 and 2025, in Ethiopia and China. The qualitative evidence is built from 200 semi-structured interviews (including life histories) with firm owners and managers, Ethiopian officials, park administrators, business associations, workers, and other relevant actors, alongside repeated factory visits, on-site observation, and informal conversations that document day-to-day operational constraints and bargaining practices as they unfolded. Documentary and administrative materials—where accessible—are used to triangulate and contextualise the field evidence, and descriptive quantitative analysis is used in a supporting role to map basic patterns (such as operational status, employment, and tax-related indicators) and to identify where administrative categories diverge from firm-level realities. Detailed discussion of the research design, data collection, data analysis, and ethical considerations is provided in Appendix A.

Conceptual Framework

To address this puzzle, Chapter 2 develops a relational-institutional framework that brings together three strands of scholarship. It draws on (1) FDI and late industrialisation, including the conditions under which FDI can support employment, technology transfer, and export capability (Page & Tarp, 2017; Whitfield et al., 2020); (2) the internationalisation of Chinese firms and the varieties of Chinese capital operating overseas, which explain differences in organisational form, market orientation, and outward strategies (Peck & Zhang, 2013; Zhang & Peck, 2016; Lee, 2017); and (3) African political settlements (PS) and SBRs, which illuminate how formal regulation interacts with informal coordination, discretion, and bargaining in policy implementation (Khan, 2018; Te Velde, 2013; Chen, 2021a, 2021b).

Together, these perspectives structure the empirical analysis of firm diversity and investment logics (Chap. 3), the operation of policy tools and bargaining mechanisms before 2020 (Chap. 4), and patterns of resilience and adaptation under post-2020 shocks (Chap. 5).

Chapter 3 operationalises this framework through a typology grounded in two dimensions: (i) market orientation (domestic/regional versus export) and (ii) position GPNs, which conditions capabilities, finance, and market discipline. It distinguishes two ideal-typical modes—MEFs and GPN-IFs—and traces how each engages Ethiopia's policy tools (e.g., industrial parks, OSS arrangements, export incentives, and FX allocation rules) as political and macroeconomic conditions shift. The categories are analytical rather than fixed: firms can hybridise strategies across modes over time.

Three terms organise the analysis in this book. Policy tools (often termed policy instruments in the policy literature) refer to the designed levers through which the state shapes incentives, compliance, and access to markets. Policy tools in practice describe how these tools actually operate on the ground—through everyday institutional practices such as routine procedures, discretionary decisions, enforcement patterns, and informal adjustments. Bargaining mechanisms refer to the formal and informal channels through which firms and state agencies negotiate how rules are interpreted, applied, adjusted, and enforced in practice. These interactions take place within institutions, understood here as the wider rule system and governance arrangements that shape and organise state–business relations.

Building on these concepts, Chapter 2 advances five propositions (P1–P5) that guide the analysis across the empirical chapters:

P1: Firm heterogeneity matters—differences in ownership structure, organisational capability, and business model shape motives, operating practices, and developmental effects.
P2: Production network position matters—firms' insertion into (or distance from) GPNs and buyer discipline conditions behaviour and upgrading possibilities.
P3: Host-country policy tools operate as sorting mechanisms—the mix of incentives, discipline, and constraints channels different firms into differentiated trajectories.
P4: Implementation is mediated by state–business relations—bargaining mechanisms, discretion, and cross-agency coordination shape how rules are interpreted and enforced in practice.
P5: Trajectories are contingent over time—learning, shocks, and political economic shifts reconfigure both firm strategies and institutional governance, producing path-dependent outcomes.

Why Ethiopia?

Ethiopia is an analytically strategic case because it pursued one of Africa's most ambitious manufacturing-led industrialisation drives during the 2010s, within a highly constrained operating environment that renders the politics of implementation visible at the level of production. Successive national plans prioritised industrial development, export expansion, and employment creation, supported by major public investment in industrial infrastructure, including power generation and industrial parks (Oqubay, 2015; Cheru & Oqubay, 2019; Hauge & Chang, 2019). Industrial parks were intended to concentrate infrastructure, simplify administration, and create a platform for export manufacturing, particularly in the LM industry.

Ethiopia presents a highly constrained operating environment for manufacturing investors. As a landlocked economy, it depends heavily on the Ethiopia-Djibouti corridor as its primary trade gateway: the World Bank (2025) reports that more than 95% of Ethiopia's imports and exports pass through this route.[8] Chronic FX scarcity further turns FX allocation rules into a powerful selection process for import-dependent manufacturers. Export-oriented firms, operating under tight buyer lead times and compliance requirements, rely on predictable customs clearance, stable corridor performance, and reliable utilities. Firms serving domestic markets are shaped more by local demand conditions, purchasing power, import competition, and the timing of public procurement. Across both groups, customs valuation, tax administration, and FX management play a decisive role in determining whether inputs can be secured, machinery maintained, and profits repatriated.

This combination of policy ambition and binding constraints also strengthens Ethiopia's value as a case for analysing industrial policy beyond "blueprint" accounts. Rapid growth during the 2000s–2010s has often been linked to a developmental-state strategy centred on structural transformation and long-term capability building through large public investment and institutional reform (Oqubay, 2019; Clapham, 2018; Martins, 2018). Yet, as a resource-scarce economy without commodity-boom windfalls, Ethiopia's industrial push relied on domestic mobilisation, concessional finance and aid, and FDI (Clapham, 2018), alongside a relatively strategic approach to managing external partnerships—engaging China while maintaining strong ties with Western development partners and multilaterals (Cheru & Oqubay, 2019).

To capture both the initial phase of accelerated industrialisation and the subsequent period of disruption and adjustment, the book adopts a two-period design. The pre-2020 period covers the rapid expansion of industrial parks and the institutional bargaining around land, licensing, labour regulation, and compliance. The post-2020 period traces how overlapping shocks—pandemic disruption, intensified FX scarcity, domestic political instability, and the termination of Ethiopia's AGOA eligibility (effective January 1, 2022)—reshaped the operating environment for firms and state agencies (USTR, 2021).

[8] Access to Eritrean ports—frequently discussed in regional political discourse—has not been operationalised as a meaningful commercial alternative, including the port of Assab (AFP Fact Check, 2025). This has reinforced reliance on a single logistics corridor for clearance and delivery.

Significance of the Book

Manufacturing, Structural Transformation, and the Return of Industrial Policy

This book concentrates on manufacturing because it sits at the core of structural transformation and because the politics of its attraction and regulation reveal most clearly how state interventions and the politics of SBRs shape foreign investment. Manufacturing remains central to long-standing debates on development because it has historically been associated with productivity growth, learning-by-doing, export diversification, and the capacity to absorb labour at scale. It generates supplier development and inter- and intra-industry linkages; it underpins FX earnings; and it supplies inputs into construction and services. These are also the reasons why states have repeatedly attempted to build productive capabilities in manufacturing through selective support, discipline, and coordination (Evans, 1995; Page & Tarp, 2017; Chen, 2025).

Across many African economies, structural transformation has been complicated by premature deindustrialisation, commodity dependence, and the limited capacity of modern services to absorb labour. Industrial policy has therefore returned—often in pragmatic rather than ideological form—as a response to employment pressures and balance-of-payments constraints (Rodrik, 2018; Page & Tarp, 2017; Cheru & Oqubay, 2019). Current strategies typically rely on policy tools that concentrate facilitation and enforcement in specific sites: industrial parks and SEZs, OSS arrangements, and export facilitation measures (Farole, 2011; Zeng, 2016; UNCTAD, 2019). What matters, however, is not only tool design but policy tools in practice—whether agencies actually deliver routine clearances, documentation, logistics coordination, and credible aftercare when problems arise. Firms encounter industrial policy through repeated, operational decisions—on customs, inspections, and access to FX for inputs—that cumulatively shape costs, delays, and production risk.

This book also concentrates on manufacturing because it makes the politics of local improvisation visible. Manufacturing depends on the routine functioning of utilities, customs and corridor logistics, labour management, and—under FX scarcity—access to foreign exchange for inputs and maintenance. These constraints are often flattened in macro indicators, but they dominate firm-level decision-making and shape whether production can be sustained.

Following Lee's (2017) relational perspective, firms are embedded in networks of social ties, buyer-driven chain governance, and state-firm linkages that travel across borders and are reworked in specific institutional settings. This requires a relational approach that examines both host-country "pulling-in" dynamics and, equally, the home-country "pushing-out" of diverse Chinese capital (Chen, 2025). Analytically, relationality directs attention to how ownership, finance, procurement, logistics, and labour management are organised through relationships that connect Chinese investors to Ethiopian industrial policy tools.

Ethiopia is a pertinent case because its industrial park strategy—alongside export-linked discipline and OSS arrangements—was designed to attract manufacturing FDI and embed it in a national development agenda (Oqubay, 2015; Industrial Parks Proclamation No. 886/2015; Industrial Parks Regulation No. 417/2017; Hauge & Chang, 2019). As documented in Chen (2021a, 2025), Chinese manufacturers—predominantly private, especially in LM and CM—offer a revealing window into how policy tools, policy tools in practice, and bargaining mechanisms shape firm behaviour and determine whether firms consolidate, adapt, or exit over time.

Manufacturing investment is therefore a useful entry point for rethinking China-Africa debates for three reasons. First, it speaks directly to the outcomes that are repeatedly placed at the centre of African policy agendas: jobs, wages, skills, productivity, FX earnings, and the prospects for structural transformation. Second, it makes policy credibility visible. A manufacturing production line forces the analysis into the routine functioning of utilities, customs and corridor logistics, labour governance, and foreign exchange allocation—constraints that are often flattened in macro indicators but dominate operational decision-making. Third, manufacturing sits awkwardly within dominant "China in Africa" narratives. It is less visible than infrastructure megaprojects and less easily captured by debt statistics or commodity export data. Treating all Chinese capital as if it operates through the same contracts and operating rules is analytically misleading: the arrangements that govern a policy bank-financed railway are not the same as those that govern a privately financed garment, footwear, or construction materials factory (Power et al., 2012; Corkin, 2013). This is also why "China" cannot be read off from state-to-state agreements alone: manufacturing outcomes depend on firm type, sector, and the local arrangements through which regulation and support are delivered.

Approaching Chinese engagement through manufacturing also directs attention to changes in China's own political economy. China's OFDI expanded after the turn of the century alongside the growth of a large, competitive private manufacturing sector. By the mid-2010s, China's economy was widely described as entering a "new normal" of slower growth, industrial upgrading, and intensified domestic competition (Naughton, 2018; Chen, 2021a). In some labour-intensive and lower-technology industries, rising costs and overcapacity pressures encouraged firms to look for spatial fixes through overseas investment and selective production relocation (Harvey, 2001). African economies—including Ethiopia—became attractive not because they offered frictionless environments, but because they combined low labour costs with policy agendas oriented towards industrialisation and, at least for some export sectors, the possibility of preferential access to major markets (Lin, 2012; Cheru & Oqubay, 2019).

Chinese policy initiatives also shaped this environment. Since the early 2010s, Chinese central and provincial authorities have increasingly framed outward investment as part of industrial upgrading and international economic strategy, including through the Belt and Road Initiative (BRI) and the discourse of "international industrial capacity cooperation" (NDRC, MOFA and MOFCOM, 2015; State Council of the PRC, 2015). These signals mattered, but they did not turn private manufacturing investors into straightforward agents of state strategy. Most were privately financed and commercially driven; they read policy signals while operating under margin pressure and working-capital constraints. State agendas and commercial calculations, therefore, intersect, but they do not coincide. In Africa, these policy signals intersected with host-country efforts to attract manufacturing investment as a route to job creation and export diversification (Ado, 2020; Wang et al., 2015).

A second motivation for focusing on manufacturing is the growing recognition that "China" is not a single actor in Africa. Chinese engagement spans SOEs operating at different levels of the state, policy and commercial banks, diversified business groups (DBGs),[9] small and medium-sized

[9] Diversified business groups (DBGs) are collections of legally distinct firms operating across at least three unrelated sectors under centralised control via equity holdings, family ownership, or financial ties (Schneider, 2009, pp. 180–81). In the China-Africa context, DBG structures often involve offshore registration and relational ownership, enabling risk buffering and cross-sectoral capital redeployment (Behuria 2021), cited in Chen (2025, p.6).

enterprises, and diaspora-linked "translocal" entrepreneurs and intermediaries (Shen, 2015; Sun, 2017; Lee, 2017; Chen, 2025). These actors differ in ownership and governance, sector, financing model, time horizon, and depth of political and institutional connections. Aggregated accounts that treat Chinese capital as homogeneous risk confuse the strategies of one subset of actors with the outcomes associated with another subset. Disaggregation, therefore, shifts attention away from aggregated investment figures to how those figures translate into different production outcomes as firms encounter different regulatory interfaces, enforcement practices, and sector-specific constraints.

The Puzzle and the Argument

A central puzzle motivates this book. During the 2010s, Ethiopia attracted an unusually visible wave of Chinese private manufacturing investors, including export-oriented light manufacturers and domestically oriented producers in construction materials. Yet their accumulation[10] trajectories diverged sharply. Some firms scaled production, renewed investment, and became anchored in industrial parks and export routines. Others stagnated, downsized, or exited. This divergence cannot be explained by national origin, by ownership form, or by a simple "good policy/bad policy" distinction. It reflects the interaction between heterogeneous firms and the combinations of industrial policy tools, enforcement practices, and bargaining arrangements that govern market access, foreign exchange, and compliance across sectors and locations. Crisis therefore becomes a revealing moment for both firm strategies and institutional governance: it serves as a pressure test that shows which strategies and governance routines hold, which break down, and why.

Methodologically, the book combines comparative ethnography with process tracing. Process tracing is used here as a within-case approach that links causes to outcomes by tracing the causal mechanism in between. In practice, I track how specific industrial policy tools (e.g., land access, FX allocation rules, customs administration, compliance enforcement) are

[10] Accumulation refers to the sequence through which advanced value is transformed into capital and expanded; production regime denotes the organisation of work, technology, and control on the shop floor; and managerial ethos refers to the norms and practices that structure authority, obligation, and reciprocity within firms (see Lee, 2017 for further discussion).

delivered in practice, how firms respond, and how bargaining mechanisms reshape both rules and routines over time. The post-2020 shocks are analytically useful because they concentrate constraints and make these mechanisms more visible: they show which strategies and governance routines hold, which break down, and why (Collier, 2011; Beach & Pedersen, 2013; Bennett & Checkel, 2014).

Existing explanations are useful starting points but insufficient. Push-pull and OLI (i.e., Ownership-Location-Internalisation) approaches highlight wage differentials, market size, and firm-specific advantages, but they typically treat institutions as background "location factors" rather than as the governance architecture within which policy tools are unevenly delivered and negotiated (Dunning & Lundan, 2008; Buckley et al., 2007). Macro political economy accounts capture state-to-state dynamics and the role of finance and infrastructure, but often under-specify how manufacturing investment is governed and contested at the level of factories, industrial parks, and local agencies (Brautigam, 2009; Lee, 2017). What is missing is a framework that links firm diversity and production network discipline to the concrete policy tools, policy tools in practice, and bargaining mechanisms through which host states shape manufacturing investment.

The book develops this account through a relational-institutional approach. It treats industrial policy not primarily as stated intent, but as policy tools administered by organisations—industrial park authorities, customs and revenue agencies, central banks, and procurement bodies—and contested through bargaining mechanisms that range from formal committees and business associations to informal problem-solving networks. These policy tools trade benefits (land access, serviced infrastructure, and—in some cases—preferential access to FX) for performance and compliance. In practice, they also operate as sorting mechanisms: they reward certain business models and capabilities while constraining others, generating differentiated investment trajectories. Their developmental effect hinges on credibility and consistency over time (Evans, 1995; Oqubay, 2015; Hauge & Chang, 2019).

To connect firm diversity to host-country governance, the book uses the MEF/GPN-IF distinction. GPN-IFs face external discipline from export buyers, standards regimes, and delivery schedules; MEFs are oriented to domestic and regional markets and are therefore more exposed to utilities reliability, procurement cycles, and day-to-day revenue enforcement. The typology is not a proxy for ownership: both private and state-linked firms can operate in either mode. It helps explain why firms from the same country engage the state through different bargaining mechanisms and, as a result, follow different trajectories of consolidation, learning, and resilience.

The post-2020 period is central because it exposes the gap between policy design and workable delivery. As global logistics were disrupted, FX scarcity tightened, conflict and insecurity interrupted production, and trade preferences shifted, firms faced constraints that managerial effort alone could not solve. Outcomes were not random. They depended on (i) the organisational capabilities firms had built under earlier conditions and (ii) whether agencies could adapt policy tools in practice—through credible rules, workable routines, and problem-solving via bargaining mechanisms—without undermining predictability.

The book makes three contributions. Empirically, it offers a longitudinal account of Chinese private manufacturing investment in Ethiopia across multiple sectors. Conceptually, it develops a relational-institutional framework that links GPN dynamics to host-country policy tools, policy tools in practice, and bargaining mechanisms. Methodologically, it demonstrates how to scale up from firm-level evidence to the level of governance and political economy through comparative ethnography and process tracing—reconstructing sequences of policy delivery, enforcement, and bargaining, and weighing competing explanations against diagnostic evidence.

Conceptualising Diversity and Heterogeneity

The book uses the terms diversity and heterogeneity deliberately. Diversity is descriptive: it captures the fact that "Chinese manufacturing firms" vary in ownership and governance, place of origin, financing, sector, organisational capabilities, and the networks through which they mobilise managers, suppliers, and intermediaries. Heterogeneity is analytical: it signals that these differences are not statistical "noise" around a typical outcome, but mechanisms that shape how firms respond to the same host-country policy tools and the same macro shocks. Disaggregation is therefore not an attempt to deny that aggregate Chinese OFDI to Africa is modest; it is a strategy for explaining why similar aggregate magnitudes can generate sharply different development paths across countries, sectors, and time periods.

Within China, regionally specific development trajectories have generated distinctive entrepreneurial strategies and operating models that travel with outward investors. For example, Zhejiang's private entrepreneurial tradition and dense business and social networks often support "going out in groups" (*bao tuan chu hai*); parts of Jiangsu have been shaped by more institutionally embedded industrial upgrading; and Guangdong's export-processing clusters have cultivated flexible subcontracting and rapid product switching (Chen, 2021a, 2025). These are not rigid types. Rather, they help explain why firms that look similar by ownership and sector can organise production differently, engage officials through different bargaining mechanisms, and sustain different time horizons in the same host-country environment.

Recognising heterogeneity also reframes how "impact" is assessed. Employment and wages depend on product strategy, workforce organisation, and buyer compliance requirements, as well as on labour-market conditions and enforcement. Technology transfer depends on production structure, the availability of skilled supervisors and technicians, and the stability of orders. Supplier linkages depend on input-market reliability, customs and logistics performance, and currency conditions. None of these outcomes can be inferred from nationality or ownership alone. They emerge from the interaction between firm strategy, sectoral regimes, and the credibility of policy tools in practice—including the bargaining mechanisms through which compliance, exceptions, and problem-solving are managed.

Unpacking the Dynamics of Chinese Capital "going out" and Contingent Investment Trajectories

The Push-pull framework helps explain why firms look abroad when domestic wages rise, regulatory enforcement tightens, and markets saturate, and why they target locations offering lower costs, incentives, and market access. The notion of a spatial fix similarly captures how surplus capacity can be relocated from over-supplied sectors (Harvey, 2001). These accounts are useful, but they leave open the question of how strategies are chosen and once firms arrive, how production is organised under new constraints, and how relations with state agencies are constructed and maintained.

The book, therefore, treats accumulation trajectories as contingent. Firms enter Ethiopia with different resource endowments, managerial capabilities, and ties to buyers and suppliers. In the pre-2020 phase, export-oriented firms could scale if they could stabilise utilities, logistics, and customs routines; domestically oriented firms could expand with demand if currency and import-licensing constraints were manageable. After 2020, overlapping shocks—including disrupted orders and logistics, intensified FX scarcity, conflict-related instability, and shifts in trade preferences—reconfigured these conditions. Firms responded by hybridising strategies (rebalancing export and domestic sales), adjusting sourcing and inventory practices, and renegotiating compliance and payment terms. Outcomes depended on both organisational capability and institutional flexibility.

State–Business Relations and Institutional Bargaining

The study also contributes to understanding how African states relate to Chinese private capital. Formal policy design matters: Ethiopia's policy tools—industrial parks, OSS arrangements, incentive regimes, labour codes, and environmental standards—made entry more readily observable and reduced some forms of uncertainty. But policy tools do not implement themselves. In practice, investment hinges on policy tools in practice: aligning land and leasing arrangements, connecting power and water, clearing machinery and inputs through customs, accessing FX, meeting labour and environmental requirements, and resolving disputes.

These tasks are handled through a combination of formal procedures and informal coordination. Firms and officials rely on interpreters, brokers, associations, and personal ties to clarify documentation, schedule inspections, and negotiate overlaps of mandate. Such practices do not replace formal rules, but they shape how rules are enacted in particular cases—and they determine whether problems become predictable processes or unpredictable confrontations. This focus on bargaining mechanisms is central to the book's account of how industrial policy is delivered—and contested—under constraint.

Structure of the Book

This book is divided into six chapters, of which this introduction is the first.

Chapter 2 develops the conceptual and analytical framework. It sets out a relational-institutional approach and advances five propositions (P1–P5) linking firm heterogeneity, production-network position, policy tools in practice, bargaining mechanisms, and temporal contingency. It also clarifies the MEF/GPN-IF typology and the book's key analytical terms.

Chapter 3 operationalises the framework by mapping the varieties of Chinese private manufacturing firms in Ethiopia and explaining their motives and determinants. It develops the MEF/GPN-IF typology empirically and addresses P1 and P2 by showing how different firm attributes and production network positions shape strategy, capability building, and performance under Ethiopia's policy tools.

Chapter 4 turns to the pre-2020 period and analyses how Ethiopia's policy tools worked in practice and how they operated as sorting mechanisms. Through the Eastern Industrial Park case, it examines bargaining mechanisms and state–business relations that mediated land access, service provision, labour and environmental compliance, and export discipline, addressing P3 and P4.

Chapter 5 analyses the post-2020 period and uses overlapping shocks—COVID-19, intensified FX scarcity, conflict-related instability, and shifting trade preferences—to examine adaptation and resilience. It shows how both firms and institutions recalibrated strategies and enforcement, directly engaging P5 while also revisiting P3 and P4 under stress.

Chapter 6 synthesises the findings and develops implications for debates on Chinese investment and African industrial futures. It discusses how different political economy settings shape investment governance and identifies priorities for industrial strategy and future research.

References

Ado, A. (2020). Informal institutions and China's BRI in Africa. *Asia Pacific Business Review, 26*(1), 86–108.

AFP Fact Check. (2025, March 17). *False claims about Ethiopia's pursuit of Red Sea access add to tensions with Eritrea.* Retrieved December 10, 2025, from https://factcheck.afp.com/doc.afp.com.372B8BR

Ahumada, J. M., & Chang, H.-J. (2025). A new international economic order for the twenty-first century: an agenda for industrial and trade policies from the Global South. *Review of Keynesian Economics, 13*(4), 562–580. https://doi.org/10.4337/roke.2025.04.06

Alden, C. (2007). *China in Africa.* Zed Books.

Allen, J. (2003). *Lost Geographies of Power.* Blackwell.

Allen, J. (2004). The whereabouts of power: politics, government and space. *Geografiska Annaler: Series B, Human Geography, 86*(1), 19–32.

Beach, D., & Pedersen, R. B. (2013). *Process-tracing methods: Foundations and guidelines*. University of Michigan Press.
Behuria, P. (2019). The domestic political economy of upgrading in global value chains: how politics shapes pathways for upgrading in Rwanda's coffee sector. *Review of International Political Economy*. https://doi.org/10.1080/09692290.2019.1625803. https://www.tandfonline.com/doi/pdf/10.1080/09692290.2019.1625803?needAccess=true
Bennett, A., & Checkel, J. T. (Eds.). (2014). *Process tracing: From metaphor to analytic tool*. Cambridge University Press. https://doi.org/10.1017/CBO9781139858472
Brautigam, D. (2009). *The dragon's gift: The real story of China in Africa*. Oxford University Press.
Brautigam, D. (2018, April 26). Chinese investment in Africa: how real is the debt trap? *Foreign Affairs*.
Brautigam, D., McMillan, M., & Tang, X. (2013). The role of the Chinese government in Africa's industrialization. *WIDER Working Paper* No. 2013/120.
Buckley, P. J., Clegg, J., Cross, A. R., Liu, X., Voss, H., & Zheng, P. (2007). The determinants of Chinese outward foreign direct investment. *Journal of International Business Studies, 38*(4), 499–518.
Burawoy, M. (1985). *The politics of production: Factory regimes under capitalism and socialism*. Verso.
Carmody, P. (2011). *The new scramble for Africa*. Polity.
Chan, S. (2008). Ten Caveats and One Sunrise in our Contemplation of China and Africa. In C. Alden, D. Large, & R. Oliveira (Eds.), *China returns to Africa: A rising power and continent embrace* (pp. 339–347). Hurst.
Chen, W. (2021a). The dynamics of chinese private outward foreign direct investment in Ethiopia: A comparison of the light manufacturing industry and the construction materials industry. PhD thesis, SOAS University of London. https://doi.org/10.25501/SOAS.00035764
Chen, W. (2021b). The dynamics of state–business relations between the Ethiopian state and Chinese private firms: A case study of the Eastern Industry Park. *WIDER Working Paper* No. 2021/122. Helsinki: UNU-WIDER. doi:https://doi.org/10.35188/UNU-WIDER/2021/890-0.
Chen, W. (2022, February 21). *China and Africa: Ethiopia case study debunks investment myths*. The Conversation Africa. https://doi.org/10.64628/aaj.jevsggshs
Chen, W. (2025). Heterogeneity and drivers of Chinese manufacturing FDI in Africa: Evidence from Angola and Ethiopia. *Journal of International Development*. https://doi.org/10.1002/jid.70038
Cheru, F., & Oqubay, A. (2019). Catalysing China-Africa ties for Africa's structural transformation: lessons from Ethiopia. In A. Oqubay & J. Y. Lin (Eds.),

China-Africa and an Economic Transformation (pp. 282–309). Oxford University Press.

Clapham, C. (2018). The Ethiopian developmental state. *Third World Quarterly, 39*(6), 1151–1165.

Clinton, H. R. (2011). Interview on Africa 360. US Department of State, Diplomacy in Action.

Coe, N. M., & Yeung, H. W.-C. (2015). *Global production networks: Theorizing Economic development in an interconnected world.* Oxford University Press.

Collier, D. (2011). Understanding process tracing. *PS: Political Science & Politics, 44*(4), 823–830. https://doi.org/10.1017/S1049096511001429

Corkin, L. (2013). *Uncovering African agency: Angola's management of China's credit lines.* Ashgate.

Dunning, J. H., & Lundan, S. M. (2008). *Multinational Enterprises and the Global Economy* (2nd ed.). Edward Elgar.

Evans, P. (1995). *Embedded autonomy: States and industrial transformation.* Princeton University Press.

Farole, T. (2011). *Special Economic Zones in Africa: Comparing Performance and Learning from Global Experience.* World Bank.

FOCAC. (2018). *Beijing Action Plan (2019–2021).* Forum on China-Africa Cooperation.

Foreign Policy. (2020). Boris Johnson's New Scramble for Africa', Stephen Paduano. *Foreign Policy,* January 29. Retrieved February 6, 2020, from https://foreignpolicy.com/2020/01/29/boris-johnsons-new-scramble-for-africa/

Gisselquist, R. M. (2017). State capability and prospects for close coordination: considerations for industrial policy in Africa. In J. Page & F. Tarp (Eds.), *The practice of industrial policy government -- Business coordination in Africa and East Asia* (WIDER Studies in Development Economics). Oxford University Press.

Gu, J., Zhang, C., Vaz, A., & Mukereza, L. (2016). Chinese state capitalism? Rethinking the role of the state and business in Chinese Development Cooperation in Africa'. *World Development, 81*, 24–34. https://doi.org/10.1016/j.worlddev.2016.01.001

Harvey, D. (2001). *Spaces of capital: Towards a critical geography.* Edinburgh University Press.

Hauge, J., & Chang, H.-J. (2019). The developmental state in Ethiopia. In C. Cramer, J. Sender, & A. Oqubay (Eds.), *African economic development: Evidence, theory, policy.* Oxford University Press.

Hurley, J., Morris, S., & Portelance, G. (2018). *Examining the Debt implications of the belt and road initiative from a policy perspective.* CGD Policy Paper. Center for Global Development, Washington, DC.

Industrial Parks Proclamation No. 886/2015. (2015). Federal Democratic Republic of Ethiopia.

Industrial Parks Regulation No. 417/2017. (2017). Federal Democratic Republic of Ethiopia.

Khan, M. (2018). Political settlements and the analysis of institutions. *African Affairs, 117*(469), 636–655. https://doi.org/10.1093/afraf/adx044

Lee, C. K. (2017). *The specter of global China: Politics, labor, and foreign investment in Africa*. University of Chicago Press.

Lin, J. Y. (2012). *New structural economics: A framework for rethinking development and policy*. World Bank.

Martins, P. M. G. (2018). Structural change in Ethiopia: an employment perspective. *Development Policy Review, 36*(S1), O183–O200.

Mohan, G., & Lampert, B. (2013). Negotiating China: Reinserting African agency into China-Africa relations. *African Affairs, 112*(446), 92–110.

Naughton, B. (2018). *The Chinese Economy: Adaptation and Growth* (2nd ed.). MIT Press.

NDRC (National Development and Reform Commission), MOFA (Ministry of Foreign Affairs) and MOFCOM (Ministry of Commerce). (2015). *Vision and Actions on Jointly Building Silk Road Economic Belt and 21st-Century Maritime Silk Road*. Beijing.

Oqubay, A. (2015). *Made in Africa: Industrial policy in Ethiopia*. Oxford University Press.

Oqubay, A. (2019). The structure and performance of the Ethiopian manufacturing sector. In F. Cheru, C. Cramer, & A. Oqubay (Eds.), *The Oxford handbook of the Ethiopian economy* (pp. 630–650). Oxford University Press.

Oya, C., & Wanda, F. (2021). Employment patterns and conditions in Angola: A comparative analysis of the infrastructure construction sector and building materials industry. IDCEA Research Report, SOAS, University of London.

Page, J., & Tarp, F. (Eds.). (2017). *The practice of industrial policy: Government-business coordination in Africa and East Asia*. Oxford University Press.

Peck, J., & Zhang, J. (2013). A variety of capitalism with Chinese characteristics? *Journal of Economic Geography, 13*(2013), 357–396. https://doi.org/10.1093/jeg/lbs058

Polanyi, K. (1944/2001). *The great transformation: The political and economic origins of our time*. Beacon Press.

Power, M., Mohan, G., & Tan-Mullins, M. (2012). *China's resource diplomacy in Africa*. Palgrave Macmillan.

Rodrik, D. (2018). New technologies, global value chains, and developing economies. *NBER Working Paper* No. 25164.

Schneider, B. R. (2009). 'A comparative political economy of diversified business groups, or how states organize big business'. *Review of International Political Economy, 16*(2), 178–201.

Scoones, I., Amanor, K., Favareto, A., & Qi, G. (2016). A new politics of development cooperation? Chinese and Brazilian engagements in African agriculture.

World Development, 81, 1–12. https://doi.org/10.1016/j.worlddev.2015.11.020

Shen, X. (2015). Private Chinese investment in Africa. *World Bank Policy Research Working Paper* No. 7318.

State Council of the PRC. (2006). *China's African Policy.* The State Council Information Office.

State Council of the PRC. (2015). Guiding opinions on promoting international production capacity and equipment manufacturing cooperation (国务院关于推进国际产能和装备制造合作的指导意见). Beijing.

Sun, I. Y. (2017). *The next factory of the world: How Chinese investment is reshaping Africa.* Harvard Business Review Press.

Taylor, I. (2006). *China and Africa: Engagement and compromise.* Routledge.

Te Velde, D. (2013, August). State-business relations and industrial policy: And introduction. In D. te Velde (Ed.), *State-business Relations and Industrial Policy: current policy and research debates'.* Growth Research Program.

Tillerson, R. (2018). Remarks - Secretary of State Rex Tillerson and African Union Commission Chairperson Moussa Faki at a Press Availability', Global Public Affairs, U.S. Department of State, March 8, 2018. Retrieved November 20, 2019, from https://translations.state.gov/2018/03/08/remarks-secretary-of-state-rex-tillerson-and-african-union-commission-chairperson-moussa-faki-at-a-press-availability/-.

UNCTAD. (2012). *World Investment Report 2012.* http://unctad.org/en/PublicationsLibrary/wir2012_embargoed_en.pdf

UNCTAD. (2019). *World Investment Report 2019: Special Economic Zones.* United Nations Conference on Trade and Development.

USTR. (2021). Statement From Ambassador Katherine Tai on the African growth and opportunity act eligibility review. press release, November 2. *United States Trade Representative.* Retrieved December 10, 2025, from https://ustr.gov/about-us/policy-offices/press-office/press-releases/2021/november/statement-ambassador-katherine-tai-african-growth-and-opportunity-act-eligibility-review

Wang, C., Du, J., & Wang, Y. (2015). International business and the new Silk Road: location choice of Chinese outward foreign direct investment. *China Economic Review, 34*, 193–208.

Washington Post. (2018, April 12). U.S. politicians get China in Africa all wrong' (Deborah Bräutigam), *The Washington Post* (TheWorldPost).

Whitfield, L., Staritz, C., & Morris, M. (2020). Global value chains and industrial policy in Ethiopia's apparel sector. *Development and Change, 51*(4), 1018–1043.

World Bank. (2025). *Implementation Status & Results Report: Trade Logistics Project (P156590)*, March 20. Retrieved December 10, 2025, from https://

documents1.worldbank.org/curated/en/099032025074024086/pdf/P156590-03d61c63-1f0a-4d14-a9bd-0c92ac7eae5c.pdf.

Yeung, H. W.-C. (2016). *Strategic coupling: East Asian industrial transformation in the new global economy*. Cornell University Press.

Zeng, D. Z. (2016). Special economic zones: lessons from the global experience. *PEDL Synthesis Paper Series*.

Zhang, J., & Peck, J. (2016). Variegated capitalism, Chinese style. *Regional Studies, 50*(1), 52–78.

CHAPTER 2

Understanding and Conceptualising Chinese Manufacturing Investment in Africa

Introduction

This chapter develops the conceptual and analytical framework that structures the book's explanation of Chinese manufacturing FDI in Africa, with Ethiopia as the core case. The chapter is motivated by a gap between how "China in Africa" is debated in public discourse and how investment is negotiated, organised, and governed in practice. Recent commentary about China's global role often shifts between "China bashing" and a more celebratory genre of "China reckonings," often framed through speculative claims about what China will "dominate" next (Ang, 2025). While these narratives shift can change how China is perceived, they do not in themselves explain how Chinese investment operates. As Ang (2025) argues, a more useful starting point is to normalise China analytically—neither treating it as an exceptional threat nor as a developmental miracle. From this comparative lens, features often portrayed as uniquely Chinese—such as rapid growth coexisting with corruption, or industrial policy pursued through decentralised experimentation—are historically familiar rather than exceptional (Ang, 2025).

Two recent syntheses sharpen what this normalising move implies for research design. Rolf and Schindler (2025) conceptualise contemporary capitalism as a system in which state intervention and corporate concentration are baseline conditions rather than anomalies, directing analytical

W. Chen, *Chinese Manufacturing Firms in Ethiopia*, Palgrave Studies in African and Development Economics,
https://doi.org/10.1007/978-3-032-24322-5_2

attention to how these power centres are organised, coordinated, and contested across sectors and jurisdictions. Oya (2025) advances a comparative synthesis of Africa–China engagements that rejects unitary "China" or "Africa" narratives and instead foregrounds the mechanisms through which outcomes are produced—policy agency, bargaining arenas, and the uneven capacities of states and firms to enforce, adapt, or renegotiate deals.

Recent scholarship has moved beyond polarised "China in Africa" narratives. Two strands are particularly relevant for this book: work that recentres analysis on firms and institutions beyond the national frame (Lee, 2017), and work that treats manufacturing as the arena in which processes of upgrading, discipline, and learning are organised and contested (Oqubay, 2015; Oqubay & Lin, 2020). Taken together, these contributions point to the need for a framework capable of explaining why ostensibly similar "Chinese" investments generate sharply divergent outcomes on the ground.

Yet much debate still reverts to simplified oppositions—win–win partnership versus neo-colonial extraction—thereby obscuring the ways in which outcomes are shaped through sectoral logics, firm strategies, and host-country governance arrangements. For a study of manufacturing investment trajectories, the key question is therefore not whether engagement is "good" or "bad" in the abstract, but how investment is shaped, governed, and transformed over time.

A second limitation concerns methodological nationalism. "China" is frequently treated as a coherent agent, and "Chinese firms" become proxies for state intent. This framing collapses differences in ownership structures, organisational capabilities, and origins—including region-specific development models within China—that shape firms' motives, operational modalities, and developmental effects.

"Africa" is too often treated in the same homogenising way. In practice, African states vary widely in industrial policy capacity, political settlements, and bargaining leverage (Whitfield et al., 2020; Oqubay, 2015). These differences condition which investors are attracted, how they are regulated and disciplined, and which are accommodated over time. Any explanation of manufacturing outcomes must therefore be relational, tracing the processes through which different types of firms engage with different host states within specific arenas of negotiation.

The chapter proceeds in three steps. Section "Literature Review and Theoretical Perspectives" critically reviews the selected literature across three dimensions: investor heterogeneity, the firm- and sector-level drivers of manufacturing FDI, and the political economy of implementation. Section "Conceptual Framework" synthesises these strands into a relational-institutional framework centred on firm heterogeneity, production network position, and the operation of policy tools in practice. Section "Conclusion" summarises the contribution and bridges to the empirical chapters.

Literature Review and Theoretical Perspectives

This section reviews scholarship on Chinese OFDI in Africa to assess how far it explains observable patterns and where gaps remain. It situates the argument developed in this book and identifies contributions aligned with its theoretical stance, questions, and empirical focus. The discussion proceeds in three steps. Section "Existing Literature on Chinese OFDI in Africa" synthesises what we know about the composition of Chinese OFDI in Africa, with attention to firm heterogeneity, sectoral contexts and data reliability; clarifies motives and determinants once firms and sectors are properly distinguished; and examines how Chinese private firms have actually internationalised. It then moves from entry to consolidation by tracing accumulation and production from installation to re-investment. Section "Chinese Capital in Global Capitalism" widens the lens to locate these firm-level dynamics within China's political economy and global capitalism, with emphasis on sub-national variation and the fractions of capital it generates. Throughout, the review keeps manufacturing at the centre because Ethiopia's policy tools—industrial parks, export-linked FX allocation, customs and standards facilitation, and public procurement—were designed most directly for this sector, and because manufacturing is where firm-level heterogeneity and state capability are most visible (Chen, 2021a, 2025). Section "Framing the Role and Trajectories of FDI" then assesses how dominant FDI and late-industrialisation frameworks conceptualise the role, trajectories, and developmental effects of manufacturing FDI—highlighting what these approaches explain well and where they under-specify the governance of consolidation and upgrading. Section "State–Business Relations: Developmental States, Political Settlements and Deals" turns to host-country politics of implementation by reviewing work on developmental states, political settlements, and state–business relations, foregrounding how policy tools operate in practice through discretion, enforcement, and bargaining. Throughout, the review keeps manufacturing at the centre because Ethiopia's policy tools—industrial parks, export-linked FX allocation, customs and standards facilitation, and public procurement—were designed most directly for this sector, and because manufacturing is where firm-level heterogeneity and state capability are most visible (Chen, 2021a, 2025).

Existing Literature on Chinese OFDI in Africa

A first strand argues that Chinese OFDI has been concentrated primarily in mining, natural resources, and construction, and is largely driven by resource-seeking and strategic asset–seeking motives (Wang, 2014; Ross, 2015; Broadman, 2007). This literature foregrounds SOE-led extraction and infrastructure—oil, hydropower, and transport—financed by policy banks and embedded in state-to-state agreements. It captures what is most visible in resource-rich or infrastructure-intensive African economies—Angola's oil-backed projects, Zambia's Copperbelt, Nigeria's power and transport sectors, and Ethiopia's corridor investments such as the Addis Ababa–Djibouti standard gauge railway and the Addis Ababa Light Rail, alongside expressways and transmission lines—but it overlooks the parallel expansion of greenfield manufacturing, telecommunications, wholesale and retail, agribusiness, and services. This omission matters because these sectors generate a large share of employment, domestic linkages, and capability building, and they engage host-country industrial policy tools in ways that differ fundamentally from large Engineering, Procurement, and Construction (EPC) projects.

Much of this early literature also treats SOEs—and a few large private "national champions" such as Huawei, Transsion, and Haier—as the primary outward investors (Lee, 2017; Wang, 2014) and thus reads Chinese OFDI as largely state-driven or politically-connected (Morck et al., 2008; Cheng & Ma, 2010). Firms are depicted as leveraging home country advantages—finance, diplomatic backing, institutional support—to secure market access and crowd out local competitors (Rugman & Li, 2007; Rui & Yip, 2008; Fu et al., 2020; Lo, 2018; Nicolas, 2017; Qu, 2014). While this captures part of the picture, such generalisations are empirically incomplete, as they rely on aggregate OFDI stock data dominated by a few state-led projects. They miss the more dispersed set of privately financed manufacturing and service firms operating outside state-backed financing arrangements and largely absent from official statistics (Chen, 2021a, 2025).

A growing disaggregated literature demonstrates that sector, ownership, and firm size profoundly influence investment dynamics (Shen, 2015; Gu, 2011; Sun et al., 2017; Sanfilippo, 2010; Calabrese & Tang, 2023). Two clarifications follow.

First, what we count matters. SOEs dominate by investment value in capital-intensive sectors, but large numbers of private firms—often small or medium—operate in labour-intensive manufacturing, construction materials and services (Shen, 2015; Gu, 2011). By 2016, construction and mining comprised 28.3 % and 26 % of recorded Chinese OFDI stock in Africa, while manufacturing and finance represented 12.8 % and 11.4 % (Lo, 2018, p. 6). These figures reflect sectoral capital intensity rather than the absence of private capital. When counting firms rather than stock values, roughly 90 % of Chinese firms in Africa are private (Sun et al. 2017 cited in Chen, 2021a). Because manufacturing concentrates private firms, generates extensive employment, and has been purposefully promoted by developmental states such as Ethiopia, it provides the clearest window into how Chinese private capital interacts with host-state policy regimes and institutional mechanisms to shape developmental outcomes (Chen, 2021a).

Second, "SOE" and "private" are not fixed categories governed by single logics. In practice, both span wide ranges of autonomy, financing arrangements, and political embeddedness (Gu et al., 2016). SOEs—often larger and more politically connected—may enter strategic sectors and absorb higher coordination costs, while private firms more often internationalise through entrepreneurial and business networks in search of market opportunities rather than through direct state direction (Lee, 2017; Calabrese & Tang, 2023). Within private capital there is further variation: family-run SMEs[1] reliant on *guanxi* (i.e., personalised ties of trust, reciprocity, and obligation); Original Equipment Manufacturer (OEM) exporters governed by buyer requirements and delivery schedules; diversified business groups (DBGs)[2] operating across multiple sectors; and

[1] In this book, small and medium-sized enterprises (SMEs) are defined according to China's official classification. While the IFC defines SMEs as non-subsidiary, independent firms below a country-specific employment threshold (IFC, 2010, p. 1), China's criteria differ. Following the Ministry of Industry and Information Technology (MIIT), the SME definition applied here removes total asset thresholds, sets an upper employment limit of 1000 workers, and caps annual operating revenue at RMB 400 million (MIIT, cited in IFC, 2010). Unless otherwise stated, SMEs in this book refer to firms defined under the MIIT classification.

[2] See Chap. 1, Footnote 9 for the definition of DBGs.

diaspora-linked "translocal" firms (Chen, 2025). Each subgroup faces distinct constraints and mobilises different advantages. Treating "private" as a single category obscures this heterogeneity.

Third, methodological design and the quality of evidence matter. Broad claims about labour practices have often relied on partial rapid appraisals and cross-firm comparisons that ignore sector-specific production regimes. By contrast, multi-year research conducted under the *Industrial Development, Construction and Employment in Africa* (IDCEA) project (2015–2019) compares firms operating in the same sectors and countries, subject to the same regulatory and labour-market conditions, but differing in ownership and management. This design documents substantial within-country and within-sector variation across ownership types and shows that workplace organisation and production discipline, rather than firm nationality per se, are central to explaining labour outcomes (Schaefer & Oya, 2019a, 2019b; Oya, 2019). The implication is both methodological and substantive: more rigorous, comparative, fieldwork-based research is needed to assess effects and evaluate labour outcomes with empirical credibility.

Fourth, temporality and macroeconomic context matter. The composition of Chinese OFDI has evolved alongside shifts in production costs, financial regulation, and global demand cycles. Rising wages, tighter environmental regulation, and overcapacity at home coincided with renewed industrial ambitions among African states under the BRI, producing a convergence of "push" and "pull" dynamics. Host-state policy tools—especially Ethiopia's industrial park programme, export-targeted FX allocation system, and OSS arrangements—enabled firms to embed export-oriented light manufacturing within structured policy environments. By contrast, sectors such as construction materials responded more directly to procurement rules, tariff protection, and local demand (Oqubay, 2015; Hauge & Chang, 2019). Global shocks, including the COVID-19 pandemic, freight-cost spikes, and intensified FX scarcity, reconfigured investment timing and firm strategies rather than merely "altering calculations." In Ethiopia, the suspension of AGOA privileges in 2022 reshaped incentives for export-oriented manufacturers, prompting some to pivot towards domestic markets or joint ventures, while capital-intensive firms faced prolonged liquidity and logistics pressures. These macro-conditions—including currency volatility, supply-chain disruption, and the reordering of export conditionalities—directly influenced firms' accumulation paths (Chen, 2025).

Finally, persistent data and visibility problems continue to constrain analysis. OFDI statistics combine equity, intra-firm loans and reinvested earnings, while many African registries fail to identify ultimate beneficial ownership. The blurred boundary between "state" and "private" in China—shaped by hybrid ownership and policy-bank linkages—makes simple dichotomies analytically unhelpful (Nolan, 2014; Jones & Zou, 2017). A more promising approach is to trace investment through scale, regional origin, and social background, and then link these to the host country's industrial policy tools, institutional mechanisms and negotiation interfaces (Chen, 2021a).

Overall, China cannot be analysed as a unitary actor with uniform motives. Ownership, sector, timing, scale, and organisational capabilities shape investment behaviour. Most Chinese private manufacturers are SMEs without the balance sheets or policy-bank ties of large SOEs; their strategies of accumulation and adaptation therefore differ significantly. Without disaggregation, analysis conflates state financed megaprojects with the day-to-day manufacturing operations that dominate many industrial parks. Rigorous assessment requires linking firm diversity to sectoral production regimes and tracing how different firms negotiate and adapt to host-country policy tools and institutional practices over time (Chen, 2021a, 2025; Oya, 2025).

Motives and Determinants

In broad terms, Chinese investors pursue profits and markets much like other foreign firms (Dollar, 2016; Sun, 2017; Lee, 2017). While the conventional push–pull framework remains a useful starting point, this book reformulates it through a relational-institutional lens that situates investment motives within the interaction between firm heterogeneity and the mediating role of host-country institutions. Rather than treating push and pull as static lists of drivers and determinants, the analysis emphasises how firm attributes, ownership structures, and policy interfaces jointly shape both the decision to invest and the subsequent process of adaptation (Chen, 2025; see also Chen, 2021a).

On the push side, rising wages, tighter environmental and safety enforcement, and persistent overcapacity in China have encouraged outward relocation. Many scholars have interpreted "Going Out" as what David Harvey (2001) terms a spatial fix—that is, the tendency of capital to resolve crises of over accumulation by constructing and revaluing fixed assets in new geographic spaces. In this view, capital establishes fixed infrastructures in one place to absorb surplus capacity, and when profitability declines or contradictions intensify, investment moves elsewhere to resume accumulation (Hung, 2008; Lee, 2017).

Section "Literature Review and Theoretical Perspectives" is structured around three analytical steps. It first demonstrates why Chinese outward investors cannot be treated as a single type, and why motives and ownership structures matter for host-country outcomes. It then evaluates dominant analytical frameworks in FDI and late industrialisation in light of the manufacturing cases examined in this book. Finally, it turns to implementation, examining how policy tools are delivered, negotiated, and consolidated through institutional practices and bargaining mechanisms.

Two analytical refinements follow from this relational framing. First, China's domestic political economy conditions are central to understanding the outward trajectory of its firms. While recognising China's industrial success, Hung (2008) shows that reforms also created structural over-accumulation pressures that required external outlets. As Lee (2017, p. 8) notes, "it is exactly such crises and imbalances in the domestic and global economies that drive Chinese investment to Africa and elsewhere." Manufacturers thus relocate segments of production to lower-cost sites abroad as wages rise, regulatory costs increase, and local market saturation constrains profitability (Eom, 2018; Knoerich et al., 2021).

Second, the configuration of motives and determinants diverges systematically once we distinguish between firms integrated into GPNs and those embedded primarily in local or regional markets. For GPN-IFs, the decisive motive is often network consolidation rather than short-term cost minimisation: securing access to lead buyers, reproducing documentation and quality routines, and coordinating suppliers in predictable institutional environments (Chen, 2025; Mudambi, 2008; Moghaddam et al., 2014). By contrast, market-embedded firms are driven by opportunities in domestic and regional markets discovered through diaspora and business networks, where guanxi and relational brokerage are crucial in navigating permits, utilities, customs, and tax administration (Song, 2011; Ado, 2020; Chen, 2025). Ethiopia illustrates both patterns under a single policy regime: park-based exporters operate under buyer-audited systems with export-linked foreign-exchange allocation, while building materials producers and light manufacturers serve domestic and the Common

Market for Eastern and Southern Africa (COMESA) markets[3] through locally embedded networks (Chen, 2025).

The international business literature identifies multiple determinants—political risk, cultural proximity, policy liberalisation, exchange rates, inflation, and distance (Buckley et al., 2017; Du & Zhang, 2017; Wang et al., 2015)—but these remain abstract until specified by sector and firm type. Over the past two decades, the landscape has changed with the rise of emerging-market multinationals (EM-MNEs). Existing theories built around mature Organisation for Economic Co-operation and Development (OECD)-based transnational corporations (TNCs) are not sufficient to explain the motives and constraints of newer investors whose ownership advantages are weaker and whose state–firm relations differ (Buckley & Hashai, 2014 cited in X. Fu et al., 2020, p. 1). X. Fu et al. (2020) highlight two differences: EM-MNEs often lack strong proprietary assets, and the state frequently incentivises or facilitates outward moves (Buckley & Hashai, 2014; Narula & Dunning, 2010; X. Fu et al., 2020). This does not make investment state-directed in any simple sense; rather, it means the pathways and supports through which firms go abroad differ. EM-MNEs bring other advantages—flexibility, the capacity to strike pragmatic bargains with host states and experience accumulated in home-market upgrading (Guillén & García-Canal, 2009).

This argument aligns with evidence on South–South FDI, where ownership advantages are relative rather than absolute. As X. Fu et al. (2020, p. 1) note, "it is the gap-filling compatibilities between investors and host economies that determine the developmental impact of FDI." Because the technological and organisational distance between Chinese and African firms is narrower than that between OECD and African counterparts, Chinese investors can operate in more institutionally imperfect settings and sustain longer horizons (Hu et al., 2021). Hence, within the same country, export-oriented factories governed by buyer standards coexist with production facilities focused on domestic markets where local supply remains insufficient.

Ethiopia's industrial experience illustrates how policy tools translate these general drivers into specific outcomes. The combination of export-linked FX allocation, coordinated OSS facilitation by the EIC and Industrial Parks Development Corporation (IPDC), and, later, the

[3] COMESA refers to the Common Market for Eastern and Southern Africa, a regional economic bloc comprising 21 member states. See https://www.comesa.int/

Home-Grown Economic Reform (HGER) programme created differentiated opportunities for firms according to their market orientation and capabilities. These policy tools mediated generic push–pull factors through a distinct developmental-state apparatus, producing divergent accumulation paths between export-integrated and market-embedded investors.

Firm's Internationalisation

Much of the China–Africa investment literature begins with national strategy and macro finance, and then treats firms as mere conduits of state objectives. This framing obscures the extent to which manufacturing outcomes hinge on how firms are organised, what capabilities they possess, and the constraints they face—particularly when investment must be sustained through routine regulatory encounters and persistent operational bottlenecks. For this reason, an account of "China in Africa" that speaks to manufacturing must begin with heterogeneous firms and their embeddedness within both home- and host-country institutional environments.

When we look at how Chinese private investors actually entered African markets, linear, stepwise trajectories travel badly. Few private firms followed gradualist models; most relied on informal institutions—above all *guanxi*—to get in (Song, 2011). At early stages these ties are typically the entrepreneur's own networks—clients, relatives, and same-origin contacts Song (2011); Luo (1997, 2007)—extended through legacies of foreign-aid projects, ethnic connections and family links.

Ado (2020, p. 86) makes a similar point about China–Africa engagement under the BRI: informal institutions continue to matter in practice. Entrepreneurship itself can function as an ownership advantage (Song, 2011), and initial investments are often triggered through word-of-mouth networks (***koukou xiangchuan***). However, these social resources are not sufficient to consolidate investment into stable production and ongoing operations. As Liu et al. (2008) note, firms must overcome "bounded drawbacks"—including uneven international experience and constraints generated by China's own institutions—if entry is to translate into sustained operations. This book therefore traces how firms attempt to address these constraints: aligning with buyers, recruiting experienced managers, training and retaining workers, and engaging Ethiopian state agencies through OSS arrangements, facilitated customs clearance mechanisms, sub-national administrative offices, and sectoral regulators, using a combination of formal procedures and relational problem-solving.

This points to a broader implication: entrepreneurship and *guanxi* should be analysed in relation to policy and institutional settings rather than treated as fixed cultural drivers. Rational choices are shaped by government policies, institutional arrangements and prevailing ideologies (Dobbin et al., 2007). Following Chang (2007, pp. 198–202), culture matters but its effects are mediated by institutions and policy: the same reliance on personal ties produces different outcomes depending on industrial park regimes and OSS delivery, labour inspection credibility, customs and tax routines, and managerial choices in production and HR. A multilayered analysis is therefore required: micro-level firm behaviour and strategy; meso-level sectoral conditions—production regimes, positions in global or domestic networks, buyer governance, and upstream inputs (power, logistics and FX); and macro-level industrial policy, institutional practice (e.g., export target instruments) and the politics of implementation. Linking these levels is necessary to account for divergent accumulation trajectories: some firms enter through aid-related facilitation legacies or buyer-led sourcing networks and consolidate, while others enter domestic markets but—facing unreliable electricity, binding FX constraints, and limited facilitation/aftercare—scale back or exit (e.g., Song, 2011; Oqubay, 2015; Whittaker et al., 2020; see also Chen, 2021a).

The crucial question is not only why firms invest but how they consolidate, adapt, and expand once in place. Explaining divergence requires a relational, processual, and path-dependent explanation: early deals, initial finance, buyer access, and first interactions with state agencies set trajectories that are hard to roll back. Following Lee's "three moments of capital"—accumulation, production, and managerial ethos—helps to trace this as a process rather than a discrete event and to connect firm choices to the politics and institutions they meet on the ground (Lee, 2017). Chen (2021a) uses this lens but pushes it further, showing how Ethiopia's policy tools and bargaining mechanisms jointly shape firm trajectories, and where Lee's distinctions travel well—and where they need qualification in specific sectors such as the LM industry.

Many analyses retain a methodological nationalism, treating the "Chinese state" and the "host state" as coherent actors and explaining outcomes through bilateral bargaining. While this approach can capture high-level deal-making, it provides a weak guide to the governance of manufacturing investment, where decision-making is dispersed across agencies and levels of government and where outcomes are shaped by routine enforcement practices, interpretive discretion, and pragmatic problem-solving in implementation.

Understanding the entire investment trajectory requires attention to firms' interactions with multiple state and non-state actors across different levels. As Lee (2017) argues, approaches that stay at the level of "varieties of capitalism" or "capitalism in China" tend to miss this eventful nature of accumulation and the primacy of politics in shaping capacity, interests, and impact.[4] In African settings, Chinese firms operate under the social and political economy conditions they find, and outcomes turn on how they bargain within those conditions. Capturing this relationality across the entire trajectory is central to the analysis that follows.[5]

Lee criticises analyses that stop at the national level and overlook how accumulation becomes political and contingent in host-country settings. The Ethiopian cases support this claim and add two refinements. First, reciprocal control mechanisms (RCMs)—notably export-linked policy tools associated with FX allocation and industrial park facilitation—discipline firms unevenly. Producers operating outside industrial parks faced a different configuration of constraints and enforcement practices than exporters located within parks. Second, shocks shift policy priorities and reconfigure the same mechanisms. COVID-19, conflict-related disruptions along corridors, and the suspension of AGOA did not only raise costs but also reshaped enforcement practices and regulatory tolerance (e.g., temporary relaxation of export conditionalities, permitted domestic sales, and shifts towards joint ventures or more capital-intensive production lines) (Chen, 2025). Together, these adjustments blur any clear-cut separation between "commercial" and "political" logics.

More recent work moves beyond treating China as a monolithic actor by tracing variation across ownership structures, financing channels, and

[4] The "Capitalism in China" literature draws primarily on economic geography and is rooted in Marxist and world-systems traditions. It treats Chinese development as shaped by processes of combined and uneven development, and foregrounds accumulation, class, crisis, contradiction, and conflict rather than institutional complementarity or equilibrium (Lee, 2017, p. 8). As Lee also recalls, drawing on Max Weber, capitalist action cannot be reduced to profit maximisation alone: "If capitalism is the pursuit of rational economic action, then profit making is just one kind of utility" (Lee, 2017, p. 12). In a similar vein, Swedberg emphasises that economic life is fundamentally about the identification, appropriation, and—where possible—the monopolisation of opportunities (Swedberg, cited in Lee, 2017).

[5] "An eventful approach to capitalism recognises the dialectical relationship between capitalism's self-reinforcing, abstract, expansive logic and its hyper eventful history" (Lee, 2017, p. 10).

political connections. However, it still often treats investor attributes as fixed "home country effects" and underplays how firms' strategies and constraints evolve once they enter specific host-country institutional environments and encounter concrete policy tools, implementation routines, and bargaining interfaces.

Another related strand of research foregrounds production networks, showing how firms' positions within supply chains—and their ties to lead firms, standards regimes, and finance—shape both their incentives and their capacity to comply with export disciplines. This perspective is particularly relevant for export-oriented manufacturing, where the credibility of host-country policy tools interacts with external market discipline to shape investment trajectories.

Lee's spectrum—from collective asceticism ("eating bitterness," *chi ku*) to looser forms of paternalism—helps to interpret authority and reciprocity in the workplace. Where managers emphasise sacrifice and long working hours, discipline tends to be tight, and remuneration leans towards basic wages supplemented by extended overtime. Where paternalism prevails, small benefits and informal understandings play a greater role. Schaefer and Oya (2019a) caution against reading "work culture clashes" through nationality; instead, outcomes are shaped by production regimes, sectoral requirements, market positioning, and enforcement contexts (see also Sun, 2017, pp. 52–55, cited in Oya, 2019, p. 26). In the Ethiopian cases, differences in market position and enforcement practices explain variation in turnover, training, and wage structures more convincingly than ownership categories alone.

Profit optimisation vs. profit maximisation—how far does the contrast travel? Lee's distinction is analytically sharp in Zambia's mining/construction: state capital often seeks profit optimisation (e.g., broader political or reputational payoffs) whereas global private capital pursues profit maximisation. Lee recalls Max Weber's reminder that capitalism cannot be reduced to profit alone: "If capitalism is the pursuit of rational economic action, then profit making is just one kind of utility" (Lee, 2017, p. 12). As Swedberg similarly argues, "Economic life is to a large extent about appropriating, and preferably monopolising, opportunities: opportunities for profit-making, market opportunities, and others" (Swedberg, 1998, p. 29, cited in Lee, 2017, p. 12). In this book, profit maximisation refers specifically to monetary profit-making, whether pursued in the short or long term, whereas profit optimisation extends beyond monetary returns to include non-economic utilities, such as the pursuit of social status, political influence, or formal titles. In Ethiopia's LM industry, the line blurs. Some private firms clearly prioritised short-term cash flow, while others were willing to trade off immediate monetary returns to secure strategic advantages—FX access, land allocation, reputational standing, or positioning for future contracts—consistent with an optimisation logic. Conversely, some state-linked firms operated under hard budget constraints and tight performance benchmarks. The point is not to flatten Lee's distinction, but to situate it: host-country policy design and enforcement can draw private firms towards optimisation strategies, while shocks and tightening constraints can push state-linked firms towards more narrowly commercial behaviour (Chen, 2021a).

After installation, firms confront a different set of demands: transitioning from initial production to sustained output, securing inputs under foreign-exchange constraints, managing labour turnover, complying with inspections and tax obligations, and maintaining relations with surrounding communities. Consolidation, therefore, depends on how installation and working capital are financed, how production is organised, and how reinvestment decisions are taken. Lee's distinction between profit optimisation ("encompassing accumulation") and profit maximisation helps to interpret these contested moments (Lee, 2017, pp. 10–11). In Ethiopia, however, whether value advanced is converted into expanding capital is shaped as much by customs and tax practices, labour administration, local politics, and industrial park governance as by firms' internal strategies and planning decisions.

Two implications follow for the conceptual framework. First, explanations that stop at macro "drivers" underplay how firms overcome bounded drawbacks and how they engage host-country actors over time. The empirical chapters, therefore, trace how firms translate *guanxi* and prior trading links into operational working relationships with OSS offices, subnational administrations, labour authorities, and environmental regulators; align production lines with buyer governance requirements; and coordinate domestic and export sales in line with FX regulations. Second, the production regime a firm adopts shapes turnover, training, wage structures, and ultimately reinvestment capacity or the likelihood of exit. The typology of Lüthje et al. (2013) guides concrete questions in the Ethiopian cases: do managers try to import a corporate-bureaucratic regime with stable employment and higher base pay because buyers demand it, or do they adopt flexible mass production with neo-Taylorist[6] control and long hours because the market is local and compliance is absent? These choices have direct consequences for learning, wages, and upgrading.

Finally, managerial ethos intersects with these choices without determining them. Ownership on its own tells us little about how a factory is run or how it performs. The analysis therefore returns to accumulation, production regimes, and managerial ethos—while grounding each in sectoral conditions and in the bargaining mechanisms through which firms navigate host-country policy tools in practice.

Taken together, these arguments point to a relational explanation of implementation. Industrial policy is not simply a set of written rules; it is enacted through interactions between firms and state agencies. This requires attention to three layers: the design of policy tools, how those tools operate in practice through institutional routines and discretion, and the bargaining mechanisms through which interpretation, sequencing, and exceptions are negotiated.

From this perspective, heterogeneity is not a residual variation around a representative investor. It is a core mechanism: different firms encounter the same policy tool in different ways, mobilise distinct capabilities in response, and gain or lose access through different bargaining channels. A framework that treats firms as homogeneous will therefore mis-specify both causal processes and outcomes.

Chen (2025) advances this claim by developing a refined typology of Chinese manufacturing FDI in Africa that distinguishes between "market-embedded firms" (MEFs), which rely primarily on local or regional demand, and "GPN-Ifs" (GPN-IFs), whose business models are organised around export markets and transnational buyer requirements. This distinction cannot be explained solely by ownership (state versus private) or size. MEFs may include SMEs, diaspora-linked translocal firms, OEM/ODM (Original Design Manufacturer) producers oriented to African markets, and DBGs that combine manufacturing with trading, construction, or services. GPN-IFs are also heterogeneous, ranging from labour-intensive apparel producers to more technology-intensive manufacturers

[6] Taylorism refers to "a factory management system developed in the late nineteenth century to increase efficiency by evaluating every step in a manufacturing process and breaking production down into specialised, repetitive tasks." Merriam-Webster Dictionary. Available at: https://www.merriam-webster.com/dictionary/Taylorism [last accessed 20 December 2020].

that plug into global supply chains through industrial parks and preferential trade regimes.

The typology helps to clarify why the same host-country incentive—for example, duty-free import of inputs, access to FX, or subsidised industrial land—can generate different outcomes across firms. For an MEF, the binding constraint may be purchasing power in the domestic market, procurement pipelines, or payment discipline; for a GPN-IF, the binding constraint is often the ability to meet delivery and compliance requirements under tight lead times while managing FX and logistics volatility. The same incentive can therefore function as a learning rent for one type of firm and as a subsidy for short-term rent seeking for another (Calabrese & Tang, 2022; Lee, 2017; Chen, 2025).

In this book, the MEF/GPN-IF distinction therefore functions as an analytical framework rather than a fixed classification. It provides a way to connect macro debates about "Chinese capital" to observable differences in workforce organisation, labour management, and bargaining with host-country agencies. It also bridges the international business literature on firm heterogeneity and the political economy literature on industrial policy: firms do not simply respond to incentives, but interpret, negotiate, and adapt to policy tools in ways shaped by their ownership structures, finance, capabilities, and networks.

Chinese Capital in Global Capitalism

To understand the motives and forms of these heterogeneous firms, we must situate them within the specific political economy from which they emerge—China's variegated capitalism.

Whether China's rapid economic development over the past four decades should be understood as driven by "capitalism" has been widely debated (Meyer, 2011; Peck & Zhang, 2013; Zhang & Peck, 2016; Gu et al., 2016; McNally, 2008; Ang, 2020; Kroeber, 2020; Naughton, 2021; Lardy, 2019). Meyer (2011) distinguishes "institutionalised GDP growth" from capitalism: "Capitalism seeks profits; institutionalised GDP growth seeks production, employment, and ultimately, social harmony" (pp. 1–15). For present purposes, two points are central: First, China is firmly integrated in global capitalism, but not in the mould of standard liberal or coordinated varieties. Second, differences within China—by region, sector, ownership, and social origin—are essential to explain how capital forms, accumulates, and internationalises. Hamilton's caution not to derive China from a theory of Europe and Fligstein and Zhang's insistence that each transition produces a distinct variety of capitalism remain salutary (Hamilton, 1985; Fligstein & Zhang, 2011, both cited in Peck & Zhang, 2013, p. 357). This book treats "China" not as a unitary model but as a set of evolving institutional arrangements that generate distinct fractions of capital, some of which internationalise under very different logics.

> [E]very transition to capitalism has produced a new variety of capitalism [...] China may be creating its own model of development...forging a new way to produce economic growth. (Fligstein & Zhang, 2011 pp.47, 59 cited in Peck & Zhang, 2013, p.357)

Political Capitalism and Variegated Capitalism

The varieties of capitalism (VoC) literature classically contrasts liberal market economies (LMEs) and coordinated market economies (CMEs) to explain national performance through institutional forms (Peck & Zhang, 2013, p. 357).[7] Zhang and Peck (2016, p. 53) locate China in a triangular relationship with the LME/CME poles and view it as closer to state capitalism than to market socialism.[8] Peck and Zhang (2013) state that the Chinese model is closer to state capitalism than market socialism. Building on this, I follow a "variegated capitalism" view in which national labels are unhelpful and the analytical work is done by tracing uneven, multi-scalar processes that link central guidance with provincial experimentation and firm repertoires (Peck & Theodore, 2007; Peck & Zhang, 2013; Zhang & Peck, 2016).

[7] Liberal market economies (LMEs) and coordinated market economies (CMEs) are the two ideal types formulated by Hall and Soskice (2001) to characterise how advanced economies organise production and coordination. In LMEs, such as the US and the UK, firms rely primarily on competitive market mechanisms to resolve coordination problems. By contrast, CMEs—exemplified by Germany and other northern European economies—depend more heavily on non-market forms of coordination, including employer associations, trade unions, and long-term bank–industry relationships, to sustain competitiveness and manage cooperation across firms and sectors.

[8] Market socialism refers to "the general designation for a number of models of economic systems in which, on the one hand, market mechanisms are used to distribute economic output, organise production, and allocate factor inputs, while on the other hand economic surplus accrues to society at large rather than to a class of private (capitalist) owners, through some form of collective, public, or social ownership of capital" (O'Hara, 2000, p. 71).

For analysing Chinese investment in Africa, this suggests that connectivity, standards, and data infrastructures are increasingly entangled with geopolitical risk management, complicating simple dichotomies of "state capitalism" versus "free markets."

Relatedly, Milanovic (2019) advances the notion of political capitalism—a system in which private-sector dynamism coexists with a one-party state and an activist, performance-oriented bureaucracy that rewards results rather than rules. He traces its intellectual lineage to Max Weber's concept of politically motivated capitalism[9]—"the use of political power to achieve economic gains" (cited in Milanovic, 2019, p. 91). In Milanovic's words, China's political capitalism "combines private-sector dynamism, efficient rule of bureaucracy, and a one-party political system" (p. 91); performance is tied to "the unique blend of political single-party centralisation and significant discretion regarding regional economic policies" (p. 124). In practice, this means central priorities set the horizon, while local states retain room to manoeuvre in selecting sectors, designing facilitation and sequencing enforcement.

Three features follow: an emphasis on state effectiveness, the absence of rule of law in a strict sense, and substantive autonomy for local and regional states (Milanovic, 2019, pp. 95–96). These are consistent with work that places sub-national governments at the centre of accumulation (Hung, 2008, 2016; Ang, 2018; Naughton, 2007, 2018; Dinh, 2017; Lee, 2017; Kroeber, 2016; Bramall, 2009). Since the early 1980s, the State Council designated SEZs and "open coastal cities," permitting streamlined approvals and land conversion; fiscal contracting (*fenzhao chifan* 分灶吃饭)[10] allowed localities to retain revenues while assuming expenditure responsibilities. The 1994 tax-sharing reform (*fenshuizhi*) recentralised key taxes but hardened local budget constraints and formalised sharing rules. Together, these changes entrenched decentralised experimentation and competition among jurisdictions (Wu, 2017, p. 281). Cadre-evaluation systems then tied promotion to economic performance and social stability, turning local leaders into "quasi-autonomous plenipotentiaries of the central authorities" (Milanovic, 2019, pp. 123–124). Beyond political loyalty and revenue remittance, boosting the local economy became a core

[9] Drawing on Max Weber's notion of *politically motivated capitalism* in *The Protestant Ethic and the Spirit of Capitalism*, this refers to "the use of political power to achieve economic gains" (Weber, cited in Milanovic, 2019, p. 91).

[10] The approach was first adopted by former Premier Zhu Rongji in 1980.

responsibility (Phillips and Yeh, in Cannon & Jenkins, 1990, p. 240). This "directed improvisation"[11] describes how central goals were pursued through local agency and experimentation, illustrating why national institutional coherence is a poor starting point for analysis: sub-national heterogeneity is both substantial and consequential.

This institutional configuration travels with firms. Central directives—"Going Out," the BRI, supply-side adjustment, and macro-prudential capital management—are filtered through provincial industrial agendas, local fiscal imperatives, and enforcement styles. Firms therefore learn to manage compliance strategically: sequencing requirements, anticipating inspections, and bargaining for phased solutions. The Ethiopian cases show how these practices play out in everyday operation. Investors anticipated negotiation over utilities, customs classification, and labour administration, and interpreted enforcement through relational signals and expectations formed in their home contexts (Chen, 2021a, 2021b, 2025). For this reason, a thin "state capitalism" label obscures more than it reveals: provincial and municipal states act as key intermediaries, while private entrepreneurship, family finance, and diaspora-led business networks remain central to many outward trajectories (Gu et al., 2016; Chen, 2021a).

The VoC dichotomy (LMEs versus CMEs) is therefore of limited use for China, where variegated capitalism (VC) approaches travel better because they emphasise uneven, relational, and multi-scalar processes (Peck & Theodore, 2007; Peck & Zhang, 2013; Zhang & Peck, 2016). Stylised regional "sub-models" make this concrete. In Guangdong's export-processing regime, district governments honed zone governance around buyer-disciplined OEM/ODM networks and vast dormitory labour systems; in Su'nan, local coordination of supplier upgrading, R&D, and linkages produced more formal Human Resource (HR) and quality assurance (QA) routines; in Wenzhou, family merchant capitalism relied on dense SME clusters, family finance and rapid product switching. These origins shape how firms internationalise: export-experienced OEMs tend to reproduce documentation-heavy lines and seek park-based platforms; Su'nan manufacturers align with host-country industrial policy and supplier co-location; Wenzhou-type "translocal" entrepreneurs target domestic or regional niches abroad and leverage diaspora distribution. In

[11] Ang (2015) characterises this mode of governance as "directed improvisation," referring to the coexistence of centralised direction and decentralised agency.

Ethiopia, I traced how Su'nan-type apparel and textile investors reproduced line discipline inside industrial parks, while Wenzhou-type firms in plastics, beverages, and construction materials pursued domestic markets through flexible mass production and personalised supervision (Chen, 2021a). Origins shape approaches to risk management, sector selection, and bargaining practices.

Against this background, approaches that emphasise variation and multi-scalar processes—variegated capitalism—are more suited to the Chinese case than the VoC dichotomy. VC rejects methodological nationalism, stresses path dependence and relational processes, and examines how provincial and municipal arrangements generate distinct patterns of development (Peck & Zhang, 2013; Zhang & Peck, 2016; Peck & Theodore, 2007). Guangdong's "dormitory regime in transition," Su'nan's "transnational technology complex" and Wenzhou's "Marshallian development in crisis" illustrate stylised regional paths and their GPN linkages (Zhang & Peck, 2016). These regional legacies travel with firms: they shape labour-management routines, supplier coordination, financing practices and state–business repertoires. As a result, origin-based differences influence risk appetite, sector choice and the bargaining styles that Chinese investors bring into African contexts. Table 2.1 summarises a stylised set of regionally differentiated "sub-models" and the firm characteristics they tend to generate.

Varieties of Chinese Private Capital and Capitalist Elites

Another way of dealing with the variegated nature of China's capitalism—while departing from VoC theory—is Lee's (2017) notion of varieties of capital, according to which Chinese state capital follows a combined logic of state imperatives and capital orientation. Building on this insight, this section introduces varieties of Chinese private capital and capitalist elites under China's political capitalism.

First, the notion of varieties has Marxist analytical roots. Appreciation of different fractions of capital can be traced back to Marx, who recognised internal segmentation within classes even if he did not fully systematise it. Subsequent work developed this insight. Bernstein (2007) theorises "classes of labour" as a heterogeneous social class whose interests depend on the specific class locations of distinct segments. Working in a related tradition, Knoerich et al. (2021) conceptualise fractions of capital along three dimensions that travel well to the Chinese case and to this book's typology (see Chap. 3): 1. the scale of business (ranging from corporate

Table 2.1 Selected regional "sub-models" of Chinese capitalism

Region/sub-model	*Core features of accumulation and governance*	*Labour/firm structure*	*GPN linkages and outward implications*
Guangdong ("dormitory regime in transition")	Export-oriented industrialisation anchored in coastal processing trade; strong district-level facilitation and zone governance	Large pools of migrant labour housed in dormitory systems; buyer-driven OEM/ODM firms	Deep ties to global buyers and logistics; firms carry buyer-governance routines abroad and prioritise park-based export platforms
Su'nan ("transnational technology complex")	Higher-tech manufacturing with local-state coordination of R&D, supplier upgrading and FIE linkages	Medium–large manufacturers with stronger formal HR/QA systems	Capability to plug into higher-value segments; outward moves often align with host industrial policy and supplier co-location
Wenzhou ("Marshallian development in crisis")	Dense private SME clustering, family finance and merchant networks; adaptive product switching	Small, flexible firms; personalised management and *guanxi*-based coordination	Translocal, diaspora-linked expansion; outward investment targets domestic/regional markets with fast product turnover

Source: Author, based on Zhang and Peck (2016); Peck and Zhang (2013); Chen (2021a, 2025).

groups to family firms); 2. spatial or regional origin (geographically rooted networks that shape accumulation and brokerage); 3.and the social origin of capital (prior statuses—such as landlord, peasant, merchant, or artisan—and trajectories formed through rapid social transformation).

These dimensions map onto the emerging fractions of Chinese private capital analysed here: DBGs, export-oriented GPN suppliers, family-run/owner-operated SMEs, and diaspora-linked translocals (see also Chen, 2021a, 2025).

In China, the formation of the first generation of private firms followed central endorsement of markets and active sub-national promotion of local business (Dinh, 2017, p. 154). The 1994 tax-sharing reform imposed hard budget constraints and incentivised local governments to build clusters and expand fiscal bases. Within their jurisdictions, local states became responsible for most public services and adopted targeted industrial facilitation. The result was a complex, regionally diverse ownership ecology—from cooperative and mixed-ownership vehicles to fully private firms—consistent with an enduring ownership maze (Nolan, 2014; Milanovic, 2019).

Deng Xiaoping's 1985 injunction to "let a few people get rich first" (让小部分人先富起来) legitimised private accumulation and emboldened emergent capitalists. As Milanovic (2019) argues, reforms catalysed the rise of new capitalist elites, most of whom started from scratch after 1978. This emergent capitalist class is, in his words, more a "class by itself" than a "class for itself," given the short historical horizon and evolving political–economic compact (p. 105).

Inter-firm relations in the private economy have been coordinated extensively through family and guanxi networks and patron–client ties, with weak legal enforcement and limited IP protection shaping practices—features consistent with political capitalism's emphasis on outcomes over legal formalism (Zhang & Peck, 2016, p. 61; Milanovic, 2019). The composition of China's urban elite shifted accordingly. Yang, Novokmet and Milanovic (2019) show that in 1988 workers, clerical staff and officials constituted 76.5% of the urban top 5% by income; by 2013, their share had halved, while business owners, the self-employed and professionals rose to 58.9%. This signals rapid social restructuring and consolidation of capitalist elites whose overseas investments reconfigure relations among state, capital, labour, and institutions (see also Chen, 2021a).

These dynamics motivate two empirical tasks pursued in this book: tracing the social origins and backgrounds of entrepreneurs who internationalise—including family histories, education, prior work experience, and *guanxi* networks—and examining how home-region trajectories of capital accumulation shape firms' financial arrangements, governance practices, negotiation strategies, and risk orientation (Chen, 2021a, 2025).

"Going Global" in the Context of China's Capitalism

These empirical objectives set up the next step: to examine how these heterogeneous firms "go global" in practice, and how domestic institutional contexts and state–business relations shape outward trajectories.

This diversity has direct implications for how firms interpret and respond to the host-country policy environment. Firms vary in their capacity to manage regulatory uncertainty, their ability to meet export targets, and the forms of support they seek from the state. As a result, policy tools—and how they operate in practice—can generate divergent trajectories even within the same sector and location.

SOEs internationalised earlier than private firms, with resource extraction and infrastructure contracting among the first policy-backed activities (Lee, 2017). "National champion" private firms (e.g., Huawei, Haier) were also encouraged to expand abroad. After 2008—and especially after the BRI—many private manufacturers joined. This sequenced expansion mirrors China's domestic reform approach of gradual experimentation, often captured by Deng's metaphor of "crossing the river by feeling the stones" (摸着石头过河). Allowing SOEs to move first contained systemic risk before private expansion at scale.

Crucially, centralised direction coexists with decentralised improvisation. Local leaders are evaluated on growth, employment, and stability, creating strong incentives to "pick winners" and tailor facilitation to sectoral priorities (Milanovic, 2019, pp. 123–124; Dinh, 2017, pp. 7–10). policy tools therefore differ across provinces and cities, producing push effects (e.g., relocation mandates and stricter environmental enforcement in coastal regions) and pull effects (e.g., targeted finance, land, tax, and trade facilitation) that shape who goes out, when, and how (Ang, 2018; Gu et al., 2016). Cost pressures (rising wages, compliance) matter, but sub-national policy often shapes these pressures into distinct outward paths (Chen, 2021a, 2025). To understand the motives and organisational forms of these heterogeneous firms, we must situate them within the specific political economy from which they emerge—China's variegated capitalism.

Summary

Both the Varieties of Capitalism and Variegated Capitalism literatures help explain how Chinese capital is inserted into global capitalism. For the purposes of this book, however, the most productive approach is a synthesis that draws selectively on three elements. First, the concept of political capitalism captures China's outcome-oriented model, in which state steering coexists with decentralised experimentation and sub-national improvisation. Second, an emphasis on fractions or varieties of capital allows the analysis to disaggregate who invests, with what endowments, and through which organisational, financial, and relational channels. Third, a multi-scalar perspective foregrounds the role of provincial and municipal states as key brokers, shaping both domestic accumulation processes and outward internationalisation trajectories.

Variegated capitalism captures the idea that China's economic transformation produced multiple, regionally distinct patterns of accumulation, governance, and firm organisation rather than a single "China model" (Peck & Theodore, 2007; Naughton & Tsai, 2015). These sub-models reflect differences in local state strategies, industrial structure, financing arrangements, labour regimes, and business networks. They shape which kinds of firms internationalise, how expansion is financed and governed, and how firms interact with the state domestically, and subsequently make sense of and manage state institutions abroad.

Framing the Role and Trajectories of FDI

These firm-level dynamics intersect with broader theories of FDI and late industrialisation. The following sections assess how well dominant paradigms explain the patterns observed.

These regionally specific trajectories matter because they shape what firms expect from the state, how they organise finance and labour, and how they manage risk. They also shape the relational capacities firms bring abroad: some rely on dense entrepreneurial networks and flexible subcontracting; others operate through more institutionally embedded industrial systems. This generates systematic variation among outward investors, even before they encounter host-country policy tools.

Neo-classical Economic Views

NCE generally takes an optimistic view of FDI's effects. At the macro level, FDI is a source of capital and foreign exchange that can relax balance-of-payments constraints; at the micro level, it is expected to raise productivity through technology transfer, managerial practices and organisational spillovers (Jenkins, 1987; Lo et al., 2016). Firms internalise cross-border transactions to lower uncertainty, policy frictions and contracting costs (Kindleberger, 1969; Hymer, 1960/1976; Cantwell, 2000).

Within this tradition, Dunning's eclectic paradigm remains the most widely used framework. The O–I–L scheme maps how firm-specific assets, internalisation incentives and host-country attractions combine to trigger internationalisation (Dunning, 1980; Dunning & Lundan, 2008). The framework is a useful organiser of questions, but its empirical core lies in large, mature OECD TNCs in capital- and technology-intensive sectors. It travels less well to latecomers. Sectoral features and institutional settings matter. As shown in Chen (2021a), many Chinese private investors—especially SMEs in greenfield manufacturing—do not begin with strong proprietary technology, brands, or global management systems. Their "ownership" advantages are relative and assembled in the course of operation: speed, flexible organisation, relational problem-solving, access to home-country finance and network-based brokerage (Rugman & Li, 2007; Rui & Yip, 2008; Buckley & Hashai, 2014; Fu et al., 2020). In industrial park settings, reproducible production discipline, reliable documentation and logistics execution—rather than patents or brands—often function as the practical assets that enable entry and underpin learning by doing.

In China's coastal regions, local governments pioneered market-creating policy tools—land leasing, credit intermediation, procurement, and industrial clustering—while tolerating a wide range of informal practices that reduced transaction costs for private firms. Over time, this produced distinct mixes of competition, coordination, and discipline across provinces and cities, and helped generate the organisational diversity observed among outward investors (Oi, 1999; Ang, 2016; Naughton, 2018).

Structuralist Development Economics

Structuralist approaches challenge NCE by re-centring power, market structure and distribution. Hymer's foundational thesis—developed in 1960 and published posthumously—explains why TNCs invest abroad and why they penetrate host markets more effectively than local firms: (i) to exploit firm-specific/monopolistic advantages over indigenous competitors, and (ii) to remove competition and reduce rivalry among dominant firms (Hymer, 1960/1976; Jenkins, 1987). The first point was absorbed into mainstream work (Dunnin, 1980, 1981); the second animated structuralist and industrial-organisation analyses of oligopolistic behaviour, including the "global reach" and "nationalist" strands (Barnet & Müller, 1974; Newfarmer, 1985; Lall, 1974). In this view, market "imperfections" are endogenous: they are created, nurtured, and exploited by TNCs to preserve rents (Jenkins, 1987; Cantwell, 2000). FDI is therefore not just a neutral resource flow but part of strategies to extend market power, sometimes producing enclaves and crowding out domestic capital.

Amsden's work on East Asia qualifies both the optimism and the pessimism. FDI can be catalytic where reciprocal control mechanisms—rents tied to performance—discipline investors and build domestic linkages; absent such policy tools, enclave formation and crowding out loom large

(Amsden, 1989, 2007, 2009). Ownership and sectoral structure matter. In monopolistic industries, foreign-owned enterprises (FoEs) backed by proprietary assets do not necessarily outperform or contribute more to development than leading private-owned enterprises (PoEs) from late-industrialising countries; indeed, top PoEs (e.g., Tata, Samsung) often show greater entrepreneurial dynamism at particular stages (Amsden, 2009, pp. 1–2). The danger is clear: promising PoEs can be displaced by FoEs before they accumulate capabilities, unless sticks-and-carrots push spillovers, localisation, and upgrading. It is also risky for a PoE to confront a dominant FoE backed by the host state without protective sequencing and learning rents (Amsden, 2009).

South–South flows complicate the standard structuralist template. When both origin and host are developing economies, technology, organisational routines and market knowledge are often closer; diffusion through everyday production becomes easier and tolerance for institutional imperfections higher (Hu et al., 2021). This helps explain why, in Africa, many Chinese manufacturers—especially in light industry and building materials—can engage productively despite thin local systems, provided that host policy reduces coordination failures and aligns incentives.

A recurrent limitation in much structuralist writing—with important exceptions, most notably Amsden—is the tendency to treat late-developing states as homogeneous and weak. This perspective under-theorises the politics of implementation and the policy tools through which governments manage rents. Evidence contradicts this. Purposeful mechanisms—skills covenants, localisation targets, coordinated customs facilitation, SS—can be built and enforced to varying degrees (Eom, 2018). Ethiopia's industrial-park regime, export-target/FX-allocation bundles, and customs/standards facilitation are concrete examples of reciprocal controls that selected, disciplined, and supported investors in practice, even if implementation remained uneven (Oqubay, 2015; Hauge & Chang, 2019; Chen, 2021a).

At the same time, changes in the organisation of international production temper simple monopoly narratives. Global production networks and modularisation have increased organisational variety and flexibility, yet buyer power persists in specific chains (textiles/apparel), where concentrated retailers and first-tier transnational producers impose standards, documentation, and delivery discipline, generating a supplier squeeze downstream. Structuralist concerns about asymmetry and control thus retain traction but must be applied with sectoral nuance and paired with analysis of host-state capability.

For Ethiopia, this implies that "Chinese investors" arrive with diverse organisational forms and expectations shaped by different region-specific trajectories from the home country. Those differences influence how firms engage Ethiopia's policy tools (e.g., industrial parks, OSS arrangements, export incentives, FX allocation rules), what kinds of problems they escalate, and which bargaining mechanisms they use to seek solutions. They also shape how firms cope when policy tools in practice become less predictable under macroeconomic stress.

Radical Political Economy and Dependency Theory

Radical political economy, often in conversation with dependency theory, offers a more pessimistic but enduringly influential assessment of FDI's developmental impact. Both traditions emerged as reactions to the optimistic tone of neo-classical economics, arguing that outward and inward FDI alike reproduce hierarchical structures of accumulation between core and periphery. In the classical dependency view, FDI causes "crowding out" of local enterprises, widening inequality, and fostering what Amin (1977) termed the "blocking of development," or what Frank (1980) called the "development of underdevelopment." Jenkins (1987) added that these processes are reinforced through labour-process degradation, or de-skilling, as capital seeks control and predictability over production.

Within this framework, the NIDL remains a key theoretical pillar. Developed by Fröbel et al. (1980), it explains the expansion of industrial production in developing countries through the geographical relocation of low-value manufacturing. Distinct from the "old" imperial division of labour—concerned with the exchange of raw materials for finished goods—the NIDL focuses on the creation of overseas production bases by TNCs from advanced economies. Two assumptions underpin this logic: first, the Lewisian notion of an unlimited supply of labour in the global periphery; second, the Babbage principle as reinterpreted by Hymer, which emphasises the intra-firm division of labour to secure efficiency and control (Lo, 2012, p. 18). The consequence is a pattern of international specialisation in low-value-added activities, sustaining structural dependency on imported technology, management, and capital.

Chinese investment has also been interpreted through dependency and structuralist lenses that emphasise unequal exchange, enclave development, and the risk of reinforcing commodity dependence (Amin, 1976;

Arrighi, 2007; Harvey, 2003). These critiques highlight real power asymmetries, but they often treat "capital" as homogeneous and pay limited attention to how firm organisation, sectoral dynamics, and host-country governance shape outcomes in manufacturing.

A manufacturing-centred analysis requires a more fine-grained account of both investors and host states. It asks how different firms respond to the same policy tools and constraints, and how the state's ability to implement, enforce, and adapt those tools shapes whether investment translates into sustained production, learning, and exports.

A third qualification comes from market-seeking motives. The NIDL framework tends to assume cost-driven relocation, but evidence from Chinese FDI shows that profit and market expansion, not merely wage arbitrage, shape investment decisions. In Ethiopia, for instance, export-oriented apparel conforms to NIDL logic through its reliance on cheap, disciplined labour, while cement, steel, and pharmaceuticals are driven by domestic demand, procurement rules and tariff protection, aligning more with state-mediated market opportunities (Oqubay, 2015; Hauge & Chang, 2019).

In the African context, radical political economy helps unpack the unequal integration of developing economies into global production, but its structural determinism requires adaptation. South–South investment—notably Chinese manufacturing FDI—challenges the binary of exploitative "core" and dependent "periphery." As Lo (2012) argues, the core analytical issue is not cheap labour per se but the configuration of labour and capital under the logic of profit maximisation. Where technological gaps between home and host economies are narrower, as in much of Chinese FDI in Africa, capital accumulation can be more reciprocal, and learning effects more attainable (Hu et al., 2021).

The OLI paradigm remains a useful starting point because it focuses attention on ownership advantages, location conditions, and internalisation choices (Dunning, 1980; Dunning & Lundan, 2008). However, for late industrialisers and manufacturing FDI, "location" is not only factor endowments or market size. It also includes the credibility of policy tools, the predictability of enforcement, and the bargaining interfaces through which firms secure clearances, exceptions, and problem-solving support.

In sum, while early dependency theory overemphasised structural inevitability and underplayed state agency, its critique of unequal exchange and labour-process subordination remains relevant. When situated in contemporary production networks, these insights invite closer scrutiny of how FDI reproduces or transforms dependency through sectoral differentiation, reciprocal control mechanisms and the strategic choices of developmental states.

Global Value Chains and Global Production Networks

As international production fragmented, the GVCs/GPNs literature brought governance and spatial organisation to the centre (Henderson et al., 2001; Coe et al., 2004; Gereffi, 2018; Escaith, 2014). In buyer-driven chains, concentrated lead firms set product, process and compliance standards and shift risks downstream to suppliers; prospects for upgrading depend on chain architecture, the strategies of transnational producers, and the institutional context of entrant sites (Gereffi, 1999; Kaplinsky & Morris, 2001; Gibbon, 2008; Azmeh & Nadvi, 2014). In apparel, retail consolidation plus production dispersion generated a supplier squeeze: higher entry requirements and risk-bearing under stable or falling prices (Whittaker et al., 2020). Since the 1990s, first-tier East Asian suppliers have upgraded and mediated triangular manufacturing that channels new locations into established buyer networks (Gereffi, 1999). Ethiopia's emergence reflects this buyer–supplier dynamic combined with proactive industrial policy and preferential market access (Brautigam et al. 2018; Staritz et al., 2016; 2019; Gebreeyesus, 2014; Oqubay, 2015).

Two clarifications refine how this lens travels to latecomer sites. First, GVCs and GPNs are complementary but not identical. GVCs emphasise value capture along vertically segmented tasks and governance types; GPNs foreground relational, multi-scalar coordination among firm and non-firm actors, including states, zones, and finance (Henderson et al., 2001; Coe et al., 2004). This shift matters in Ethiopia, where park authorities, customs, labour inspectorates and export FX policy tools are integral nodes in production networks rather than mere "context." Second, localisation benefits are conditional: they hinge on the type of buyers and transnational producers engaged, their embeddedness, the capabilities of local firms, and the design and enforcement of industrial policy (Whitfield et al., 2020; Yeung, 2016).

Building on strategic coupling (Yeung, 2016), regional economies must align their assets, institutions, and coalitions with lead-firm requirements to enter and remain in GPNs. This logic extends beyond tradables to infrastructure investment: mega-projects require temporary coalitions across central and regional governments, park developers, policy banks, EPC contractors and regulators to make territories investible and to manage construction risk, land, permits, and community relations (Dawley et al. 2019; Phelps & Wood, 2006; Kleibert, 2014). In Ethiopia, anchor-tenant strategies in parks (e.g., brand-led clusters), "green-channel" customs routines, and export-linked FX allocation exemplify coupling devices that translate generic locational advantages into operational reliability (Brautigam et al. 2018; Staritz et al., 2016; Oqubay, 2015).

Recent work adds geopolitical stress to the strategic coupling framework. Trade–security agendas increasingly trigger decoupling/recoupling and friend-shoring, while investment-screening and due-diligence requirements layer security logics onto investment selection (Kalvelage & Tups, 2024). These screening and sorting mechanisms are formalised at the level of states, but they are implemented and negotiated in specific places—city-regions, ports, industrial zones and parks—where coalitions assemble assets and bargain over compliance. The result is a mix of "hard" de-risking (legal screening, sanctions) and "soft" de-risking (procurement preferences, due-diligence standards) that can reshape where and how GPNs land (Schaefer et al., forthcoming).

The GPN literature also treats the state as more than passive "context." On the host side, central agencies act as pivots that refract global pressures through procurement rules, tariff schedules, FX allocation and park regimes; regional administrations supply last-mile facilitation or—under political contestation—become bottlenecks (Henderson et al., 2001; Yeung, 2016). On the home side, Chinese outward investment highlights state orchestration via policy banks, export credits and BRI platforms, while scholarship on state fragmentation cautions against reading "China" as a monolith; incentives, supervision, and autonomy vary across ministries, provinces and SOE groups (Jones & Hameiri, 2021; Gambino & Franceschini, 2025; Lim, 2025). Western home states, by contrast, wield weaker levers over private lead firms, which conditions their ability to direct geopolitically desirable siting (Raco et al., 2023).

Two implications follow for this book's approach. First, GVCs/GPNs frames are necessary but insufficient without a firm-type and institutional decomposition. In Ethiopia, GPN-integrated exporters couple through lead-firm oversight, logistics discipline and park routines; market-embedded producers couple through domestic demand, procurement cycles and tariff structures (Chen, 2025). The same state deploys reciprocal control mechanisms—export-target-linked FX, OSS arrangements, "green-channel" customs—that select and discipline these firm types differently (Oqubay, 2015; Staritz et al. 2019; Chen, 2021a). Second, coupling is eventful and reversible: shocks such as Covid-19, corridor disruptions or AGOA suspension reorder priorities, loosen export conditionality and shift sales towards domestic markets, prompting joint ventures or more capital-intensive pivots among some firms while others exit.

In sum, GVCs/GPNs perspectives explain who governs, how risks are allocated, and where value is captured. Read with strategic coupling, geopolitical de-risking, and a granular view of host- and home-state roles, they provide a workable scaffold for analysing Ethiopia's manufacturing FDI. The empirical chapters, therefore, combine GPNs logics with a relational-institutional account of state–business bargaining to track how firm variety, sector conditions and policy tools co-determine entry, consolidation, and outcomes.

Summary

Global production network perspectives add two further insights. First, firms' network positions shape the forms of discipline they face (e.g., standards, delivery schedules, oversight by lead firms) and the resources they can mobilise (e.g., finance, know-how, supplier access) (Gereffi, 1994; Coe & Yeung, 2015). Second, because value chains are governed through lead-firm strategies and regulatory regimes, the same host policy tool can have different effects depending on whether firms are embedded in export networks or primarily serve domestic markets.

Structuralist analysis recentres market power, rents, and distribution. It travels to Ethiopia when read with sectoral nuance and reciprocal control mechanisms: enclave risks in buyer-driven chains are real, yet targeted policy tools can discipline investors and build linkages. Radical/dependency insights keep unequal exchange, labour-process control and the NIDL in view, but must be shaped by South–South specificities and market-seeking dynamics evident in domestic-market industries such as cement, steel, and pharmaceuticals.

GVCs/GPNs perspectives explain who governs, how risk is allocated and where value is captured. For latecomers, their payoff rises when combined with (i) a firm-type decomposition—distinguishing GPN-integrated exporters from market-embedded producers—and (ii) a relational-institutional analysis of policy implementation. Strategic coupling clarifies how regional assets, institutions, and coalitions are aligned to lead firm requirements; it also travels to infrastructure via temporary coalitions among central and regional states, policy banks, developers, and EPC contractors. Recent geopolitical de-risking/friend-shoring pressures reframe admissible couplings and require tracking both host-end and home-end state roles.

Second, the analysis traces processes (i.e., mechanisms) and trajectories (i.e., outcomes over time) rather than discrete events. It follows accumulation from installation through consolidation to reinvestment or exit, showing how early deals, working-capital arrangements, buyer access, and initial interactions with state agencies generate path-dependent outcomes over time.

Third, the book embeds policy tools in the analysis of firm behaviour. It examines how Ethiopia's industrial parks, export-linked FX allocation, OSS arrangements, customs "green channels," procurement rules, and localisation requirements select, discipline, and support different types of firms, and how shocks—such as COVID-19, corridor disruptions, and the suspension of AGOA—reconfigure these same mechanisms.

Fourth, the study links shop-floor regimes to policy implementation. It connects production regimes and managerial ethos to sectoral requirements and enforcement practices in order to explain variation in labour turnover, training, wage structures, and reinvestment decisions.

Read together, these strands provide the analytical scaffold for the empirical chapters: a disaggregated, relational-institutional analysis that explains entry, consolidation, and outcomes for Chinese private manufacturing FDI in Ethiopia across both export-oriented and domestic-market trajectories.

State–Business Relations: Developmental States, Political Settlements, and Deals

Ultimately, these firm-level strategies and macro-level policy and institutions play out in concrete arenas of negotiation. A final lens—focusing on state–business relations and political settlements—is therefore essential to understand implementation.

Recent work on Africa–China engagements emphasises that industrialisation outcomes depend on policy agency, bargaining, and contestation, not simply on the nationality of capital (Oya, 2025). This makes SBRs a core analytic lens for unpacking how Chinese firms operate in African political economy.

Industrial Policy and Developmental States

The operations of Chinese private firms in Africa are inseparable from how they bargain with host states and, to a lesser degree, with Chinese state institutions. SBRs can cover the whole economy or target specific sectors, types of firms or policy processes. In some situations they involve highly organised relationships, in others they are loose relationships between the state and business' (te Velde, 2013, p. 9). SBRs therefore sit at the core of the explanatory framework in this book. They illuminate why similar policy tools yield different outcomes across sectors, firms, and moments, and why the same investor can face different "institutional practices" across sites. In what follows, I integrate insights from the developmental state/industrial policy (DS/IP) literature with political-settlements (PS) and deals perspectives and link them to evidence on Chinese private manufacturing in Ethiopia drawn from my previous work (Chen, 2021a, 2021b) and the empirical chapters of this book.

In late-industrialising settings, industrial policy aims to accelerate structural change by moving labour into higher-productivity activities and by building firm-level capabilities, especially in manufacturing (Page & Tarp, 2017; Hauge & Chang, 2019). The DS/IP repertoire emphasises capable bureaucracy, embedded autonomy[12] and RCMs in which support ("carrots") is tied to monitorable performance (Amsden, 1989, 2001; Evans, 1995). Ethiopia's programme of industrial parks, export promotion and OSS arrangements sits squarely in this tradition (Oqubay, 2015). In practice, however, implementation has too often leaned towards carrots without commensurate discipline, so learning and linkage effects have been weaker than intended (Hauge, 2019; Chen, 2021a, 2021b).

Policy design choices matter. The comparative advantage following (CAF) versus comparative advantage defying (CAD) debate frames priorities and sequencing differently across sectors (Lin & Chang, 2009). Apparel and footwear fit CAF logics; pharmaceuticals, machinery, or upstream chemicals require CAD-type bets. Ethiopia experimented with both: park-based apparel exporters built standardised routines quickly under buyer-governed regimes; more complex bets in building materials

[12] Peter Evans (1995). first introduced the term "embedded autonomy" when studying South Korea. It refers to a state's capacity to coordinate closely with business while retaining enough independence to discipline rent seeking; see Evans (1995). "Embedded autonomy" describes a way of attaining a balance between coordination and capture (Gisselquist, 2017, p. 82).

and pharmaceuticals depended on tariff design, procurement regimes and input localisation, with mixed consequences for linkages and learning (Oqubay, 2015; Hauge & Chang, 2019).

Where DS/IP writing is strongest on policy tools, it is thinner on the political processes through which they are bargained, coordinated, and enforced. It says relatively little about who negotiates rents, exemptions, and compliance; how monitoring is sustained or undermined inside bureaucracies; how coordination failures across agencies (investment, customs, tax, labour, utilities) reshape the effective operating rules firms face; and why similar toolkits produce divergent outcomes across places and time (Chibber, 2014; Fine & Pollen, 2018; Gisselquist, 2017). These omissions matter for Ethiopia: the same device—for example, a customs "green channel," a park one-stop or an export-linked FX allocation—worked very differently across sites depending on the credibility of follow-up, the coherence of local administration, federal–regional relations and leadership stability. In this sense, SBRs are not merely the interface where policy meets firms; they are constitutive of the policy itself (te Velde, 2013, p. 9). Evidence from Vietnam and East Asia similarly underlines that effective collaboration requires not only firm–state coordination but also coordination within the state (Vu-Thanh, 2017; Dinh, 2017).

Ethiopian experience also Thanh highlights a second point developed in Chen (2025): park policy tools compress some entry frictions for GPN-integrated suppliers, but they rarely substitute for sector-specific capability building or for cross-agency coordination. Conversely, market-embedded producers oriented to domestic and regional demand depend more on procurement rules, tariff design and access to inputs and foreign exchange outside parks. In both cases, outcomes turn on how policy tools are implemented—by whom, with what follow-up—not on design alone.

Political Settlements and Deals: Holding Power and Informal Institutions

The political settlements framework addresses these blind spots by foregrounding holding power, elite bargains,[13] and the interplay of formal and informal institutions (Khan, 2010, 2018; Di John & Putzel, 2009). In

[13] Elite bargains refer to "[a] discrete agreement, or series of agreements, that explicitly sets out to re-negotiate the distribution of power and allocation of resources between elites" (Di John & Putzel, 2012, cited in Cheng et al. 2018, p. 11).

clientelist settings, enforcement is often discretionary; formal rules and outcomes diverge; and rents are allocated and policed along political lines.

Settlements are reproduced through punctuated renegotiations over offices, resources, and coercive capacities—elite bargains that cumulatively sustain or alter the overarching settlement. Institutions are thus sustained not by design alone but by the distribution of power and the rent flows that bind coalitions.

In this context, it is analytically more informative to study the deals firms actually receive than to treat formal rules as predictive (Pritchett et al., 2013; Kar et al., 2019). Deals vary in how predictable and generalised they are. Where predictability is low, firms gravitate to bespoke fixes rather than lobby for rule changes. Ang's (2020) "unbundled corruption" framework helps classify exchanges without collapsing them into a single judgement: "speed money" to move routine files; "access money" to enter exclusive opportunities; and distinct theft pathologies at petty and grand scales. Growth can coincide with corruption depending on who benefits and how exchanges are structured; the harms and benefits are unevenly distributed (Deller, 2018). The analytical point is not to normalise corruption but to specify mechanisms—how rents are created, allocated, and policed—and their consequences for learning, linkages, and re-investment.

Political settlements approaches direct attention to the distribution of power and the bargains that underpin institutional arrangements (Khan, 2010; Goodfellow, 2018). For industrial policy, the key implication is that credibility depends on enforceable commitments: whether agencies can coordinate, apply discipline, and sustain predictable rules over time. Implementation, therefore, hinges on both the broader political settlement and the state–business relations that structure bargaining mechanisms at the point of delivery—within industrial parks, OSS stations, customs posts, and FX allocation routines.

Ethiopia's political settlement since 1991 has combined ambitious state-led industrialisation with shifting patterns of coalition management, reform, and conflict.[14] These shifts matter because changes in political authority and fiscal–external constraints reshape which policy tools remain feasible, which implementation practices can be sustained, and which bargains between firms and state agencies endure over time. To render these

[14] Ethiopia's political trajectory is "relatively tight with authoritarian control by a dominant party" (Matfess, 2015, cited in Goodfellow, 2018, p. 215).

dynamics empirically observable, the analysis focuses on three questions: whether agencies can coordinate and deliver core services and clearances (including permits, customs, utilities, and logistics); whether policy commitments are reliable and predictable over time—particularly access to incentives, foreign exchange, and export facilitation—or are frequently revised and unevenly applied; and whether firms and agencies possess effective bargaining mechanisms to negotiate interpretation, sequencing, and exceptions without undermining discipline.

Two implications follow. First, policy tools must be analysed in relation to political settlements: reciprocal control mechanisms operate as intended only where monitoring coalitions have both the authority and the incentives to enforce them. Without such alignment, incentives risk becoming open-ended transfers, one-stop services may turn into new chokepoints, and sectoral strategies remain largely declarative. Second, firm types must be treated relationally. Different fractions of Chinese private capital—varying in scale, origin, and social endowments—bring distinct practices into bargaining practices. Family-run SMEs embedded in merchant networks bargain differently from mid-tier suppliers integrated into buyer-governed chains, and both differ from large group companies with provincial backing. As shown in my earlier work, these differences map onto Ethiopia's institutional interfaces in systematic ways, shaping installation processes, production models, and reinvestment trajectories (Chen, 2021a, 2025).

Relational Power and Mediated Bargaining

The DS and PS literatures emphasise that industrial policy success depends on the ability of state actors to discipline capital and coordinate across agencies. Yet they often under-specify how power is exercised through the everyday interactions in which rules are interpreted, contested, and enforced. Building on Allen's work, this book treats power not as a possession or a simple "capacity," but as something that becomes consequential through relationships and institutional mediation (Allen, 2003, 2004). On this view, what matters is not only the formal authority or resources an agency holds formally, but how authority, coercion, persuasion, and other modalities are deployed in particular sites and moments.

For Pritchett et al. (2013), "deals" are inseparable from institutions: they are negotiated channels through which actors access rents, manage risk, and coordinate investment. For manufacturing FDI, the practical question is how such deals interact with formal policy tools, and whether they reinforce credible discipline or instead generate ad hoc exemptions that erode predictability.

Actors with different structural positions and resources can shape rules, enforce them unevenly, and secure exceptions. These mechanisms are central to explaining why similar policy tools produce different outcomes across firms and sectors (Allen, 2018).

Mohan et al. (2025) develop this relational approach in the context of Chinese overseas investment, arguing that outcomes depend on mediated interactions among Chinese firms, host-state actors, and other intermediaries rather than on a straightforward projection of state strategy. Although their cases concern European port investments, the conceptual point travels: Chinese capital—like other cross-border investment—is shaped through domestic political economies and institutional contexts. Apparent "leverage" is therefore an empirical outcome of bargaining, accommodation, and resistance, not an assumption.

For manufacturing investment, the relevant points of contact are often located in everyday administrative and regulatory settings—industrial-park administrations, customs posts, tax offices, local labour authorities, and public procurement bodies. Within these settings, state authority may be exercised through licensing, inspections, and sanctions; through facilitation and selective problem-solving; and through informal arrangements or uneven enforcement. Firms, in turn, mobilise their own relational resources—business associations, diaspora brokers, and group-level finance—to manage uncertainty and contest unfavourable decisions. Treating these encounters as sites of relational power complements, rather than replaces, the focus on political settlements: it links macro configurations of authority to micro-level implementation and helps explain why similar policy blueprints can generate divergent investment trajectories.

Summary

The DS/IP literature specifies what states can do and why sectoral strategies must differ. But it under-specifies how, by whom, and for whose benefit these policy tools are bargained and enforced. Political settlements and deals perspectives supply that missing political content by tying policy tools to holding power, elite bargains and informal institutions, and by directing attention to the actual deals firms receive. Read together, these approaches provide a multi-layered frame for Ethiopia: sectors differ in feasible production regimes; agencies differ in coordination capacity; and shifting settlements at national, regional, and local levels shape whether

Chinese investors encounter consistent enforcement and reliable facilitation or more shifting, case-by-case practice. The empirical chapters operationalise this lens, comparing GPN-integrated and market-embedded firms as they work through parks, procurement channels, and FX constraints under evolving settlements, and tracing how these configurations shape installation, production choices, and decisions to re-invest or withdraw.

Conceptual Framework

This chapter develops the analytical framework for explaining variations in outcomes among Chinese manufacturing investors in Africa. It links firm heterogeneity to policy tools in use through the lens of SBR, drawing on a relational and process-oriented approach that follows firms over time as they interact with institutional mechanisms and political settlements in Ethiopia. The framework rests on the idea that both firms and states are heterogeneous, adaptive, and relationally embedded. Outcomes are therefore not determined by nationality or sector alone, but by the intersection between firm attributes, host-country institutions, and the bargains that emerge at their interface. Linking lenses to mechanisms. For later examination, I treat three mechanisms as central: (i) GVCS under lead firm governance selects for park siting and standardised production systems with formal quality controls; (ii) procurement-centred demand and tariff schedules select for domestic-market producers with flexible mass production; (iii) RCMs only bind where sanctions are credible and cross-agency coordination is stable.

The analysis adopts a relational-institutional approach, recognising that the behaviour of Chinese investors cannot be explained through static notions of "China" or "Africa." Instead, it focuses on how policy tools—industrial parks, OSS arrangements, export-linked FX allocation, customs and standards regimes, procurement rules, and tariff schedules—function in practice as institutional bargaining mechanisms. These mechanisms are implemented through a series of formal and informal deals, whose predictability, scope, and stability vary depending on bureaucratic coherence, political settlements, and macroeconomic conditions. As such, rules on paper matter less than how they are interpreted and enforced through negotiation between firms and state agencies.

The framework distinguishes between two enduring firm orientations: GPN-IFs and MEFs. GPN-IFs invest to consolidate relationships with global buyers, reproducing quality and documentation standards in stable industrial park environments. Their aim is often to secure predictable contracts, reliable logistics, and compliance systems consistent with lead-firm monitoring. In contrast, market-embedded firms are driven primarily by local and regional demand. They operate outside export parks and depend on personal and business networks to access land, utilities, and licences, as well as to navigate customs and tax systems. MEFs are particularly exposed to fluctuations in procurement policies, tariffs, and foreign-exchange rationing. Both categories are fluid, reflecting adaptive strategies rather than fixed firm types, but they capture consistent differences in capital intensity, market orientation, and relational dependence.

Operationalising the typology. Empirically, I classify firms as GPN-IFs where more than 60% of output is under lead-firm monitoring and delivered to export markets, documentation requirements are externally defined, and access to export-linked FX is substantive. I classify firms as MEF where more than 60% of sales are domestic or regional, procurement and tariff schedules shape demand, and the firm operates outside parks (Chen, 2025). Dual-orientation groups are treated as separate firm-site pairs; when one plant serves export buyers and another serves domestic markets, the plants are coded separately. For switching cases, the coding follows the dominant governance mode in the period under analysis.

Within the broader universe of Chinese private capital, fractional diversity matters as much as the public–private divide. Chinese private capital consists of multiple fractions differentiated by scale, sectoral orientation, and social origin. Their origins in China's region-specific development models shape how they organise production, manage labour, coordinate suppliers, and negotiate with host states abroad (Zhang & Peck, 2016; Chen, 2021a). These variations travel across borders, structuring how firms bargain, mitigate risk, and build relationships in new institutional environments.

Accumulation is treated here as a process and a trajectory, rather than a discrete event. Firms are followed from opportunity discovery and decision-making through installation, production, and re-investment or withdrawal, drawing on Lee's (2017) "three moments of capital." Early deals and financing arrangements, first buyer contracts or procurement links, and initial encounters with investment or park authorities often set trajectories that are difficult to reverse. Production regimes also vary. In export parks, buyer-audited firms tend to adopt standardised production systems with formal quality controls that meet external delivery schedules.

Outside parks, domestically oriented firms typically operate under more flexible mass-production systems characterised by long working hours, personalised supervision, and rapid product switching. Managerial ethos further differentiates these operations: some managers rely on collective discipline and long overtime, while others use paternalistic systems built on informal reciprocity. Crucially, these management choices interact with the credibility of local enforcement and the structure of labour markets to shape turnover, wage structures, and training outcomes.

Ethiopia's policy tool provide a "typical case" (Seawright & Gerring, 2008) to observe these interactions. Industrial parks, OSS arrangements, export-target FX allocation, customs "green-channel" procedures, and public procurement systems were designed as reciprocal control mechanisms (Amsden, 1989, 2001) linking incentives to measurable performance. Their success, however, depends on coordination among agencies—investment, customs, tax, labour, utilities—and on credible monitoring coalitions. When institutional coherence is high, these tools select capable investors and promote learning; when coordination falters, they become fragmented or selectively enforced, weakening developmental outcomes (Oqubay, 2015; Hauge & Chang, 2019; Chen, 2021a). In practice, GPN-IFs benefit most from export-linked FX allocations and park-based facilitation, while market-embedded firms rely on domestic procurement systems, tariff protection, and access to inputs through informal or sub-national channels.

Shocks between 2020 and 2025—the COVID-19 pandemic, global freight-cost spikes, FX scarcity, and the suspension of AGOA preferences—did not simply raise costs; they reconfigured how these policy tools were applied. Export enforcement was temporarily relaxed, domestic sales allowed, and closed-loop dormitory regimes tolerated to sustain production. Procurement contracts, especially in health and defence, became stabilisers for firms that could meet qualification criteria. Meanwhile, customs valuations tightened and tax enforcement became more revenue-driven. Firms with diversified buyers or dual domestic–export strategies adapted by reallocating orders and sustaining throughput; those dependent on single markets faced severe disruptions. In all cases, resilience was negotiated: survival depended less on ownership or nationality than on the ability to mobilise relationships and rework supply chains under evolving policy conditions.

From these observations, several analytical propositions follow. First, park-based export policies tend to select and stabilise GPN-IFs, while procurement- and tariff-based systems favour market-embedded producers. Second, stability in policy tools—such as multi-year schedules for FX allocation, tariffs, and export rules—encourages re-investment, whereas abrupt changes deter it. Third, firm resilience under macro shocks increases with either diversified buyer networks or access to protected procurement channels. Fourth, localisation policies ease FX shortages but simultaneously heighten firms' exposure to local rent-seeking and environmental enforcement. Finally, the structure of production regimes—lead firm-oversight versus flexible domestic—explains variations in turnover, training, and upgrading more accurately than ownership categories.

P1: Firms' heterogeneity matters—differences in ownership, capability, and region-specific development model shape motives, operation models, and development effects.
P2: Production network position matters—firms' insertion into GPNs and exposure to external regulatory requirements condition behaviour and upgrading possibilities.
P3: Host-country policy tools operate as sorting mechanisms—the mix of incentives, discipline, and constraints channels different firms into differentiated trajectories.
P4: Implementation is mediated by state–business relations—various bargaining mechanisms within political settlements shape how policy tools are interpreted, enforced, and renegotiated.
P5: Trajectories are contingent over time—learning, shocks, and phase shifts reconfigure constraints and bargains, producing path-dependent outcomes.

In sum, this conceptual framework integrates firm diversity, sectoral regimes, and host-country policy tools into a unified analytical architecture. It retains useful insights from classical FDI theories such as OLI and staged learning, while re-specifying them for latecomer manufacturing in South–South contexts where ownership advantages are relative and often accumulated through operation. It incorporates structuralist concerns about buyer power and dependency but extends them to account for African state agency and policy experimentation. It also draws on GPN theory to trace how industrial policies, regulatory practices, and bargaining mechanisms shape developmental outcomes.

Two clarifications sharpen how this framework is used in the empirical chapters. First, the book treats "policy tools" as institutional practices: not only the formal policy or legal context, but the bundle of administrative routines, discretionary practices, and enforcement patterns through which firms experience the state. An industrial park incentive, for example, is inseparable from the functioning of OSS arrangements, the predictability of customs clearance, and the credibility of export-linked foreign exchange access. This focus on implementation is what makes it possible to analyse why policy mixes that appear similar on paper generate different outcomes across regions, sectors, and time periods.

Second, the framework is operationalised through firm-level investment trajectories traced over time. Outcomes are measured not only by entry or approval, but by survival, scale (employment and output), reinvestment, upgrading and local linkages, and the capacity to maintain production under shocks. Chapters 3, 4, and 5, therefore, combine mapping of the investor landscape with process tracing of how firms and agencies interact around specific policy tools (industrial parks, FX allocation, customs valuation, tax and labour enforcement, and procurement calendars) and how these interactions shape learning, conflict, and bargaining. The aim is to connect macro constraints to observable changes in factory routines and institutional practice.

Conclusion

This chapter has demonstrated that outcomes in Chinese manufacturing investment are produced through relational processes: heterogeneous firms enter with different motives and capabilities, occupy different positions in production networks, and confront distinct bundles of host-country policy tools in practice. Section "Conceptual Framework" distilled this logic into five propositions that structure the empirical chapters.

On the firm side, investor heterogeneity is central: GPN-integrated exporters and market-embedded producers face different constraints and opportunities, and they respond differently to discipline, learning, and risk. The former consolidates buyer relationships and upgrade through standards, speed, and process control; the latter relies more on local markets and navigate a different set of capabilities and cash-flow pressures.

On the state side, performance hinges less on announced policy and more on implementation. Policy tools shape outcomes only when enforcement is credible and bargaining mechanisms are coordinated across agencies.

Finally, trajectories are contingent over time. Shocks such as COVID-19, FX scarcity, logistics disruptions, and geopolitical tensions recalibrate policy tools and firm strategies, producing phase shifts that can lock in, redirect, or unwind earlier pathways.

This framework, grounded in the realities of manufacturing, now guides the empirical investigation of divergent Chinese firm trajectories in Ethiopia, beginning in Chap. 3 with a mapping of firm diversity and the formative logic of the MEF/GPN-IF typology.

The implications are twofold. For host governments, the priority is to build institutional capability to deploy policy tools coherently and sustain credible discipline; without this, industrial policy becomes either symbolic or selectively enforced. For firms, the analysis highlights how capability accumulation depends not only on markets and finance but also on production network position and local bargaining environments.

More broadly, the framework reinterprets classical FDI and late-industrialisation debates for contemporary manufacturing. It retains the insight that ownership and internalisation matter, but shows that trajectories in the Global South are co-produced by policy tools in practice, bargaining, and temporally shifting constraints.

References

Ado, A. (2020). Informal institutions and China's BRI in Africa. *Asia Pacific Business Review, 26*(1), 86–108.

Allen, J. (2003). *Lost geographies of power*. Blackwell Publishing.

Allen, J. (2004). The whereabouts of power: Politics, government and space. *Geografiska Annaler: Series B, Human Geography, 86*(1), 19–32.

Allen, J. (2018). The circulation of financial elites. In M. Coleman & J. Agnew (Eds.), *Handbook on the geographies of power* (pp. 178–202). Edward Elgar.

Amin, S. (1976). *Unequal development: An essay on the social formations of peripheral capitalism*. Monthly Review Press.

Amin, S. (1977). *Imperialism and unequal development*. Monthly Review Press.

Amsden, A. (1989). *Asia's next giant*. Oxford University Press.

Amsden, A. (2007). *Escape from empire*. MIT Press.

Amsden, A. (2009). *The rise of "the rest"*. Oxford University Press.

Amsden, A. H. (2001). *The rise of "The Rest": Challenges to the west from late-industrializing economies*. Oxford University Press.

Ang, Y. Y. (2016). *How China escaped the poverty trap*. Cornell University Press.

Ang, Y. Y. (2018). Decentralization and development in China. *Studies in Comparative International Development, 53*(4), 449–471.

Ang, Y. Y. (2020). *China's gilded age*. Cambridge University Press.

Ang, Y. Y. (2025, May 25). China in Africa is neither neocolonialism nor altruism. *LinkedIn*. Retrieved December 19, 2025, from https://www.linkedin.com/pulse/china-africa-neither-neocolonialism-nor-altruism-yuen-yuen-ang-4hype/.

Arrighi, G. (2007). *Adam Smith in Beijing: Lineages of the twenty-first century*. Verso.

Azmeh, S., & Nadvi, K. (2014). Asian firms and the restructuring of global value chains. *World Development, 63*, 127–140.

Barnet, R. J., & Müller, R. E. (1974). *Global reach: The power of the multinational corporations*. Simon & Schuster.

Bernstein, H. (2007). Capital and labour from centre to margins. Paper presented at *Living at the Margins* conference, Stellenbosch, 26–28 March.

Bramall, C. (2009). *Chinese economic development*. Routledge.

Brautigam, D., Tang, X., & Xia, Y. (2018). What kinds of Chinese "geese" are flying to Africa? Evidence from Chinese manufacturing firms. *Journal of African Economies, 27*(suppl_1), i29–i51.

Broadman, H. G. (2007). *Africa's silk road*. World Bank.

Buckley, P. J., & Hashai, N. (2014). Is competitive advantage a necessary condition for the emergence of the multinational enterprise? *Global Strategy Journal, 4*(1), 35–48.

Buckley, P. J., et al. (2017). The determinants of Chinese outward FDI: New empirical evidence. *Multinational Business Review, 25*(1), 1–25.

Calabrese, L., & Tang, X. (2022). Chinese manufacturing investments in Africa. *The Journal of Modern African Studies, 60*(3), 371–398.

Calabrese, L., & Tang, X. (2023). Economic transformation in Africa: What is the role of Chinese firms? *Journal of International Development, 35*(1), 43–64.

Cannon, T., & Jenkins, A. (Eds.). (1990). *The geography of contemporary China: The impact of Deng Xiaoping's decade*. Routledge.

Cantwell, J. (2000). A survey of theories of international production. In C. Pitelis & R. Sugden (Eds.), *The nature of the transnational firm*. Routledge.

Chang, H.-J. (2007). *Bad Samaritans*. Random House.

Chen, W. (2021a). The dynamics of Chinese private outward foreign direct investment in Ethiopia: A comparison of the light manufacturing industry and the construction materials industry (PhD thesis). SOAS University of London. Retrieved December 10, 2025, from https://doi.org/10.25501/SOAS.00035764.

Cheng, L. K., & Ma, Z. (2010). China's outward foreign direct investment. In R. C. Feenstra & S.-J. Wei (Eds.), *China's growing role in world trade* (pp. 545–578). University of Chicago Press.

Cheng, C., Goodhand, J., & Meehan, P. (2018). *Synthesis paper: Securing and sustaining elite bargains that reduce violent conflict*. UK Stabilisation Unit.

Chen, W. (2021b). *The dynamics of state–business relations between the Ethiopian state and Chinese private firms: A case study of the Eastern Industrial Park.* (*UNU-WIDER Working Paper, No. 122*), 10.35188/unu-wider/2021/062-7.

Chen, W. (2025). Heterogeneity and drivers of Chinese manufacturing FDI in Africa: Evidence from Angola and Ethiopia. *Journal of International Development, 0*, 1–18. https://doi.org/10.1002/jid.70038

Chibber, V. (2014). The developmental state in retrospect and prospect. In M. Williams (Ed.), *The end of the developmental state?* Routledge.

Coe, N. M., & Yeung, H. W.-C. (2015). *Global production networks: Theorizing economic development in an interconnected world.* Oxford University Press.

Coe, N., Dicken, P., & Hess, M. (2004). Global production networks. *Journal of Economic Geography, 4*(4), 437–464.

Dawley, S., MacKinnon, D., & Pollock, R. (2019). Creating strategic couplings in global production networks: Regional institutions and lead firm investment in the Humber region, UK. *Journal of Economic Geography, 19*(4), 853–872.

Deller, N. (2018). *Business associations, deals and development* (IDS Working Paper 519).

Di John, J., & Putzel, J. (2009). *Political settlements* (GSDRC Issues Paper).

Dinh, H. T. (2017). *Light manufacturing in Africa.* World Bank.

Dobbin, F., Simmons, B., & Garrett, G. (2007). The global diffusion of public policies: Social construction, coercion, competition, or learning? *Annual Review of Sociology, 33*, 449–472.

Dollar, D. (2016). China's engagement with Africa. *Brookings Papers.*

Du, J., & Zhang, Y. (2017). Does One Belt One Road initiative promote Chinese overseas direct investment? *China Economic Review, 47*, 189–205.

Dunning, J. H. (1980). Toward an eclectic theory of international production. *Journal of International Business Studies, 11*(1), 9–31.

Dunning, J. H., & Lundan, S. (2008). *Multinational enterprises and the global economy* (2nd ed.). Edward Elgar.

Eom, J. (2018). *China's manufacturing investment in Sub-Saharan Africa* (CGD Working Paper 493).

Escaith, H. (2014). *Mapping value chains* (WTO Working Paper).

Evans, P. (1995). *Embedded autonomy: States and industrial transformation.* Princeton University Press.

Fine, B., & Pollen, G. (2018). Development policy in the twenty-first century. *Development and Change, 49*(2), 570–591.

Frank, A. G. (1980). *Crisis in the Third World.* Holmes & Meier.

Fröbel, F., Kreye, O., & Heinrichs, J. (1980). *The new international division of labour.* Cambridge University Press.

Fu, X., Buckley, P. J., & Fu, X. M. (2020). The growth impact of Chinese direct investment on host developing countries, International Business Review, 29(2), article 101658.

Gambino, E., & Franceschini, I. (2025). Flexible embeddedness: How Chinese lead firms develop and embed overseas state-SOE relations. *New Political Economy*. https://doi.org/10.1080/09692290.2025.2538187

Gebreeyesus, M. (2014). A natural experiment of industrial policy: Floriculture and the metal and engineering industries in Ethiopia (WIDER Working Paper No. 2014/163). UNU-WIDER.

Gereffi, G. (1994). The organization of buyer-driven global commodity chains: How U.S. retailers shape overseas production networks. In G. Gereffi & M. Korzeniewicz (Eds.), *Commodity chains and global capitalism* (pp. 95–122). Praeger.

Gereffi, G. (1999). International trade and industrial upgrading in the apparel commodity chain. *Journal of International Economics, 48*(1), 37–70.

Gereffi, G. (2018). *Global value chains and development.* Cambridge University Press.

Gibbon, P. (2008). Governance, entry barriers, upgrading. *Competition & Change, 12*(1), 29–48.

Gisselquist, R. M. (2017). State capability and prospects for close coordination: Considerations for industrial policy in Africa. In J. Page & F. Tarp (Eds.), *The practice of industrial policy: Government–business coordination in Africa and East Asia*. Oxford University Press.

Goodfellow, T. (2018). Seeing political settlements through the city: A framework for comparative analysis of urban transformation. *Development and Change, 49*(1), 199–222.

Gu, J. (2011). *The Last Golden Land? Chinese Private Companies Go to Africa* (IDS Working Paper No. 365). Institute of Development Studies.

Gu, J., et al. (2016). *The BRICS in international development.* Palgrave.

Guillén, M. F., & García-Canal, E. (2009). The American model of the multinational firm and the "new" multinationals from emerging economies. *Academy of Management Perspectives, 23*(2), 23–35.

Hall, P. A., & Soskice, D. (Eds.). (2001). *Varieties of capitalism: The institutional foundations of comparative advantage.* Oxford University Press.

Harvey, D. (2001). *Spaces of capital.* Edinburgh University Press.

Harvey, D. (2003). *The new imperialism.* Oxford University Press.

Hauge, J. (2019). Should the African lion learn from the Asian tigers? A comparative-historical study of FDI-oriented industrial policy in Ethiopia, South Korea and Taiwan. *Third World Quarterly, 40*(11), 2071–2091.

Hauge, J., & Chang, H.-J. (2019). The developmental state in Ethiopia. In C. Cramer, J. Sender, & A. Oqubay (Eds.), *African economic development.* Oxford University Press.

Henderson, J., et al. (2001). Global production networks. *Review of International Political Economy, 9*(3), 436–464.

Hu, A., et al. (2021). South–South FDI and technological upgrading. *World Development, 139*, 105316. https://doi.org/10.1016/j.worlddev.2020.105316

Hung, H.-f. (2008). Rise of China and the global overaccumulation crisis. *Review of International Political Economy, 15*(2), 149–179.

Hung, H.-f. (2016). *The China Boom: Why China will not rule the world*. Columbia University Press.

Hymer, S. H. 1960/1976. *The international operations of national firms: A study of direct foreign investment*. PhD thesis. Massachusetts Institute of Technology.

International Finance Corporation (IFC). (2010). *How do economies define micro, small and medium enterprises (MSMEs)?* (MSME Country Indicators Note). Retrieved March 27, 2017, from http://www.ifc.org/wps/wcm/connect/624b8f804a17abc5b4acfddd29332b51/msme-ci-note.pdf.

Jenkins, R. (1987). *Transnational corporations and uneven development*. Methuen.

Jones, L., & Hameiri, S. (2021). *Fractured China: How state transformation is shaping China's rise*. Cambridge University Press.

Jones, L., & Zou, Y. (2017). Rethinking the role of state-owned enterprises in China's rise. *Review of International Political Economy, 24*(2), 307–328.

Kalvelage, H., & Tups, A. (2024). Friend-shoring and supply-chain politics. *Journal of Economic Geography, 24*(2), 255–278.

Kaplinsky, R., & Morris, M. (2001). *A handbook for value chain research*. IDRC.

Kar, S., Pritchett, L., Raihan, S., & Sen, K. (2019). Political settlements and growth episodes. In A. Noman & J. Stiglitz (Eds.), *Efficiency, finance and varieties of industrial policy*. Columbia University Press.

Khan, M. (2010). *Political settlements and the governance of growth-enhancing institutions* (SOAS Working Paper).

Khan, M. (2018). Political settlements and the analysis of institutions. *African Affairs, 117*(469), 636–655.

Kindleberger, C. (1969). *American business abroad*. Yale University Press.

Kleibert, J. M. (2014). Strategic coupling in "next wave cities": Local institutional actors and the offshore service sector in the Philippines. *Singapore Journal of Tropical Geography, 35*(2), 245–260.

Knoerich, J., et al. (2021). Fractions of capital in India. *Economy and Society, 50*(3), 433–461.

Kroeber, A. R. (2016). *China's economy*. Oxford University Press.

Kroeber, A. R. (2020). *China's economy: What everyone needs to know* (2nd ed.). Oxford University Press.

Lall, S. (1974). Less-developed countries and private foreign direct investment: A review article. *World Development, 2*(4–5), 43–48.

Lardy, N. R. (2019). *The state strikes back: The end of economic reform in China?* Peterson Institute for International Economics.
Lee, C. K. (2017). *The specter of global China*. University of Chicago Press.
Lim, K. F. (2025). The firm as a geoeconomic actor. *Environment and Planning A: Economy and Space, 57*(1), 138–143. https://doi.org/10.1177/0308518X24123456
Lin, J. Y., & Chang, H.-J. (2009). Should industrial policy in developing countries conform to comparative advantage or defy it? *Development Policy Review, 27*(5), 483–502.
Liu, X., Xiao, W., & Huang, X. (2008). Bounded entrepreneurship and internationalisation of indigenous Chinese private-owned firms. *International Business Review, 17*(4), 488–508. Retrieved December 10, 2025, from http://eprints.bbk.ac.uk/3910/1/3910.pdf
Lo, D. (2012). Alternative perspectives on industrialization (*SOAS Department of Economics Working Paper* 171).
Lo, D. (2018). China in the global economy. *Journal of Chinese Economic and Business Studies, 16*(1), 1–20.
Lo, D., Hong, F., & Li, G. (2016). Assessing the role of inward foreign direct investment in Chinese economic development, 1990–2007: Towards a synthesis of alternative views. *Structural Change and Economic Dynamics, 37*, 107–120.
Luo, Y. (1997). Guanxi and business . World Scientific.
Luo, Y. (2007). Guanxi and business (2nd ed.). World Scientific.
Lüthje, B., et al. (2013). *Beyond the iron rice bowl?* Campus.
McNally, C. (2008). *China's emergent political economy*. Routledge.
Meyer, M. W. (2011). Is it capitalism? *Management and Organization Review*. https://doi.org/10.1111/j.1740-8784.2011.00211.x
Milanovic, B. (2019). *Capitalism, alone*. Harvard University Press.
Moghaddam, K., et al. (2014). Global value chain governance and EM-MNEs. *Journal of International Management, 20*(4), 359–372.
Mohan, G., Hu, R., Katsinas, P., & Rogers, S. (2025). A tale of two ports: Relational power in COSCO's European port investments. *Territory, Politics, Governance*. https://doi.org/10.1080/21622671.2025.2449756
Morck, R., et al. (2008). Corporate governance, economic entrenchment and growth. *Journal of Economic Literature, 46*(3), 655–720.
Mudambi, R. (2008). Location, control and innovation. *Journal of Economic Geography, 8*(5), 699–725.
Narula, R., & Dunning, J. H. (2010). Multinational enterprises, development and globalization: Some clarifications and a research agenda. *Oxford Development Studies, 38*(3), 263–287.
Naughton, B. (2007). *The Chinese economy*. MIT Press.
Naughton, B. (2018). *The Chinese economy: Adaptation and growth*. MIT Press.

Naughton, B. (2021). *The rise of China's Industrial Policy, 1978 to 2020*. Universidad Nacional Autónoma de México.
Naughton, B., & Tsai, K. S. (Eds.). (2015). *State capitalism, institutional adaptation, and the Chinese miracle*. Cambridge University Press.
Newfarmer, R. (1985). *Profits, progress and poverty*. University of Notre Dame Press.
Nicolas, F. (2017). *Chinese investors in Ethiopia: The perfect match? Notes de l'Ifri*. Institut français des relations internationales.
Nolan, P. (2014). *Chinese firms, global firms*. Routledge.
O'Hara, P. A. (Ed.). (2000). *Encyclopedia of political economy*. Routledge.
Oi, J. C. (1999). *Rural China takes off: Institutional foundations of economic reform*. University of California Press.
Oqubay, A. (2015). *Made in Africa*. Oxford University Press.
Oqubay, A., & Lin, J. Y. (Eds.). (2020). *The Oxford handbook of industrial hubs and economic development*. Oxford University Press.
Oya, C. (2019). Labour regimes and multinational firms in Africa. *Journal of Agrarian Change, 19*(2), 251–264.
Oya, C. (2025). *China for Africa's industrialization?* Cambridge University Press. https://doi.org/10.1017/9781009347679
Page, J., & Tarp, F. (Eds.). (2017). *The practice of industrial policy : Government–business coordination in Africa and East Asia.*. Oxford University Press.
Peck, J., & Theodore, N. (2007). Variegated capitalism. *Progress in Human Geography, 31*(6), 731–772.
Peck, J., & Zhang, J. (2013). A variety of capitalism with Chinese characteristics? *Journal of Economic Geography, 13 (3)*, 357–396. https://doi.org/10.1093/jeg/lbs058
Phelps, N. A., & Wood, A. M. (2006). Lost in translation? Local interests, global actors and inward investment regimes. *Journal of Economic Geography, 6*(4), 493–515.
Pritchett, L., Sen, K., & Werker, E. (2013). *Deals and development*. Overseas Development Institute.
Qu, F. (2014). Jiangsu pattern change and structural adjustment. In S. Fan, R. Kanbur, S.-J. Wei, & X. Zhang (Eds.), *The Oxford companion to the economics of China* (pp. 540–550). Oxford University Press.
Raco, M., Sun, Y., & Brill, F. (2023). Relational regulation and Chinese real estate investment in London: Moving beyond the territorial trap. *Territory, Politics, Governance, 11*(2), 354–376. https://doi.org/10.1080/21622671.2021.1987225
Rolf, S., & Schindler, S. (2025). *State platform capitalism: The United States, China, and the global battle for digital supremacy*. Cambridge University Press. https://doi.org/10.1017/9781009446594

Ross, A. G. (2015). An empirical analysis of Chinese outward foreign direct investment in Africa. *Journal of Chinese Economic and Foreign Trade Studies, 8*(1), 4–19.

Rugman, A., & Li, J. (2007). Will China's multinationals succeed globally? *European Management Journal, 25*(5), 333–343.

Rui, H., & Yip, G. S. (2008). Foreign acquisitions by Chinese firms. *Journal of World Business, 43*(2), 213–226.

Sanfilippo, M. (2010). Chinese FDI to Africa: What is the nexus with foreign economic cooperation? *African Development Review, 22*(S1), 599–614.

Schaefer, F., Chen, W., Katsinas, P., & Mohan, G. (Forthcoming). Geoeconomics, strategic coupling, and local development: The multi-scalar politics of Chinese investment in Duisburg and London. *Journal of Economic Geography.*

Schaefer, F., & Oya, C. (2019a). Labour regimes and global production. *World Development, 113*, 1–12.

Schaefer, F., & Oya, C. (2019b). Employment patterns in Ethiopian manufacturing. *Journal of Development Studies, 55*(7), 1–21.

Seawright, J., & Gerring, J. (2008). Case selection techniques in case study research: A menu of qualitative and quantitative options. *Political Research Quarterly, 61*(2), 294–308.

Shen, X. (2015). *Private Chinese investment in Africa* (World Bank Policy Research Working Paper No. 7318). World Bank.

Song, H. (2011). Chinese private direct investment and overseas Chinese network in Africa. *China & World Economy, 19*(4), 109–126.

Staritz, C., Plank, L., & Morris, M. (2016). *Global value chains, industrial policy, and sustainable development—Ethiopia's apparel export sector.* ICTSD.

Staritz, C., Plank, L., & Morris, M. (2019). A different path of industrial development? Ethiopia's apparel export sector. In S. Scholvin, A. Black, J. Revilla Diez, & I. Turok (Eds.), *Value chains in Sub-Saharan Africa: Challenges of integration into the global economy* (pp. 79–93). Springer.

Sun, I. Y. (2017). *The next factory of the world.* Harvard Business Review Press.

Sun, I. Y., Jayaram, K., & Kassiri, O. (2017). *Dance of the Lions and Dragons: How are Africa and China engaging, and how will the partnership evolve?* McKinsey & Company.

te Velde, D. W. (2013, August). State–business relations and industrial policy: An introduction. In *State–business relations and industrial policy: Current policy and research debates.* Growth Research Programme, Overseas Development Institute (ODI).

Vu-Thanh, T. A. (2017). The political economy of industrial development in Viet Nam: Impact of state-business relationship on industrial performance, 1986–2013. In J. Page & F. Tarp (Eds.), *The practice of industrial policy: Government–business coordination in Africa and East Asia.* Oxford University Press.

Wang, C., Du, J., & Wang, Y. (2015). Belt and Road and OFDI location. *China Economic Review, 34*, 193–208.

Wang, M. (2014). The political economy of China's OFDI. *International Review of Economics & Finance, 29*, 106–121.

Whitfield, L., Staritz, C., & Morris, M. (2020). Global value chains and industrial policy in Ethiopia's apparel sector. *Development and Change, 51*(4), 1018–1043.

Whittaker, D. H., et al. (2020). *Compressed development.* Oxford University Press.

Wu, J. (2017). *China's fiscal system.* CITIC Press.

Yang, J., Novokmet, F., & Milanovic, B. (2019). *From workers to capitalists?* (World Inequality Lab Working Paper 2019/11).

Yeung, H. W.-C. (2016). *Strategic coupling.* Cornell University Press.

Zhang, J., & Peck, J. (2016). Variegated capitalism, Chinese style. *Regional Studies, 50*(1), 52–78.

CHAPTER 3

Varieties, Motives, and Determinants of Chinese Manufacturing Firms in Ethiopia

Introduction

Common perceptions regarding Chinese engagement in Africa are that it is one-dimensional and sometimes biased. One common problem with this perception is the seeming acceptance of methodological nationalism, whereby the national origin of a firm or agency is treated as if it determines outcomes. The main issue with this tendency is that it conceals the highly significant heterogeneity of Chinese actors overseas. As argued in this chapter, it ignores the variety of Chinese capital, not only in terms of the familiar state-private distinction, but also the substantial variation within each of these groups. Moreover, methodological nationalism attached to "Chinese" firms also obscures the importance of the African host-country context, as if African states and societies were not able to shape how foreign firms operate through policy tools, enforcement routines, and day-to-day bargaining.

In Ethiopia, both official statistics and the empirical evidence collected for this study show that the Chinese private sector plays a dominant role in manufacturing OFDI—by project numbers and by value (see Section "The Presence of Chinese OFDI in Ethiopia"). Not only is there the economic impact of Chinese private firms to consider, but also their social and political effects, which are consequential enough that they should not be treated as minorities or "exceptions." Following Lee (2017), the point is

W. Chen, *Chinese Manufacturing Firms in Ethiopia*, Palgrave Studies in African and Development Economics,
https://doi.org/10.1007/978-3-032-24322-5_3

not to deny the relevance of ownership categories, but to avoid treating "Chinese" as an explanatory shortcut. What matters is how different fractions of capital pursue accumulation and how they relate to state agencies, workers, and markets—through the everyday points of contact that make production possible (or interrupt it).

This chapter has two objectives. First, it identifies varieties of Chinese private capital in Ethiopian manufacturing and develops a typology based on empirically relevant criteria. Second, it examines the concrete motives and drivers that lead different types of firms and entrepreneurs to invest in Ethiopia, and to choose particular sectors and market orientations. Capturing both similarities and differences across firm types is necessary for understanding how investment trajectories unfold in practice, and why some firms consolidate while others stagnate, shift market(s) or exit.

The chapter argues that Chinese private OFDI in Ethiopia is part of an ongoing learning process. It is diverse and fluid, and it involves interaction among various actors, between capital and the state, and between capital and labour, with substantial variations within each group. Methodological nationalism obscures this variation and produces an empirical trap: similarities are over-interpreted as national attributes, while differences are flattened or treated as "exceptions." Consistent with Lee (2017), Sun (2017), Schaefer and Oya (2019), and my own findings, the chapter shows that ownership and nationality alone do not explain the dynamism of Chinese manufacturing investment (also see Chen, 2021a, 2022, 2025). Sector-specific requirements, firm characteristics, and the host-country political economy—at both national and local levels—are more decisive for explaining variation in motives, drivers, and investment trajectories.

The data in this chapter draws mainly on evidence collected up to late 2019, in order to document the pre-COVID period. The evidence presented in this chapter is based on a combination of data sources, including: (a) primary and secondary data collected from government agencies and firms through interviews and visits; (b) a survey of 16 Chinese private manufacturing firms (14 based in the Eastern Industrial Park, EIP)[1] conducted between January and April 2018; and (c) 96 semi-structured interviews, including 86 interviews with 20 firms (74 interviews with 15 firms in the EIP) and 10 interviews with Chinese and Ethiopian government

[1] Eastern Industry Zone PLC officially changed its name to Eastern Industry Park PLC on 14 June 2018 (internal document provided by the Eastern Industry Park, 20 July 2018). For consistency, this book refers to the Eastern Industry Zone as EIP throughout.

agencies and business associations (see Appendix A for more details). Frequent follow-up visits took place between October 2018 and June 2019. Firms were selected as analytically relevant and generally exemplified cases of Chinese private investment in Ethiopian manufacturing in the post-2008 period (Chen, 2021a, 2021b, 2025).

Following this introduction, Section "The Presence of Chinese OFDI in Ethiopia" provides an overview of Chinese OFDI in Ethiopia. Section "A Variety of Chinese Manufacturing Firms in Ethiopia" documents firm diversity and develops the typology used in the book. Section "Why Are Chinese Firms Investing in Ethiopia's Manufacturing Sector?" then compares motives and determinants across LM and CM, showing where firm interests converge and diverge and why.

Analytically, this chapter operationalises the framework and propositions set out in Chap. 2. It speaks most directly to P1 and P2 by exploring firm heterogeneity and by distinguishing MEFs from GPN-IFs as different production network positions with different constraints and upgrading options. It also prepares the ground for P3 and P4 by identifying the concrete points where Ethiopian policy tools are encountered in practice—licensing, land access, industrial parks and aftercare, customs and standards routines, utilities provision, and foreign exchange allocation—which later become arenas of bargaining and enforcement. Finally, by focusing on evidence up to late 2019, the chapter establishes a pre-2020 baseline against which the post-2020 phase shift analysed in Chap. 5 (P5) can be assessed.

The Presence of Chinese OFDI in Ethiopia

By the late 2010s, China had become Ethiopia's largest source of investment by number of licensed projects and a major trade and infrastructure partner. Official EIC data show that, over the two decades to 2019, China ranked first by number of projects—1149 in total, including joint ventures with local and third-country partners—and also ranked first in terms of projects in operation (stock) (EIC, 2019, 2020). Between 1998 and 2018, there were 839 Chinese projects in operation, with a cumulative value of ETB 37.07 billion (approximately US$1.34 billion), accounting for 31.8% of Ethiopia's total inward FDI (EIC, 2019, 2020). China also led in both project numbers and investment value between 2010 and

2018. Measured by projects in operation, China (460) was followed by India (111), Turkey (55), the UK (32), and the US (27) (see Fig. 3.1).[2]

In value terms, China accounted for 42.3% of total FDI between 2010 and 2018. China ranked first with US$1060 million, followed by the UK (US$360 million), Saudi Arabia (US$205 million), Turkey (US$165 million), and India (US$91 million) (Fig. 3.2).

Geographical Distribution (pre-2020)

Chinese manufacturing FDI is concentrated in Oromia and Addis Ababa. By stock value, Oromia received ETB 18.28 billion and Addis Ababa ETB 16.01 billion, with Amhara a distant third at ETB 1.57 billion (EIC, 2019) (Fig. 3.3). This pattern reflects Ethiopia's market geography and its main transport corridor. Addis Ababa is the primary consumption market and administrative hub. Neighbouring Oromia offers proximity to the capital and easier access to land and labour for manufacturing sites. Connectivity also improved with the Adama expressway (opened September 2014) and the Addis-Djibouti Railway (operational since January 2018). These changes matter because they affect the everyday logistics of manufacturing -- how quickly inputs move in, and how

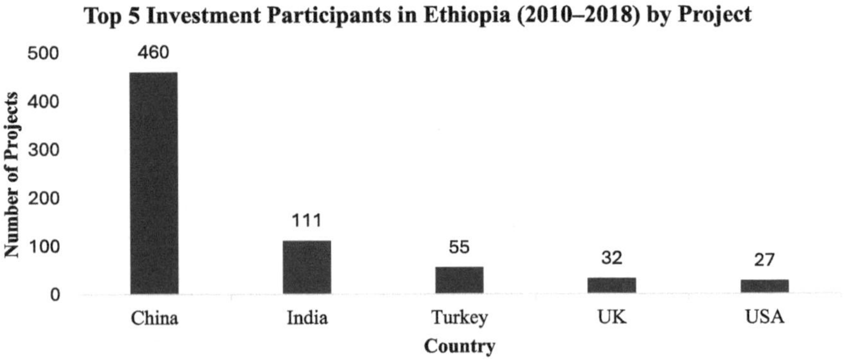

Fig. 3.1 Top 5 investment participants in Ethiopia (2010–2018) by project. (Source: Author, analysis based on data collected from the EIC (2018, cited in Chen (2021a))

[2] This section draws on EIC records and updates the overview presented in Chen (2025, pp. 8–9).

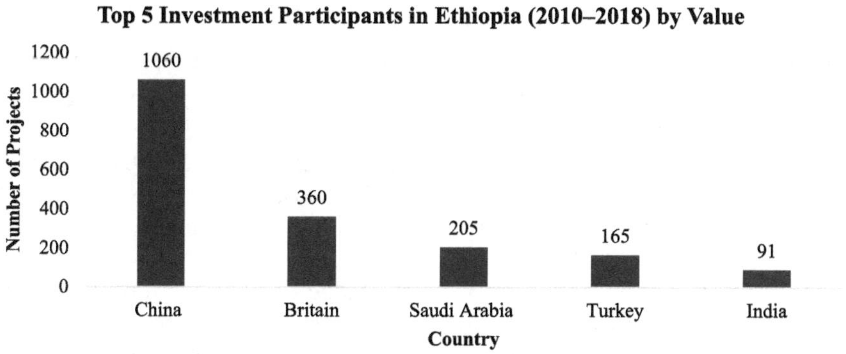

Fig. 3.2 Top 5 investment participants in Ethiopia (2010–2018) by value. (Source: Author, analysis based on data collected from the EIC (2018), cited in Chen (2021a))

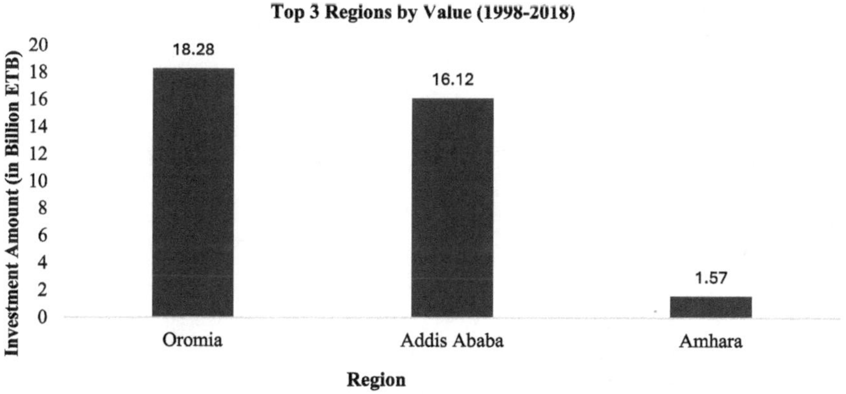

Fig. 3.3 Geographical distribution of Chinese FDI in Ethiopia's manufacturing industry: Top 3 regions by value. (Source: Author, calculated and compiled based on the data collected from EIC (2019))

predictably exports can move out. The corridor passes through and anchors industrial parks (IPs) such as the EIP and Adama IP, which helps explain why Chinese manufacturing investment clusters in and around these locations (*Addisfortune* 2014; CG2; CCM2-4-b; CCM3-1-b; CCM17-1-b).

Sectoral Distribution (pre-2020)

Manufacturing accounts for the largest share of Chinese FDI recorded by the EIC (Fig. 3.4). Construction follows at some distance, then real estate and machinery leasing/consulting. Over roughly two decades to 2019, Chinese investment stock in manufacturing reached ETB 29.17 billion (78.69%) (Chen, 2025, p. 8). Construction stood at ETB 6.73 billion (18.15%). Real estate/machinery leasing/consulting reached ETB 0.92 billion (2.45%) (EIC, 2019 cited in Chen, 2025, p. 8).

These FDI figures do not capture the value of construction contracts undertaken by Chinese firms, which are highly visible in Ethiopia's infrastructure boom. As Brautigam (2015) cautions, it is misleading to "mix apples and elephants." Conflating contracts with FDI overstates the role of Chinese state capital in FDI stocks and flows. In Ethiopia's FDI statistics, the private sector -- particularly private manufacturers -- accounts for the bulk of recorded Chinese investment (Chen, 2025, p.2). This challenges popular narratives that emphasise SOE dominance in mining and infrastructure (see Chap. 2).

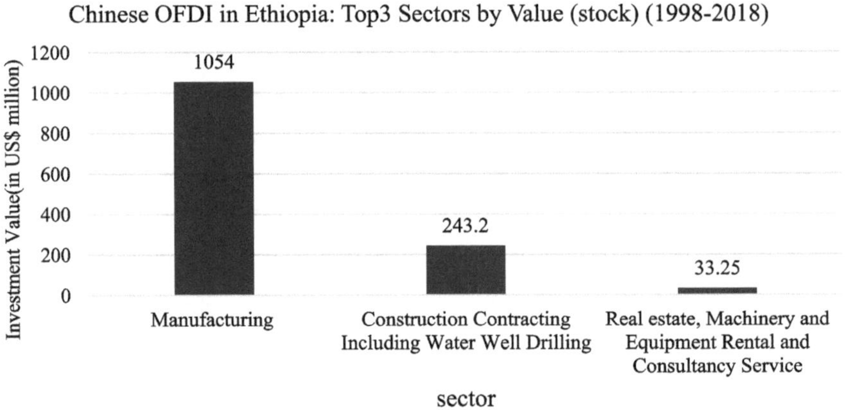

Fig. 3.4 Chinese OFDI in Ethiopia: Top 3 sectors by value (stock) (1998–2018). (Source: Author, calculated and compiled based on data collected from EIC (2019), cited in Chen (2025, p.10). The exchange rate refers to the average conversion rate for 2018 https://www.exchangerates.org.uk/USD-ETB-spot-exchange-rates-history-2018.html (accessed Aug 23, 2022))

Since 2020, official EIC data indicates a re-composition of Chinese manufacturing capital. There has been a shift towards fewer, larger, more capital- and technology-intensive projects, with greater local equity participation. (These post-2020 shifts are analysed in Chap. 5).

Summary

Overall, China leads by both the number of projects and recorded investment value in Ethiopia, and manufacturing accounts for the largest share of this investment. This pattern is closely linked to Ethiopia's industrial policy priorities, particularly the use of industrial parks to promote export-oriented manufacturing alongside selective support for import-substituted manufacturing. The concentration of Chinese investment in Oromia and Addis Ababa reflects where these parks are located and where access to transport infrastructure—especially along the Addis-Adama-Djibouti corridor—makes it easier for firms to organise production, source inputs, and move goods to market.

Within these aggregates, private manufacturers account for most recorded Chinese investment in Ethiopia's FDI statistics. By contrast, the prominent presence of Chinese firms in infrastructure largely reflects construction and engineering contracts rather than FDI. This distinction is important because it corrects a common assumption—often made in policy and media debates—that equates highly visible construction activity with accurately reflecting the composition of inward FDI.

At the same time, official databases have clear limitations. Smaller and diaspora-linked firms are often undercounted, and investment announcements circulated by firms and intermediaries can overstate investment when projects do not actually realise (Chen, 2025, p. 2). Checking the official record against firm-level evidence nevertheless supports the conclusion that Chinese private investment in Ethiopian manufacturing is both significant in scale and diverse in form—and that its distribution follows where industrial parks, land, and logistics are concentrated, rather than simply where wages are low.

To explain why firms facing similar macro "push" and "pull" conditions pursue different strategies and leave different trajectories, we move from aggregates to varieties of firms. Section "A Variety of Chinese Manufacturing Firms in Ethiopia" develops a refined typology and maps characteristics of firms that are prominent in Ethiopia's manufacturing sector (see also Chen, 2025, pp. 8–9).

A Variety of Chinese Manufacturing Firms in Ethiopia

Chinese manufacturing investment in Ethiopia expanded sharply after 2008, and it did so through a wide range of private firms rather than a single "Chinese" actor. This section there asks a simple set of questions: which kinds of Chinese private firms were present in Ethiopian manufacturing (up till 2019), where do they come from, what do they produce, which markets do they serve, and how do they organise finance and management?, which markets do they serve, and how do they organise finance and management?

Drawing on firm surveys, interviews, participant observation, and industrial park and agency records (see Appendix A), the section describes the main patterns and then summarises them in a typology. The aim is not classification for its own sake. It is to show how firm diversity maps onto the practical conditions emphasised in Section "Introduction": the everyday processes through which firms obtain licences, land and sheds, utilities, customs clearance, and access to foreign exchange for inputs and maintenance.

The typology developed here builds on my earlier work on region-specific business models (e.g., Zhejiang/Wenzhou, Guangdong/Dongguan, Jiangsu/Su'nan) (Chen, 2021a), but it is reorganised around the two categories used throughout this book: MEFs and GPN-IFs. This framing is consistent with the approach developed in my article, which distinguishes market-embedded firms from those organised around export buyers and compliance routines (Chen, 2025, pp. 6, 10–11).

Who Are They? Where Are They From?

Unlike SOEs, it is difficult to track the geographical origin of Chinese private firms in Ethiopia. Central SOEs must obtain an Overseas Investment Permit through the Ministry of Commerce (MOFCOM). Provincial and municipal SOEs obtain permits from their respective Commerce Departments. Firms involved overseas engineering projects typically register and report through formal channels. This enables MOFCOM to track the domestic locations of these SOEs via their licences. Private firms are different because registration is not mandatory. Many small projects have not been accurately tracked by MOFCOM or by African investment authorities (Xia, 2019, p. 2). In recent years, MOFCOM shifted from registration to a filing system to ease procedures for overseas investment (CG2). Although all investors register at the EIC and the Ministry of Industry (MoI), those records do not include the Chinese regions of origin. In practice, learning where private firms come from requires asking investors directly.

A further complication is the presence of "translocal" arrangements, where investors operate through locally registered entities or local partners while maintaining effective control. There have also been cases in which foreign investors married Ethiopian citizens to access rights or sectors otherwise closed to foreigners (Chen, 2021a). Authorities have occasionally identified sham marriages. These arrangements can be difficult to identify in official datasets and tend to be undercounted in standard FDI records (Sun et al., 2017; Chen, 2025, p. 2). The implication is not that official figures are unusable, but that they must be cross-checked with firm-level evidence.

Presence of Chinese Manufacturing Firms in Ethiopia

By number of firms, the private sector is much more important. A MOFCOM official based in Ethiopia estimated that around 95% of Chinese firms operating in the country were private (CG2). Two groups, however, were likely to be missing even from this estimate.

First, some early investors—mainly SMEs—entered through informal channels, including third-country routing or cash transfers, especially in the earlier phase of post-2008 expansion. Second, "translocals" were also easy to miss for the reasons noted above. Both issues reinforce the broader warning already made in Section "Introduction ": aggregate datasets tend to undercount smaller and mobile private firms, especially when ownership is layered or routed through offshore and third-country structures (Sharman, 2010; Sun et al., 2017; Chen, 2025, p. 2).

The Main Characteristics of Chinese Private Firms in Ethiopia

Tracking all private firms in Ethiopia is unrealistic within limited time and budget to conduct fieldwork (Chen, 2021a). As a compromise, the EIP was used as a core research site and an empirical lens on firm diversity. The EIP is analytically useful because it is the first industrial park in Ethiopia constructed, developed, operated, and managed by a Chinese private firm, the EIP has attracted a mix of Chinese investors—both early investors and latecomers—mainly from the private sector. It is a mixed park with various manufacturing sectors.

Evidence for this section draws on: (i) secondary data collected from the EIC and EIP Management Committee (EIPMC);[3] (ii) approximately six months of participant observation in the EIP; (iii) a firm survey conducted in early 2018 (14 surveyed firms in the EIP, 2 were in other state-led IPs); and (iv) semi-structured interviews with firms and relevant state and business bodies (see Appendix A for more details).

As of September 2018, there were 86 firms operating in the EIP, of which 79 were Chinese. The Chinese presence was overwhelmingly private: 78 of the 79 Chinese firms were private, with only one municipal SOE recorded. By sector, Chinese firms in the EIP clustered in LM and CM. Of the 79 Chinese firms, 38 were in LM and 28 in CM. Within LM, most firms were in textiles and garments (35 of 38), with a small remainder in leather products and footwear. Most LM firms moved into the EIP after 2013. CM firms were more dispersed across grinding stations, steel products, aluminium products, ceramics, and gypsum boards.

According to internal EIP data (2018), Chinese firms in the EIP created 14,794 jobs for locals, with an average localisation rate of 92.57% (Table 3.1). The rate is consistent with Schaefer and Oya's finding of around 90% (2019, p. 22). Sectoral composition matters for job creation and localisation. In the same location, localisation rates are higher in LM

Table 3.1 Employment status and localisation rates in the EIP

Context of the firm	*Number of firms*	*Job creation (Local)*	*Localisation rate*
All firms in EIP	86	15,032	92.54%
Chinese firms in EIP	79	14,794	92.57%
Chinese LM firms	38	11,371	95.41%
Chinese CM firms	28	2671	86.24%

Source: Author calculated and compiled based on EIP Committee data collected in October 2018.

[3] Data were collected from the EIC and the EIPMC. These host-country sources differ from MOFCOM statistics and provide a more accurate reflection of sectoral distribution. Firm origins were manually verified, including entities registered in Hong Kong and the British Virgin Islands, which are classified here as part of Chinese OFDI. See SAIS–CARI, *Statistical Bulletin of China's Outward Foreign Direct Investment* (updated March 12, 2024).

firms (95.41%) than in CM firms (86.24%). This reflects the different factor intensities and skill requirements of each sector.

By size, most Chinese firms in the EIP are SMEs by Chinese criteria. Almost all LM firms (37 of 38) were small or medium-sized; one footwear exporter (pseudonymised as Fujin Footwear)[4] was the only large LM firm in the park. Among the 28 CM firms, even Xinhua Cement and Dongxin Steel (both were pseudonymised)—regarded as the largest Chinese cement plant and steel mill in Ethiopia—were SMEs by Chinese standards when measured by investment value and employment. By origin, Zhejiang ranks first by number of firms in the EIP, with Jiangsu second (CCM2-3-a). There were fewer firms from Guangdong, but Fujin Footwear was an exemplary case of large-scale export-processing relocating industrial capital to Ethiopia. By market orientation, in the 2018 survey, only one of eight surveyed LM firms was fully export oriented. Most LM firms primarily served Ethiopia's domestic market and later began exporting a smaller share (around 15–40%), partly in response to Ethiopian government requirements and to strengthen access to incentives and foreign exchange. In CM, the pattern was clearer: surveyed CM firms produced entirely for the domestic market, consistent with Ethiopia's import-substitution stance in these sub-sectors. This market contrast was important for the chapter's later analysis. It pointed to two broad operating logics: firms that build their position through domestic and regional markets, and firms that were organised around export buyers and their requirements and delivery schedules.

By ownership, survey findings show that most firms were legally registered as private limited companies (PLCs) (11 of 14), with one public limited company and one sole proprietorship. Despite different legal forms, most firms in practice adopt family or owner-operated models. Ownership and management were rarely separated. In many cases, the owner also acts as manager. This was more common in LM than in CM. In textiles and garments, many Chinese managers and expatriates were family members or friends (author's observation). In CM, more capital-intensive lines such as cement and steel tended to hire salaried professional managers and expatriates with higher qualifications and skills, while smaller aluminium, steel pipe, and wood factories rely more on acquaintances. The

[4] Fujin was established in Dong'guan, Guang Dong Province, China, in 1996. By 2017, Fujin's parent company had 11,000–12,000 employees worldwide and 40 production lines (CCM1-4-a).

only firm reported to adopt a management regime with international standards was a publicly listed company that started operations in November 2017.

By finance, most surveyed firms (13 of 14) relied primarily on self-financing (retained earnings, savings, and personal loans). Firms reported that local borrowing was rarely used because interest rates were high. Bank loans in China were either difficult to obtain for private firms or too expensive due to discriminatory regulation (survey, 2018). Beijing launched support programmes for private "Going Out" under the BRI. Firms, however, reported limited impact of Chinese government finance on their investment decisions (survey, 2018; see also Xia, 2019). In principle, all firms could seek equity finance through the China–Africa Development Fund (CADFund) if two criteria are met: firm's background and credit meet CADFund standards, and the project value exceeds US$50 million (CG3). In practice, this excludes most SMEs in Ethiopia. Either the firm does not qualify, or the project is too small (CG3). Due diligence challenges further constrain CADFund, which prioritises SOEs, listed firms, or large private firms.

According to the 2018 survey, LM firms typically had longer prior experience in their sector in China—often 15–20 years—and several had long-standing trade relations with Ethiopian clients before investing. In terms of the CM industry, 4 out of 6 firms have relevant experience in China. The remaining two firms stated that they engaged in different sectors in China, and their investment in Ethiopia is solely for opportunity and market seeking. They were enticed by friends telling them profitability was potentially much higher in Ethiopia than in China (where competition is more significant). They expected profits to be exceptionally high in Ethiopia, offsetting all the risks of setting up there with no previous experience. Across both LM and CM, *guanxi* and prior trading ties shaped how opportunities were discovered, how information circulated, and how early learning occurred.

As discussed in Chap. 2, *guanxi* networks play an important role in Chinese firms' internationalisation. Consistent with Chap. 2, *guanxi* (especially Type 3-social network relations) remained central to opportunity discovery. Firms used three types of networks (Table 3.2).

In the survey, 10 of 14firms learned of investment opportunities primarily through social networks (i.e., 4 LM; 6 CM). CM firms relied particularly heavily on social networks; in the survey sample, all CM firms reported this as their main network ties. LM firms used a broader mix of

Table 3.2 Main guanxi networks to discover investment opportunities

Type A. Official networks (Formal)	Invitation from high government officials, state-led Chinese business council(s), such as (CCPIT)
Type B. Business networks (Formal)	Invitation from clients, business partners, or private business association(s)
Type C. Social networks (Informal)	Family members, friends, and/or Chinese overseas network ties

Source: Author's elaboration

guanxi networks: some entered through official invitations and support, others through long-term client relations, and others through social networks.

Typology of Firms

This section proposes a typology of Chinese private firms based on empirically observable criteria (see Appendix A for the full elaboration). The typology uses the following criteria: scale, origin, sector, main market, the main networks for opportunity discovery, and the main reason to invest in Ethiopia (Table 3.3).[5]

The typology recognises three recurrent patterns linked to China's regional development trajectories (Chen, 2021a) and consistent with the dimensions used in my 2025 analysis of manufacturing FDI (Chen, 2025, pp. 6, 10–11). These region-specific development models (Table 3.3) are not treated as deterministic "Chinese" traits. Rather, they serve as descriptive reference points for how firms' ownership structures, management practices, and network repertoires shape entry and adaptation abroad over time.

To align this regional typology with the book's core analytical focus—how firms operate through Ethiopia's institutions and policy tools—these three types are reclassified into the two categories used throughout the remaining chapters:

[5] The firm typology developed in this book is based on three pre-selected criteria: (i) firms that invested in Ethiopia between 2008 and 2017; (ii) firms operating in LM or CM; and (iii) firms that were fully operational during the main fieldwork period (2017–2018). Newer projects in Hawassa, Adama, and Kombolcha IPs were still at the construction or trial-production stage during 2017–2018 and are therefore excluded from the typology.

Table 3.3 Typology of Chinese manufacturing firms

	Type 1	*Type 2*	*Type 3*
Scale	SME	Large	SME
Origin	Zhejiang province	Guangdong province	Jiangsu province
Sector	Family business / merchant-evolved LM; Small–medium CM	Large-scale export-processing LM for global brands/retailers	Comparatively larger-scale LM; Owner-operated CM
Region-specific development model	"Wenzhou model": private-sector dominant; long entrepreneurial history; emigre merchant networks; *baotuan chuhai*; dense guanxi	"Dongguan model": export-processing ecosystems; "world factory" labour-intensive OEM	"Su'nan model": capability-rich manufacturing; stronger local-state linkages
Main market	Domestic market	Export market	Ethiopia domestic (and mixed for some LM)
Main source of knowing investment opportunity	Business + social networks	Official networks (often)	Social networks (often)
Main reason to invest in Ethiopia	Host-country market	Access to international markets	Host-country market
Representativeness	Highly exemplary	Exemplary but more unique	Highly exemplary

Source: Author's elaboration

- MEFs: mainly family/owner-run SMEs (including translocal and diaspora-linked firms) oriented towards Ethiopia's domestic and regional markets. They often rely more heavily on social and business networks and on municipal and sectoral offices for permits, utilities, land access, and problem-solving.
- GPN-IFs: mainly medium to large firms oriented to export markets and shaped by buyer requirements (e.g., standards, environmental compliance, delivery schedules). They are more likely to cluster in industrial parks and to work closely with park-based services and agencies (e.g., customs, banks, and other parts in one-stop services).

Table 3.4 Mapping from region-specific development models to the MEF/GPN-IF categories

Region-specific model	*Ownership/ financing*	*Sectoral specificities*	*Market orientation*	*Ethiopian institutional embedding*
Zhejiang / "Wenzhou"	Family/owner-run; self-financed; informal management	LM (low-end consumer goods); CM (small–medium)	Domestic	Social/business networks; Municipal/ sectoral interfaces; Off-park/mixed
Guangdong / "Dongguan"	Medium–large private exporters; some listed	LM (textiles/ apparel/ footwear)	Export	Park-based; customs/ standards; Buyer requirements; Preference policies
Jiangsu / "Su'nan"	Medium–large private firms; more formal management	LM (exporters); CM (higher capital)	Mixed	Park/buyer governance for LM; State facilitation for CM

Source: Author's elaboration; see Zhang and Peck (2016), Qu (2014), Chen (2021a, 2025)

This MEF/GPN-IF distinction follows the logic set out in Chen (2025, pp. 6, 10–11): it connects firm characteristics to how production is organised and governed, and how firms interact with state institutions and markets in practice.

Survey (2018) findings show that three region-specific development models were prominent in the EIP: the Wenzhou model, the Dongguan model, and the Su'nan model. Based on surveys, interviews, and observation, three types of private firms are present in Ethiopian manufacturing (Table 3.3). As noted earlier, 29 of 38 LM firms in the EIP (76%) were SMEs focused on the domestic market, mainly from Zhejiang.

Taken together, the EIP patterns—firm size, sector, market orientation, ownership and management practice, financing, and network channels—show why "Chinese private capital" cannot be treated as a single category. They also clarify what is at stake for the next section: different types of firms enter Ethiopia for different reasons, and they face different practical constraints once they start operating. The next section, therefore, turns from "who was here" to "why they came" and "what conditions shaped their investment trajectories" across LM and CM (Table 3.4).

Why Are Chinese Firms Investing in Ethiopia's Manufacturing Sector?

This section compares Chinese Sections "The Presence of Chinese OFDI in Ethiopia" and "A Variety of Chinese Manufacturing Firms in Ethiopia", which show that Chinese manufacturing firms in Ethiopia were not a homogeneous type of investor. They ranged from owner-operated or family-run SMEs producing for domestic and regional markets, to larger firms whose production was organised around export buyers, compliance, and delivery schedules. In all cases, firms still needed to make money, but they did so through different strategies shaped by different motives and constraints. As set out in Chap. 2, Lee (2017) argues that Chinese state capital often follows a logic of profit optimisation, while global private capital tends towards profit maximisation. Although Lee does not focus on Chinese private capital in Africa, the distinction is still useful here because it helps clarify why firms facing similar conditions can make different choices.

This section compares Chinese investment in LM and CM to identify the main motives and drivers, and to show how these vary by firm type and sub-sector. It asks three questions: what factors in China pushed firms to go overseas; what features of Ethiopia pulled them in; and how Ethiopia's policy and institutional contexts shaped what firms could actually do once they arrived.

As elaborated in Chap. 2, firms' "Going Out" is pushed by domestic pressures in China and pulled by host-country opportunities. Shen's (1990) Push–Pull lens—first applied to early FDI into China—remains useful for mapping broad determinants. Yet, as Chen (2025) discussed, these analytical frameworks (e.g., push–pull, OLI, flying-geese) were developed around OECD-based TNCs and often through M&A. They under-specify ownership variety, sectoral specificities, and informal practices such as guanxi that shape Chinese private FDI in Africa; they also travel poorly to predominantly greenfield manufacturing (Dunning & Lundan, 2008; Hymer, 1976; Porter, 1998; Chen, 2025; Shen, 2015; Moghaddam et al., 2014). In what follows, Push–Pull is used to structure the evidence (Table 3.5), while a relational-institutional lens explains outcomes by firm type and embedding mode (see also Chen, 2025).

Chinese private investment in LM and CM is heterogeneous in a concrete sense. In LM, two patterns stand out: early investors who targeted Ethiopia's domestic market, and firms that invested to export to the US

Table 3.5 Push and pull factors

"Push" factors	*"Pull" factors*
A. Rising production costs (e.g., labour cost; energy cost) B. Regulatory/legal cost of doing business C. Environmental compliance cost	A. Lower production costs (abundant, inexpensive, trainable labour; low energy cost; abundant raw materials[a]) B. Market factors (bundled export-oriented incentives; high profit margins in certain segments) C. Political economic factors (bundles of preferential investment incentives (for export); committed government; political stability; supportive macroeconomic conditions)

Source: Author's elaboration based on interviews and surveys; see also Chen (2025, p. 13)

[a]Raw materials here refer to inputs required for manufacturing, including tannery inputs, sandstone, pumice, and limestone used in clinker production

and European markets under buyer requirements and third-party compliance regimes (Chen, 2025, p. 9). In CM, entry is more varied and does not follow a simple relocation story: some firms moved outward from related activities in China, while others entered CM in Ethiopia with limited prior sector experience, drawn by domestic demand and price margins—cement being the clearest example (Chen, 2025, pp. 13–14). Discovery channels also differ: LM investors often drew on broader business ties (including long-standing trading relations), while CM investors relied more heavily on family- and friend-based networks and word of mouth (Chen, 2025, pp. 13–14). The analysis proceeds by sector: (a) LM and (b) CM.

"Push" and "Pull" Factors of Investing in Ethiopia's Light Manufacturing Industry

Push Factors

Rising Unit Production Costs in China

Rising unit costs—especially labour—are a common push factor, but the pressure is strongest for export-oriented manufacturers because their orders are sensitive to cost and delivery performance in buyer-driven production networks. Where brands and major retailers govern cross-border production through purchasing, lead times, and compliance routines, firms that cannot keep costs down or meet delivery schedules risk losing orders (Gereffi, 1994; Zhang, 2014). The "flying geese" logic still applies in a basic sense: labour-intensive segments tend to move to lower-cost sites over time (Lo, 2012), and rising costs in China[6] have encouraged a shift first inland and then outward to lower-wage locations in Asia and Africa (Knoerich et al., 2021).

Fujin Footwear (Type 2, pseudonym) illustrates how cost pressure interacts with a firm's position in export markets. After two decades (since 1996) as a traditional OEM, Fujin had not developed a strong brand and relied heavily on agents for orders rather than partnering directly with lead firms (mainly buyers from the US) (CCM1-1). This made it more vulnerable when costs rose: if unit costs were not reduced, agents could divert orders to cheaper suppliers. Fujin moved part of its production from coastal China (Dongguan, Guangdong) to inland China (Ganzhou, Jiangxi) in 2002, but wage gaps narrowed over time (CCM1-6). By 2017, basic monthly pay was about 2000 CNY in Dongguan and 1600–1700 CNY in Ganzhou. China became a high-cost location for low-end OEM segments even after accounting for productivity differences. Fujin reduced its workforce in China while expanding in Ethiopia: combined employment fell from 21,200 (2012) to 12,747 (2017) (Table 3.6), indicating stagnation or scale-down in China alongside a search to restore cost competitiveness through Ethiopian production (CCM1-6; CCM1-2).

Ethiopia's attraction in this case is not wages alone, but the overall unit-cost calculation. In 2012, the nominal wage ratio between Chinese and Ethiopian line workers at Fujin was roughly 1:6–1:7 and persisted for at least six years. By 2018, the average wage for production line workers in

Table 3.6 Employment (China vs Ethiopia)

Year	*Employment (China)*	*Employment (Ethiopia)/ (Chinese)*	*Localisation rates (Ethiopia)*
2012	21,200	1000 (100)	90.90%
2015	9500	4619 (179)	96.27%
2017	6000	6747 (204)	97.07%

Source: Author calculated and compiled based on CCM1-2 and CCM1-1 (2018)

[6] For example, average hourly wages in China increased from US$0.43 in 2000 to US$2.88 in 2013, an average annual growth rate of approximately 16% (McKinsey, 2018, p. 55).

China was around 3600 CNY (CCM1-2), while ETB 2000–2500 (roughly 500–600 CNY) was typical for Ethiopian workers (CCM1-11). Fujin paired lower wages with process investment—importing more advanced machinery (including from Germany) and investing in training—to raise Ethiopian productivity towards 50–60% of the China benchmark, with scope to improve.

Over time, production was differentiated across sites. Higher-end or smaller-production lines remained in Dongguan; Ganzhou ran mid-range volumes; Ethiopia began with simpler, high-volume products and—after training—moved into more demanding lines such as boots and vulcanised shoes (CCM1-7-c).[7]

Cost pressure is not limited to low-end OEM firms. More advanced producers can absorb rising costs longer, but they also reach a point where labour costs and recruitment become challenging. Rongxin Garment (Type 3, pseudonym)—a listed firm from Jiangyin, Jiangsu, founded in 1986—entered Ethiopia only in 2017/2018, later than early movers, because its brand, distribution channels, and higher-value products sustained competitiveness in China. Yet even Rongxin faced growing wage burdens ("even at 8,000 CNY/month for an operator"), expanded social insurance and pension costs, and recruitment difficulties, which changed the calculus (CCM14-1-a). As the General Manager put it:

> [I]t is inevitable that labour-intensive industries will move to places with lower labour and production costs. Even if Ethiopia does not have the advantage of zero tariffs on exports, we will still relocate here. It is just like how the textile industry relocated from Japan, South Korea and SEA countries to China two, three decades ago. During that period, China did not have a preferential policy such as zero tariffs to export textile products to the US and European markets either. (CCM14-1-a)

Late Commercial Payment Costs

Late payments are a second push factor for some family-owned SMEs. Where transactions rely heavily on *renqing* (i.e., trust-based relations and personal networks), late payments can be hard to enforce through formal legal channels without damaging business relationships. Haicheng Garment (Type 1, pseudonym), established in 2015, illustrates this

[7] This finding is based on a combination of interviews, survey data, and the author's observations.

mechanism: a six-month payment term stretched to 18 months. Legal action might have recovered cash sooner, but the perceived reputational costs were high. Delays created working-capital stress and forced repeated borrowing from family and friends; several clients went bankrupt, and invoices were never recovered (CCM3-1-a). Chapter 2 documents how "family, *guanxi* networks and patron–client ties together play a dominant role for private economy coordination" (Zhang & Peck, 2016, p. 56). The consequence is uneven enforcement that pushes some SMEs to seek alternative markets and operating environments.[8]

Environmental Compliance Costs

A third push factor is the cost of meeting tightening environmental standards in China. *The Atmospheric Pollution Prevention Action Plan* (2013) aimed to reduce harmful particulates and improve air quality by 2017 (Mazars, 2018). Many factories faced surprise inspections, fines, or closures pending compliance; over 14,000 factories reportedly closed in 2018, with knock-on supply-chain effects (Mazars, 2018). In LM, environmental compliance pressures are especially relevant for textile firms with dyeing and spinning stages. As discussed in Chap. 2, China's "centralised control, decentralised improvisation" produces fragmented, uneven enforcement. Coastal governments implemented stricter measures to expel low-end, high-polluting firms (Ang, 2018). In recent years, textile mills in the Yangtze River Delta (Zhejiang/Jiangsu) were barred from using coal-fired boilers; firms had to electrify or relocate (CCM5-2-a).

Dongsheng Dyeing (CCM5) (Type 3could not expand under tighter caps in China. It pursued partial relocation, pseudonym) and upgrading. After starting with wood-fired boilers in Ethiopia in 2013, Dongsheng invested ETB 200–300 million in improved boiler and dust-removal systems in 2016. Meanwhile, headquarters focused on higher-end products and R&D, maintaining profitability even as the number of textile mills in China fell. The motivation combined relocation of specific production stages with expansion (including three new factories in Ethiopia in later years).

Large "national champions" such as Rongxin Garment, have also faced stricter standards but met them more easily thanks to stronger financing

[8] Firms from Zhejiang account for the majority and therefore constitute a typical example of Type 1 businesses; however, similar models have also been adopted by firms from other regions since late 2020s.

and continuous process upgrading (CCM14-a). This highlights that the composition of unit cost varies by firm: some (e.g., Fuxin Footwear, Rongxin Garment) are most exposed to labour costs; others (Dongsheng Dyeing) face greater pressure from environmental compliance. Overall, tighter regulation raises production costs in China and tends to widen the gap between firms. Better-capitalised firms are more able to upgrade and comply; thinner SMEs often relocate more polluting stages, adjust product lines, or exit.

Pull Factors

Growing Demand and High Margins in Ethiopia's Domestic Market

Ethiopia's robust growth, urbanisation, and demography generate strong domestic demand for locally produced substitutes. Domestic market opportunity is a major pull factor for many early LM investors—predominantly Zhejiang SMEs—who leveraged pre-existing trading relations with Ethiopian clients. These ties gave them practical knowledge of local preferences, seasonality, and operating conditions. Interviews and surveys repeatedly described the domestic market as "high margin and fast moving," especially in basic apparel, footwear, and plastics (Chen, 2025, p. 12).[9] Several firms noted that machinery considered obsolete or too polluting in China was still relatively advanced in Ethiopia, which reduced set-up costs and shortened the time to first orders. One manager noted that long-term employees (more than seven years) now made up about 70% of the line and that Ethiopian supervisors had been trained, linking steadier local demand with retention and internal promotion (CCM3-4-a). These observations align with the timing point: early domestic-market entrants captured margins first; export-oriented firms scaled later as policy windows opened (Chen, 2025).

Trading restrictions also shape incentives. Retail, import, and wholesale are reserved for Ethiopian nationals and the diaspora; many merchants sourced goods cheaply in China (e.g., Yiwu and Guangzhou) and sold at high margins domestically. By relocating production to Ethiopia, Chinese manufacturers could compete with importers on price and responsiveness, capture part of the trading margin, and stabilise orders. Several firms

[9] Based on survey findings and interviews (CCM3-1-a; CCM4-1-a; CCM6-1-a, see Appendix C Interview Code for more details).

described a shift from opportunistic shipments to more regular orders once local production or finishing began (Chen, 2025, p. 12).

Even when firms shared the same profit motive, strategies diverged. Some pursued rapid high profits; others prioritised market share and steadier margins. Some treated the move as relocation (downsizing production in China), while others treated it as expansion.

Preferential Market Access, Investment Incentives, and a Committed Host Government

Cost pressure in China helps explain why firms looked outward, but it does not explain why relocation becomes durable in one particular place rather than another. In Ethiopia, the pre-2020 period offered a policy window for export-oriented LM: industrial parks and related bespoke services (utilities, compliance, customs) combined with preferential market access (notably the African Growth and Opportunity Act (AGOA)[10] and Everything But Arms (EBA)[11]) to reduce the operational risks that export firms face (Chen, 2025, pp. 12–13).

Thus, for export-oriented LM firms, the key pull factor is the combination of preferential market access (e.g., AGOA/EBA), investment incentives, and industrial park infrastructure. Under strained Sino–US trade relations, relocating to Ethiopia also enabled some firms to bypass trade barriers more quickly (Lim & Kimura, 2010). For instance, apparel/textile exports from China to the US faced tariffs of roughly 30–40%; the same products exported from Ethiopia enjoyed zero tariffs and no quota restrictions. Thirty-eight Sub-Saharan African countries benefit from AGOA (AGOA, 2019) and 34 from EBA (Chen, 2021a).

Beyond market access, the GoE offered bundles of preferential incentives—corporate income-tax holidays, duty- and tax-free import of equipment, machinery and spares, and pre-shipment financing (Whitfield et al., 2020, p. 13). These measures mattered most where they reduced operational frictions: predictable utilities, clearer customs procedures, and support for meeting buyer compliance requirements (Chen, 2025, pp. 12–13).

Field evidence converges on a basic mechanism: when park services and state facilitation reduce uncertainty around customs, standards, and utilities, export-oriented firms find it easier to meet buyer lead times and compliance demands (EIC, 2017, p. 12; Chen, 2025, pp. 12–13). This is why

[10] See https://agoa.info/about-agoa.html for more details.

[11] See https://trade.ec.europa.eu/tradehelp/everything-arms for more details.

industrial parks are not simply "locations"; they are part of the operating model that can make export production possible.

Attracting the "Leading Goose"

Ethiopia's industrial development vision aspires to make the country the leading manufacturing hub in Africa by 2025 (EIC, 2018). The first Growth and Transformation Plan (GTP I (2010–2015)) was established in 2010, aiming to drive growth and transformation by developing a vibrant manufacturing and industrial base. The export-oriented manufacturing industry had been prioritised as a key strategic industry and benefited from policy reform. The GoE identified which sectors were a priority and what were the most promising sources for better quality FDI. They had also targeted firms as "leading geese." This came from their realisation that they needed to attract technologically advanced firms from countries with higher costs that could benefit from Ethiopia's cost advantages (Brautigam et al., 2018, p. 164).

Ethiopia's industrial strategy sought to attract large, export-oriented manufacturers that could demonstrate feasibility and encourage follow-on investment. Under the GTP I (2010–2015), export-oriented manufacturing was prioritised, and policymakers sought "leading goose" investors from higher-cost locations (Brautigam et al., 2018, p. 164).

As the first large-scale, export-oriented Chinese manufacturer in Ethiopia, Fuxin Footwear played a demonstration role, signalling feasibility to followers (Chen, 2021a). Its investment was facilitated by then-Prime Minister Meles Zenawi and supported by Chinese authorities. Fuxin's Deputy Chairman cited preferential export policies (especially the AGOA) as the critical determinant—for example, high tariffs (i.e., 37.5%) on shoes exported from China versus zero tariffs from Ethiopia (CCM1-1). While market access was central, political recognition associated with being a successful "leading goose" also mattered (Brautigam et al., 2018). Fuxin thus exemplifies a profit-optimisation logic (i.e., economic plus political returns).

Cluster Building Through Supply Chains and Buyer–Supplier Co-location

Under GTP II (2016–2020), policy shifted from reactive to proactive: the GoE approached global buyers, transnational producers, accessory suppliers and textile mills, tailoring park design to their needs (Staritz & Whitfield, 2017, p. 17; EIC, 2017, p. 12). With abundant labour, cheap electricity and scope for forward/backward linkages, the textile/apparel sector was positioned for comparative advantage (EIC, 2017, p. 14). The intent was not only to attract individual factories, but to draw in more complete supply chains—buyers, first-tier suppliers, and supporting firms—in order to reduce coordination failures and improve the chances that export manufacturing could scale (Oqubay, 2019a, 2019b; Chen, 2025, p. 12). Quota-free access, incentive bundles and the "Made in Africa" brand became key selling points to integrate Ethiopia into GPNs/GVCs.

A new wave of Chinese exporters followed this buyer-led model since GPT II. A major US apparel buyer (hereafter, the Lead Buyer)—as both investor and buyer- played a stabilising role by encouraging its long-term strategic suppliers (including Chinese firms) to co-locate and by providing confidence that extra orders would be available during the transition.

Jintai Textile (Type 3, pseudonym) established in 2016 (operations from late 2017), was invested by its parent company, a long-term supplier of its Lead Buyer. According to Jintai's senior manager, the Lead Buyer encouraged the move and indicated that orders to the China operation would not be reduced during the transition (CCM13-1-a; CCM13-1-b). As the Chairman of Jintai summarised, the project reflected cooperation among three parties—the Lead Buyer, the GoE at the federal and local levels (land and sheds at HIP), and Jintai—where the buyer's purchasing commitments helped reduce demand uncertainty during the relocation process (CCM13-1-a; Chen, 2025, p. 12).

Strategically, such export-oriented firms often retain buyer-facing functions in China during the early phase of relocating industrial capital (e.g., quality control, design, buyer liaison). Durable export embedding then depends on whether Ethiopian plants stabilise productivity and compliance under local constraints—utilities, logistics, and customs clearance. Several exporters reported prioritising the US market for larger, more standardised orders, while European buyers tended to place smaller and more varied orders (CCM13-1-a; CCM14-1-b; Chen, 2025, p. 12).

Firms such as Jintai invested in Ethiopia primarily for profit maximisation, with a focus on industrial upgrading and market expansion. With increasing internationalisation, leading manufacturers diversify their product lines and seek new markets. As of late 2018, Jintai's main business was garments (56% of overall exports); pet products (such as pet beds, crate mats, toys, apparel, and accessories) accounted for a further 22%. Organisationally, Jintai belongs to the "Department of Textiles" in its parent company (ibid.). In the past, the Lead Buyer was its biggest customer, accounting for 50% of Jintai's total exports. As Jintai expanded, its product range and customers grew increasingly diversified. Although the Lead Buyer remains Jintai's largest client, its share of Jintai's total export volume had declined as the firm had expanded into the European market (CCM13-1-a).

Taken together, the LM evidence indicates that relocation is not driven by "low wages" alone. Firms respond to cost and regulatory pressures in China, but Ethiopia becomes a viable destination when domestic demand is strong (for domestic-market firms) or when export access, buyer commitments, and park-based facilitation make reliable production and delivery possible (for export-oriented firms) (Chen, 2025, pp. 12–13).

The above implies that the industrial relocation of Chinese LM firms to Ethiopia has been driven by both buyers and the host-country government. Even for firms focused on exporting, firms' motives and determinants of investing in Ethiopia differ significantly, depending on firms' positions in GPNs, the type of firm and sector specificities and the host country's political economy conditions. HIP (at least during the post-2020 period) can be seen as a hub for buyer-led cluster building: park services, promised orders and supplier co-location reduce coordination failures and compress learning curves (Chen, 2025).

"Push" and "Pull" Factors of Investing in Ethiopia's Construction Materials Industry

The CM industry is generally more capital- and energy-intensive than LM. It has been a core import-substitution (ISI) priority in Ethiopia since 2005 (Gebreeyesus, 2014, 2017; Oqubay, 2015; see also Chen, 2025, pp. 10, 13–14). As Xia (2019, p. 3) notes, the movement of CM firms to Africa has been pulled by infrastructure-led demand for materials and pushed by China-side pressures to deal with overcapacity and pollution. However, the push–pull framework is only partly applicable for explaining Chinese private investment in Ethiopia's CM industry, because many CM investments are not straightforward relocation from an existing cement or steel business in China. Some firms moved out of related sectors; others entered CM in Ethiopia with little prior sector experience, after seeing domestic demand and margins.

Consistent with the typology developed earlier, most CM entrants in Ethiopia were closer to MEFs: they mainly sold into Ethiopia's domestic market, and their day-to-day business depended less on export-buyer governance than on whether production can be kept running under practical constraints such as FX access, power reliability, and the ability to secure key inputs and permits (Chen, 2025, pp. 13–14).

Two broad manufacturing firm groups are present in Ethiopia's CM industry: (i) investors with related operations in China; and (ii) investors without such experience. For the second group, China-side "push" factors are less relevant (see Table 3.7). Sub-sector variations also matter. Clinker production and large steel mills require large upfront capital, stable electricity, and long investment cycles. Other sub-sectors—such as steel pipe, cement grinding stations, aluminium products, ceramic products, and gypsum boards—have lower entry barriers. How investors learn about CM opportunities also differs from LM: early CM moves, especially in cement, often spread through word of mouth via family and friends (fieldwork, 2016–2018; see also Chen, 2025, pp. 13–14).

This section argues that four main factors have driven Chinese private firms to invest in Ethiopia's CM industry: (i) growing demand and generous profit margins in the domestic market; (ii) lower production costs (especially energy); (iii) a committed host government and political stability; and (iv) Ethiopia's macroeconomic conditions, especially FX

Table 3.7 Push and pull factors of investing in the construction materials industry

Sector	*Type of factors*	*Factors*	*Comment*
Construction materials	Push	Increasingly difficult operational climate in China	Specific to firms with related business in China
	Pull	Growing domestic demand and generous margins	Common to all firms
		Lower production costs (especially energy)	Common to all; strongest for capital-/energy-intensive sub-sectors
		Committed host government and political stability	Common to all firms
		Macroeconomic conditions (notably FX availability)	Common to all; binding for import-dependent lines

Source: Author's elaboration based on interviews and survey data (see also Chen, 2025, pp. 13–14).

availability. These drivers do not operate uniformly: they play out differently across steel, cement, ceramics, and related products (Chen, 2025, pp. 13–14).

Push Factors

Increasingly Difficult Operational Climate in China

An increasingly difficult operational climate in China is a specific push factor for private SMEs that already operated in CM-related sectors. Parts of CM have been targeted for restructuring under *guo jin min tui* ("the state advances, private retreats") (Kroeber, 2016). Measures accelerated after 2008 and into the "New Normal" (from 2013), squeezing many SMEs (Lüthje et al., 2013). The outward movement of "overcapacity" industries to developing economies is consistent with China's structural transformation agenda. Managers repeatedly linked outward movement to "thin margins plus tighter enforcement," especially in steel, where capacity controls and environmental compliance raised fixed costs (CCM15-1; CCM2-1-b).

At the EIP, Zhenxing Steel (Type 1, pseudonym) and Dongxin Steel (Type 3, pseudonym) both cited falling profitability and policy pressure in China as key pushes. Ethiopia's price differential also mattered: in 2014, rebar sold at roughly CNY 5000/tonne in Ethiopia versus CNY 2000–2200/tonne in China, leaving around CNY 1000/tonne net even after higher logistics; by 2017, net profit could reach around CNY 3000/tonne in favourable conditions (CCM15-1; CCM2-1-b). Both firms framed "Going Out" as a way to restore margins under stronger local demand and pricing.

Pulls Factors

Growing Demand and Generous Margins in the Domestic Market

Unlike LM, which can target both domestic and export markets, CM in Ethiopia was primarily oriented to Ethiopia's domestic market. Large-scale infrastructure programmes and urban construction had generated sustained demand for cement, steel, and related construction materials. In practice, this domestic demand—together with the selling-price margin it can sustain—helps explain both entry timing and firm behaviour in CM (survey, 2018; CCM2-1-b; CCM17-1-a; Chen, 2025, pp. 13–14).[12]

Zhenxing and Dongxin were pulled by the Ethiopia–China price spread noted above. Even allowing for Ethiopia's higher logistics and coordination costs, privately financed mills could restore margins when domestic demand supported selling prices and capacity utilisation (CCM15-1; CCM2-1-b). One steel firm claimed that by 2014 it still realised around CNY 1000/tonne net profit (CCM15-1). By 2017, net profit on rebar in Ethiopia could reach CNY 3000/tonne under favourable conditions, as confirmed with another private steel mill (CCM2-1-b). These figures clarify why relocation could make sense for privately financed mills facing a tightening cost and regulatory environment in China.

Cement shows an even clearer demand-led pull. Many early cement investors lacked prior cement experience in China. Their motives ranged from speculative entry to incremental capability building, but most shared the belief that local demand outstripped capacity.

Entrepreneur background matters. Mr Zhou (pseudonym), a Zhejiang entrepreneur, established a cement plant in 2006 (production in 2007) when only three plants operated in Ethiopia; prices at CNY 2000–2300/tonne—roughly ten times China's—prompted investment (CCM17-1-a).[13] Mr Ma (pseudonym), a Jiangsu entrepreneur, entered cement after initially exploring steel pipe; cement's demand/price signal and perceived resemblance to Su'nan development patterns shaped the choice (CCM2-1-b). Both investments started before the BRI and proceeded without special incentives except for a two-year tax exemption. And both were discovered via social networks and amplified by word of mouth. As noted before, most early investors had no relevant experience in China, indicating that entry decisions were driven more by network position and perceived demand than by pre-existing firm capabilities.

Rapid entry under a generous price umbrella also brought risks and policy response. By 2009, five more Chinese privately owned (mostly small in scale) plants started. Ill-prepared entrants lacking sectoral knowledge distorted prices and created further coordination problems. In 2013,

[12] This finding is based on a combination of interviews, surveys, and the author's observations (2016–2018).

[13] "First" here refers to the first investment project that became operational. All interviewees provided informed consent and agreed that the information they shared could be used for research purposes (see Appendix E for a sample consent form). For confidentiality, the names of all firms and interviewees have been pseudonymised.

the GoE closed cement to new foreign investors (National Planning Commission, 2016; Gebreeyesus, 2014; Oqubay, 2015). Post entry trajectories then diverged. Mr Zhou sold and reinvested downstream (real estate, from 2011) with a Chinese mixed ownership enterprise (CCM17-1-a); Mr Ma stayed in cement while diversifying into industrial park development and other CM sub-sectors.

Two recurring patterns emerge in CM, consistent with the MEF repertoire outlined earlier. First, discovery channels are overwhelmingly social (i.e., family, friends, and diaspora ties) networks, unlike the official/business networks common in export-oriented LM. Second, most CM firms are owner-operated, and entrepreneur characteristics (origin, education, prior experience, network position) shape risk appetite (speculative vs incremental), scale and diversification pace.

Lower Production Costs (Especially Energy)

Lower production costs—especially energy—are another common pull factor for CM. This matters most for capital and energy intensive sub sectors such as cement, steel, and ceramics. Although average wages in CM can be higher than in LM, labour often makes up a smaller share of total costs (Oqubay, 2015). Instead of low wages, overall cost efficiency—especially energy—is more important. In cement, for example, labour costs are modest compared to energy and raw materials. For Ordinary Portland Cement (OPC), energy costs account for nearly 46% of total production costs (coal 43% and fuel power 3%), while labour accounts for approximately 15% (FCM1-3) (see Fig. 3.5). To produce one tonne of OPC, approximately 110 kWh of electricity and 110 kg of coal are required (FCM1-1).

Ethiopia's industrial electricity tariffs are low by African standards (Oqubay, 2015; National Planning Commission, 2016). Industrial power in China ranges from CNY 0.78–0.81/kWh (around US$0.11–0.12),[14] whereas Ethiopia charges roughly ETB 0.3664–0.7426/kWh (around US$0.019–0.039) (MOFCOM) (Eth) (2018, p. 35). This matters directly for energy-intensive lines such as medium/large cement (clinker), steel and ceramics. Yuande Ceramics (Type 1, pseudonym)—a medium-scale plant set up by Wenzhou entrepreneurs in 2016 (production from December 2017)—explicitly cited market demand, low production costs,

[14] Author calculated based on CEIC data, available at: https://www.ceicdata.com/en/china/electricity-price (accessed January 10, 2019).

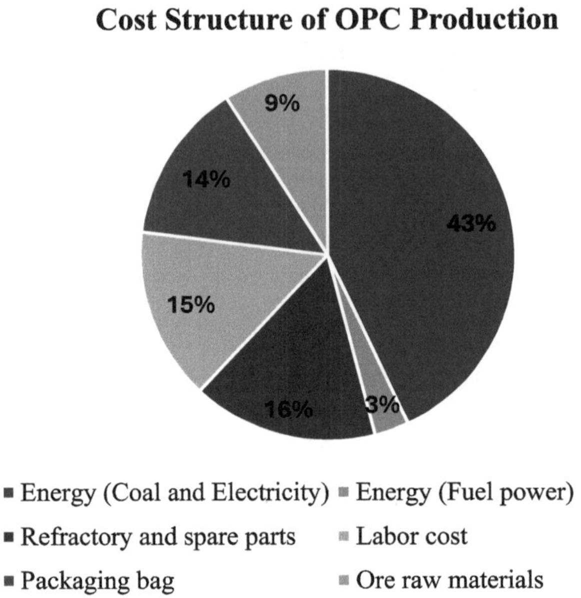

Fig. 3.5 Cost structure of OPC production. (Source: Author, compiled based on data provided by a non-Chinese foreign cement firm (FCM1-3))

and the availability of local raw materials as key determinants during an FX shortage period (CCM11-1; CCM11-2).

Low electricity prices, however, are not enough on their own. For CM plants with high fixed capital and continuous processes, what matters is also whether power supply is reliable and whether key inputs can be secured consistently. Entry and exit are harder than in LM because sunk costs are larger and the production cycle is less flexible.

A Committed Host Government and Political Stability

Another driver is the GoE's commitment to supporting investors. This is especially important in sub-sectors with complex input chains and high sensitivity to domestic political–economic conditions. Cheap energy is necessary but not sufficient for CM: cement and steel require consistent power; coordination across upstream inputs (e.g., mining rights, fuel logistics), FX prioritisation for strategic imports; and workable downstream distribution. High fixed capital and scale economies also make entry/exit far harder than in LM, raising the value of predictable facilitation (Oqubay, 2015).

Survey evidence indicates that firms consistently cite political stability as an important determinant, and GoE facilitation as a common driver—particularly in clinker and steel where coordination needs are greatest. Subsector dynamics matter: clinker production typically requires more coordination (covering mining rights, fuel logistics, FX prioritisation for key inputs, and distribution) than, for example, gypsum boards or wood products. As Oqubay notes, "to improve energy efficiency and support cement producers, the government imported bulk coal" (2018, p. 17).

Macroeconomic Conditions

Ethiopia's macroeconomic setting, characterised by capital controls and chronic FX scarcity (Senbeta, 2013), makes binding FX ceilings pivotal for import-dependent CM subsectors. The size and timing of FX allocation directly affected whether firms can open letters of credit, import inputs, keep plants running near full capacity, and maintain cash flow. Beyond a few lines—such as ceramics, gypsum, and wood—that can source most inputs locally, many CM activities relied heavily on imported materials (survey, 2018). This helps explain why some high-margin niches still see limited new entry.

In practice, FX scarcity constrains CM through three linked aspects:

- Access to FX approvals, which determines whether firms can import raw materials, spare parts and equipment.
- Import intensity, since sectors that rely heavily on imported inputs face sharper output disruptions when FX tightens.
- Government prioritisation, where some inputs (e.g., fuel for cement) may receive higher priority than others (e.g., billet for rebar), reshaping which CM lines remain viable.

Cement is partly insulated (see Table 3.8). Core raw materials—limestone, sandstone, clay, gypsum, and pumice—are domestically available, while coal and heavy fuel oil (HFO) must be imported but are often prioritised because cement is treated as strategic. Prioritisation eases exposure to FX and logistics but does not remove it; plants still depend on timely allocations to sustain clinker and grinding operations.

Steel, by contrast, is highly FX-exposed (see Table 3.8). To meet rebar quality standards, Dongxin Steel imported 100% billet (formerly from

Table 3.8 Examples of raw materials that rely heavily on importation in the construction materials industry

Sector	*Imported items specific to the sector*	*Imported items common across CM*
Steel products	Billet; cold-rolled coil; structural steel	Chemicals; accessories; high-quality coal
Cement	Fuel inputs (coal/HFO); selected chemicals	Selected chemicals
Ceramic products	Glaze	Selected chemicals
Wood products	Selected accessories	Selected accessories

Source: Author, calculated and compiled based on a survey conducted in April 2018

Ukraine). Despite attractive Ethiopia–China price spreads, FX shortages forced a half-year shutdown in 2017 (CCM8-1-a). In steel, FX availability can become the binding constraint on throughput and profitability, even when market demand and selling prices are favourable.

Ceramics illustrates how local inputs can reduce FX exposure. Yuande Ceramics cited market demand, low production costs and the ready availability of local raw materials as decisive during an FX shortage period (CCM11-1; CCM11-2). More broadly, import dependence varies across CM: steel products typically require imported billet and coils; cement relies mainly on domestic minerals but still depends on imported fuel inputs and some chemicals; ceramics often import glazes; wood products source core materials locally and import only selected accessories.

The implication is that CM sector choice correlates with import intensity and expected FX access. Investors tend to gravitate towards lines with domestic inputs (ceramics/gypsum/wood) or lines where key imports are more likely to be prioritised (cement fuel), and away from lines such as steel where billet, FX can become a hard constraint. In CM, these practical constraints—FX, input logistics and power reliability—often matter more for plant performance than the headline selling price or profit margin (see also Chen, 2025, pp. 13–14).

Summary

This section has shown that motives and determinants vary systematically by firm type and by sub-sector, and that "push" and "pull" factors only become meaningful once they are linked to how firms actually operate in Ethiopia.

In LM, cost and regulatory pressures in China are common pushes, but firms translate them differently. MEFs—often SMEs with prior trading ties—typically entered through domestic-market opportunities and relied on established relationships and flexible routines to manage practical constraints such as FX shortages, uneven utilities, and logistics delays (Chen, 2025, pp. 10–12). GPN-IFs—export-oriented manufacturers—expanded where Ethiopia's trade preferences, industrial park services, and customs/standards facilitation could support lead firm (e.g., buyer) requirements, including monitoring cycles, documentation, delivery schedules, and compliance routines (Chen, 2025, pp. 9–13). In this sense, what matters is not "low wages" only, but whether production can be organised reliably under buyer time schedules and standards, and park-level service delivery.

In CM, the dominant pull is domestic demand and price margins, but viability is filtered by the practical cost structure of each line—especially energy intensity and dependence on imported inputs—and by macro constraints such as FX access and power reliability (Chen, 2025, pp. 13–15). Cement is partly buffered because core raw materials are local and fuel imports may be prioritised, while steel is more exposed to FX constraints when key inputs such as billet depend on imports. Ceramics and some allied lines can reduce FX pressure where local inputs are available, but still depend on stable electricity and reliable logistics (Chen, 2025, pp. 13–15).

Taken together, the evidence supports a "combination" view of causality: outcomes hinge less on any single determinant (wages, incentives, or "Chinese" origin) than on whether sector requirements, firm capabilities, and Ethiopia's operating arrangements—industrial parks and aftercare, customs/standards routines, utilities, logistics, and FX allocation—line up in practice over time (Chen, 2025, pp. 12–15).

Conclusion

This chapter's core move is to shift analysis away from methodological nationalism and towards firm heterogeneity and host-country operating conditions. "Chinese private capital" in Ethiopia is not a single actor, and outcomes are shaped through the concrete settings where firms meet the state and the market—licensing, land access, utilities, customs and standards routines, labour administration, and, under FX scarcity, access to foreign exchange for inputs and maintenance.

The MEF/GPN-IF distinction developed in Section "A Variety of Chinese Manufacturing Firms in Ethiopia" clarifies why similar macro conditions can produce different strategies and trajectories. MEFs tend to build their position through domestic and regional markets, using prior trading ties, informal and business networks, and flexible production decisions to cope with uneven service delivery and FX constraint (Chen, 2025, pp. 10–12). GPN-IFs are organised around export buyers and compliance requirements, and their viability depends heavily on whether industrial-park services and administrative routines can support predictable throughput—utilities, clearance, standards, and logistics—under time-sensitive delivery schedules and lead firm-monitoring (Chen, 2025, pp. 9–13).

The chapter also demonstrates that single-factor explanations travel poorly. In LM, the decisive issue is not simply cheaper labour, but whether firms can rebuild unit costs while meeting buyer discipline and operating reliably under Ethiopia's production and logistics constraints (Chen, 2025, pp. 9–13). In CM, domestic demand and margins are central pulls, but the binding constraints often sit in the interaction between energy intensity, import dependence, and FX allocation, with power reliability and input logistics determining whether plants can run at viable capacity (Chen, 2025, pp. 13–15). These sector differences help explain why CM entry can be attractive yet uneven, and why export-oriented LM becomes durable only under specific combinations of buyer governance and credible facilitation.

The practical implications follow from this logic. For export-oriented LM, attracting and retaining GPN-IFs is mainly an execution challenge: predictable utilities, faster and more reliable customs/standards procedures, and logistics performance matter at least as much as headline incentives because they determine whether buyer requirements can be met in practice (Chen, 2025, pp. 9–13). For domestic-market oriented LM, lowering routine operating frictions—licensing, land and workspace access, and FX constraints on inputs—matters for sustaining margins and stabilising production. For CM, credibility hinges on the ability to stabilise power supply and to make FX prioritisation rules legible and predictable for strategic inputs, so investors can price risk in capital- and energy-intensive lines (Chen, 2025, pp. 13–15).

If investment performance depends on how policy tools are enacted in practice—industrial parks, one-stop services, export discipline, and the routines governing FX, customs, and standards—then the next step is to examine how these arrangements are negotiated, implemented, and enforced. Chapter 4 therefore focuses on the institutional bargaining mechanisms and day-to-day practices through which firms and state agencies in and around the EIP deal with land, services, export expectations, labour administration, and environmental compliance, and how these interactions shape firm trajectories over time.

These conclusions lead directly to Chap. 4. If investment performance depends on how policy tools are enacted in practice— industrial parks, one-stop services, export discipline, and the routines around FX, customs, and standards—then the next step is to examine how those arrangements are actually negotiated, implemented, and enforced. Chapter 4 therefore focuses on the institutional bargaining mechanisms and day-to-day practices through which firms and state agencies in and around the EIP deal with land, services, export expectations, labour administration, and environmental compliance, and how these interactions shape firm trajectories over time. Put differently, the evidence in this chapter substantiates P1 and P2 and sets up the institutional mechanisms examined under P3 and P4.

References

Addisfortune. (2014, September 14). Ethiopia's Addis Abeba–Adama Expressway finally open. *Addis Fortune*. Retrieved February 12, 2019, from https://addisfortune.net/articles/ethiopias-addis-abeba-adama-expressway-finally-open/.

AGOA.info. (2019). *Annual review of country eligibility for benefits under AGOA for 2021* [PDF]. Retrieved February 16, 2019, from https://agoa.info/images/documents/15769/ustrfrdoc0001-0610content.pdf

Ang, Y. (2018). Domestic flying geese: Industrial transfer and delayed policy diffusion in China. *The China Quarterly*. Retrieved February 24, 2019, from https://doi.org/10.1017/S0305741018000516.

Brautigam, D. (2015, December 7). Chinese investment in Africa: How not to mix apples and … elephants. *China Africa: The Real Story (Blog)*. Retrieved December 20, 2018, from http://www.chinaafricarealstory.com/2015/12/chinese-investment-in-africa-how-not-to.html

Brautigam, D., Tang, X., & Xia, Y. (2018). *What kinds of Chinese "geese" are flying to Africa? Evidence from Chinese manufacturing firms* (Working Paper No. 2018/17). China Africa Research Initiative, Johns Hopkins University SAIS. Retrieved December 10, 2025, from http://www.sais-cari.org/publications.

Chen, W. (2021a). The dynamics of Chinese private outward foreign direct investment in Ethiopia: A comparison of the light manufacturing industry and the construction materials industry. PhD thesis, SOAS University of London. https://doi.org/10.25501/SOAS.00035764.

Chen, W. (2021b). The dynamics of state–business relations between the Ethiopian state and Chinese private firms: A case study of the Eastern Industrial Park, WIDER Working Paper, No. 2021/122. Helsinki: UNU-WIDER. https://doi.org/10.35188/UNU-WIDER/2021/062-7.

Chen, W. (2022). China and Africa: Ethiopia case study debunks investment myths, The Conversation Africa, 21 February. https://doi.org/10.64628/aaj.jevsggshs.

Chen, W. (2025). Heterogeneity and drivers of Chinese manufacturing FDI in Africa: Evidence from Angola and Ethiopia. *Journal of International Development*. https://doi.org/10.1002/jid.70038

Dunning, J. H., & Lundan, S. M. (2008). *Multinational enterprises and the global economy* (2nd ed.). Edward Elgar.

Ethiopian Investment Commission (EIC). (2017). *Industrial Parks in Ethiopia: Incentives package*. Ethiopian Investment Commission.

Ethiopian Investment Commission (EIC). (2018). *Ethiopian Investment Report 2017*. Ethiopian Investment Commission.

Ethiopian Investment Commission (EIC). (2019). *Summary of licensed total foreign direct investment projects by sector and status since August 22, 1992–January 24, 2019 (GC)*. Internal document.

Ethiopian Investment Commission (EIC). (2020). *Ethiopian Investment Report 2019*. Ethiopian Investment Commission.

Gebreeyesus, M. (2014). *A natural experiment of industrial policy: Floriculture and the metal and engineering industries in Ethiopia* (WIDER Working Paper 2014/163). UNU-WIDER. Retrieved December 10, 2019, from https://www.wider.unu.edu/sites/default/files/wp2014-163.pdf.

Gebreeyesus, M. (2017). The private sector in Ethiopia's transformation. In J. Page & F. Tarp (Eds.), *The practice of industrial policy: Government–Business coordination in Africa and East Asia* (pp. 687–703). Oxford University Press.

Gereffi, G. (1994). The organization of buyer-driven global commodity chains: How U.S. retailers shape overseas production networks. In G. Gereffi & M. Korzeniewicz (Eds.), *Commodity chains and global capitalism* (pp. 95–122). Praeger.

Hymer, S. (1976). *The international operations of national firms: A study of direct foreign investment*. MIT Press.

Knoerich, J., Mouan, L., & Goodburn, C. (2021). Is China's model of SEZ-led development viable? A call for smart replication. *Journal of Current Chinese Affairs*. https://doi.org/10.1177/1868102621993487

Kroeber, A. R. (2016). *China's economy: What everyone needs to know*. Oxford University Press.

Lee, C. K. (2017). *The specter of global China: Politics, labour, and foreign investment in Africa*. University of Chicago Press.

Lim, H., & Kimura, F. (2010). The internationalization of small and medium enterprises in regional and global value chains. ADBI Working Paper No. 231. Asian Development Bank Institute.

Lo, D. (2012). *Alternative to neoliberal globalization: Studies in the political economy of institutions and late development.* Palgrave Macmillan.

Lüthje, B., Luo, S., & Zhang, H. (2013). *Beyond the Iron Rice Bowl: Regimes of production and industrial relations in China.* Campus Verlag.

Mazars. (2018, June 19). Increased environmental regulations on Chinese manufacturing: Considerations for U.S. companies.

McKinsey & Company. (2018). *Africa's business revolution: How to succeed in the world's next big growth market.* McKinsey & Company.

Ministry of Commerce of the People's Republic of China (MOFCOM). (2018). *Country guide for foreign investment and cooperation: Ethiopia* (2018th ed.). MOFCOM.

Moghaddam, K., et al. (2014). Global value chain governance and EM-MNEs. *Journal of International Management, 20*(4), 359–372.

National Planning Commission. (2016). *Growth and Transformation Plan II (GTP II), 2015/16–2019/20.* National Planning Commission.

Oqubay, A. (2015). *Made in Africa: Industrial policy in Ethiopia.* Oxford University Press.

Oqubay, A. (2018). Industrial policy and late industrialization in Ethiopia, Working Paper Series No. 303. Abidjan: African Development Bank.

Oqubay, A. (2019a). Industrial policy and late industrialization in Ethiopia. In F. Cheru, C. Cramer, & A. Oqubay (Eds.), *The Oxford Handbook of the Ethiopian Economy* (pp. 605–629). Oxford University Press.

Oqubay, A. (2019b). The structure and performance of the Ethiopian manufacturing sector. In F. Cheru, C. Cramer, & A. Oqubay (Eds.), *The Oxford Handbook of the Ethiopian Economy* (pp. 630–650). Oxford University Press.

Porter, M. E. (1998). Clusters and the new economics of competition. *Harvard Business Review* (November–December issue).

Qu, F. (2014). Jiangsu pattern change and structural adjustment. In S. Fan, R. Kanbur, S.-J. Wei, & X. Zhang (Eds.), *The Oxford companion to the economics of China* (pp. 540–550). Oxford University Press.

Schaefer, F., & Oya, C. (2019). *Employment patterns and conditions in construction and manufacturing in Ethiopia: A comparative analysis of the road building and light manufacturing sectors* (IDCEA Research Report). SOAS, University of London.

Senbeta, S. (2013). *Foreign exchange constraints and macroeconomic dynamics in a small open economy* (Working Paper 2013023). University of Antwerp, Faculty of Business and Economics.

Sharman, J. C. (2010). Shopping for anonymous shell companies: An audit study of anonymity and crime in the international financial system. *Journal of Economic Perspectives, 24*(4), 127–140.

Shen, X. (1990) *Foreign direct investment and economic development: A study of the Chinese experience, 1978–88.* PhD thesis, Johns Hopkins University, School of Advanced International Studies, Washington, DC.

Shen, X. (2015). *Private Chinese investment in Africa* (World Bank Policy Research Working Paper No. 7318). World Bank.

Staritz, C., & Whitfield, L. (2017). *Made in Ethiopia: The emergence and evolution of the Ethiopian apparel export sector.* Roskilde University.

Sun, Y., Jayaram, K., & Kassiri, O. (2017). *Dance of the lion and dragons: How are Africa and China engaging, and how will the partnership evolve?* McKinsey & Company.

Whitfield, L., Staritz, C., & Morris, M. (2020). Global value chains and industrial policy in Ethiopia's apparel sector. *Development and Change, 51*(4), 1018–1043.

Xia, Y. (2019). *Assessing Chinese manufacturing investments in East Africa: Drivers, challenges, and opportunities* (SAIS-CARI Briefing Paper No. 2). China Africa Research Initiative, Johns Hopkins University SAIS.

Zhang, J., & Peck, J. (2016). Variegated capitalism, Chinese style: Regional models, multi-scalar constructions. *Regional Studies, 50*(1), 52–78.

Zhang, W. (2014). The future of private and state-owned enterprises in China. In S. Fan, R. Kanbur, S.-J. Wei, & X. Zhang (Eds.), *The Oxford companion to the economics of China* (pp. 285–290). Oxford University Press.

CHAPTER 4

The Dynamics of State–Business Relations Between the Ethiopian State and Chinese Private Firms: A Case Study of the Eastern Industrial Park (Pre-2020)

Introduction

This chapter uses the Eastern Industrial Park (EIP) as a case study of the pre-2020 period to examine the dynamics of state–business relations between Ethiopian government agencies (the EIC in particular) and Chinese private firms. It focuses on the bargaining mechanisms through which firms seek permits, services, and problem-solving support, and on the role of tacit networks in day-to-day negotiation. It traces how these mechanisms emerged, the institutional forms they took, and how they evolved as the park expanded. Set against Ethiopia's "Made in Ethiopia" industrial agenda, the EIP case highlights how national ambitions met everyday frictions over land, services, labour relations, and regulatory compliance in Dukem, Oromia.

By analysing how firms lobby, adapt, and bargain with host country state actors at multiple levels, this chapter complements Chap. 3's focus on who invested, with what motives, and with what market priorities and investment logics. Tracing what firms do after entry is essential for understanding how Chinese private FDI operates in practice and why outcomes diverge across firms.

The chapter also shows that Chinese official institutions had limited capacity to represent the diversity of private firms. Many private investors therefore relied more on local improvisation and built their own

W. Chen, *Chinese Manufacturing Firms in Ethiopia*, Palgrave Studies in African and Development Economics,
https://doi.org/10.1007/978-3-032-24322-5_4

bargaining channels, even when official platforms existed. This is where the distinction between state and private capital matters (Lee, 2017), because it shapes which channels are effective, for whom, and on what issues. In the EIP, relations between Chinese private firms and Ethiopian agencies were not uniformly cooperative: they were complex, context-specific, and fluid, shifting across issues such as land and services, labour conflict, and export targets.

The chapter is structured as follows. Section "The Bargaining Mechanisms of Chinese Businesses in Ethiopia" outlines the main types of institutional bargaining mechanisms used by Chinese firms in Ethiopia. Section "Chinese Business Institutional Bargaining Mechanisms in the EIP" traces how bargaining mechanisms evolved within the EIP and introduces the key institutions involved. Section Dealing with the Local Government, Labour Conflict and Export Targets" examines three areas of recurrent friction in the pre-2020 period—land and local services (including environmental governance), labour conflict, and export targets—and identifies the instruments and bargaining processes used to address them. Section "Ways Forward" draws out practical implications and "ways forward." Section "Conclusion" concludes and links the pre-2020 configuration to the post-2020 period discussed in Chap. 5 and to the wider arguments developed in Chap. 6.

Analytically, this chapter speaks most directly to P3 and P4 in Chap. 2. It shows how a core policy tool—the industrial park and its associated one-stop service arrangements—shaped investors and structured expectations, but also how outcomes depended on bargaining over how rules were interpreted, implemented, and enforced in practice. It also revisits P1 and P2 by showing how MEFs and GPN-IFs used different collective platforms and brokers, reflecting their market orientation and production-network position. Finally, by reconstructing the pre-2020 configuration, the chapter provides a baseline for the post-2020 phase shift analysed in Chap. 5 (P5).

The Bargaining Mechanisms of Chinese Businesses in Ethiopia

This section brings empirical evidence to show that there are various Chinese business bargaining mechanisms in Ethiopia, which can be divided into two main types: the first is a formal, legitimate institutional bargaining mechanism. Firms establish relatively formalised mechanisms, such as associations (there are different kinds of business associations, such as the Chamber of Commerce (CCCE) in Ethiopia). The names of these associations differ, depending on the different meetings, reporting, mandates, and remits. The second mechanism is an informal one (what I refer to as "tacit networks"). Tacit networks can be any type of *guanxi* networks (including official, business, and social networks, as discussed in Chap. 3). However, they are manifested in a highly implicit and subtle way to establish, develop and maintain *guanxi* with political elites and bureaucrats. This type of bargaining mechanism sometimes operates in groups, and at other moments is applied on an individual basis.

Both of the above are bargaining mechanisms. They are the main interlocutors between Chinese businesses and the state. Within those business bargaining mechanisms, firms have different levels of engagement. Some are just for information sharing. Others are managed by Chinese institutions, while still more are truly independent.

Chinese Business Associations in Ethiopia

A growing literature on state–business relations highlights the role of business associations in channelling firms' collective demands and influencing how policies are implemented in practice (Pritchett et al., 2013). However, associations vary in whose interests they represent and how effectively they can speak for different categories of firms (Deller, 2018). This section examines Chinese business associations in Ethiopia and assesses how they operated and for whom they worked.

Central Government-Led Business Association

The China Chamber of Commerce in Ethiopia (CCCE) was the largest formal Chinese business association in Ethiopia during the period covered by this chapter. It was established in 2008 under the supervision of MOFCOM (China).[1] Initially, the CCCE did not provide a bargaining

[1] According to the CCCE website, the organisation is formally registered as a non-state entity. In practice, however, it functions as the Chinese business association most closely linked to the Chinese government in Ethiopia. See State Council of the PRC, "China Chamber of Commerce in Ethiopia" (April 30, 2025), available at: https://english.www.gov.cn/news/202504/30/content_WS6811757cc6d0868f4e8f2342.html (accessed 9 December 2025).

channel focused on manufacturing-specific issues. It was not until December 15, 2017, that it was formally recognised by the EIC (CBA-1).[2]

The organisational politics of the CCCE and the EIC differ significantly. The main focus of the EIC is attracting investors (to manufacturing sectors in particular). The CCCE was initiated in 2007 by several state-owned contractors, and most members were SOEs (CBA-1). The establishment of the CCCE was meant as a way to manage Chinese firms in Ethiopia and their activities with a particular focus on the construction sector. Therefore, its initial remit was more limited and focused as its main objective was to coordinate bids between Chinese SOEs to avoid vicious competition. Early members of the CCCE were not investors, strictly speaking, but construction contractors, that is, providers of construction services. This kind of issue-driven association was not set up for bargaining with the Ethiopian government (such as the EIC). Therefore, the EIC had no particular interest in the CCCE at the beginning, as, during this period, the CCCE was catering for the needs of these types of companies (construction contractors).

As Chinese investment in Ethiopia increased, more private firms entered. Because the CCCE already existed, some of its functions became relevant beyond construction, including as a source of information and a platform for raising general concerns. However, it remained only loosely sector-specific. A branch called the "Investment in the Chamber of Commerce"(投资商会)was established in 2010 under the CCCE (CBA-1). Any Chinese firm with legal status and a decent reputation (in the eyes of the Chinese government) was eligible to apply for membership. During the period of this research, the CCCE was most useful for collective lobbying on cross-cutting constraints (such as safety issues and tax policy), where a unified voice could carry more weight with host-country agencies than isolated firm complaints.

By late 2018, the CCCE's priorities had been shifting from policy coordination towards information sharing and practical support for Chinese firms, including translation and guidance on labour and tax regulations. For instance, the CCCE drafted investment guides periodically to provide updated investment information. In addition to the MOFCOM (Ethiopia) website, the CCCE also set up official accounts on social media (e.g., QQ and WeChat) to circulate updates (CBA-1). Translating local tax and labour law was particularly valuable, and it was difficult for individual firms

[2] All interviews have been coded. See Appendix A Interview Code for more information.

or informal groups to do this work, given the cost and workload. In this sense, the CCCE functioned more as a service provider than as a dedicated manufacturing bargaining mechanism.

However, the influence of private firms in the CCCE remains limited despite the increase of their presence at the decision-making level. A number of private firms claimed that the key benefit of joining the CCCE is to receive up-to-date information. However, most SMEs are not members of it because they found that problems facing individual firms (SMEs in particular) have little chance of being resolved through this channel due to the divergent interests of the main players (SOEs and large private firms) (CCM20-1-a).

However, the influence of private firms within the CCCE remained limited despite their increased presence in some decision-making roles. Several private firms described the main benefit of membership as access to up-to-date information (CCM10-1-b, CCM11-1, CCM18-1-b, CCM20-1-a). Many SMEs did not join because they felt that firm-specific problems—especially those faced by smaller investors—were unlikely to be resolved through a channel dominated by larger firms and state-owned enterprises (CCM20-1-a).

Regional and Local Government-Led Business Associations

The formation of some Chinese business associations also has region-specific characteristics and strong connections with Chinese provincial and municipal governments (see Chap. 3 for more details). These associations were often effective at resolving problems for firms from particular regions. Prime movers—entrepreneurs who had accumulated experience in Ethiopia—sometimes acted as focal points for subsequent investor delegations, including visiting officials. As noted in Chap. 3, Zhejiang entrepreneurs (浙商) (Type1) were well known for "going out" in groups and for maintaining dense overseas networks. Zhejiang province ranked first in terms of the number of Chinese FDI projects in Ethiopia, but many Zhejiang firms were small or medium in scale, and their voice remained limited within the CCCE.

Since 2016, when Ethiopia experienced its first state of emergency, the increasing uncertainty of safety and political instability in Ethiopia (especially in the Oromia region, where Chinese manufacturing FDI was concentrated)[3] had become private firms' top concern. However, private

[3] Oromia is the top recipient region of Chinese manufacturing FDI (see Chap. 3).

firms' investments had already been severely impeded by the host country's political uncertainties, and solving this kind of problem was beyond individual firms' capabilities. In response to investors' uncertainties, a new association—the Promotion of the Peaceful National Reunification (CCPPNR)—was established on August 26, 2018. Mr Zhou (pseudonymised) was appointed by the Chinese government as the Chief Representative of the Joint Office for the CCPPNR (Ethiopia).[4] Mr Zhou's appointment was not accidental. He was a successful Zhejiang entrepreneur who had invested in Ethiopia since 2007 (see Chap. 3). With the experience that Mr Zhou accumulated and close connections that he established with Ethiopian government agencies, he was elected as the Chairman of the Hangzhou Business Association to promote FDI in Ethiopia (CCM17-1-a). Whenever government delegations and potential investors from Zhejiang province come to Ethiopia, they would visit Mr Zhou first.

In China, the CCPPNR (Ethiopia) is supported by the Zhejiang provincial government and related bodies (CCPIT, Zhejiang). Mr Zhou leveraged his connections with Ethiopian agencies and his standing within the overseas Chinese community to link provincial government actors with the CCPPNR. In Ethiopia, the association falls under the supervision of the Chinese Embassy (Consular Section). Unlike the CCCE, which reported through MOFCOM (Ethiopia), the CCPPNR (Ethiopia) could report directly to Beijing, which gave it greater leverage. Its establishment illustrates how central and provincial government linkages, together with influential entrepreneurs, could create regionally oriented bargaining mechanisms in the host country.

Successful "Leading Geese"

The type of firm and entrepreneur's background also matter and reveal another layer of differentiation between Chinese firms that has an impact on institutional arrangements. As discussed in Chap. 3, Fujin (Type 2, pseudonym) offers a unique case of Chinese private investment in Ethiopia. Being a successful "leading geese," Fujin's investment in Ethiopia has received great support from both the Chinese and the Ethiopian governments. Because political influence is one of the top agendas for Fujin to

[4] The Ethiopia Trade and Investment Fair was organised by the China Council for the Promotion of International Trade (CCPIT) Zhejiang Sub-Council and held in Addis Ababa on August 26, 2018. See CCPIT Zhejiang Sub-Council (2018).

invest in Ethiopia, this accumulation logic has leveraged it to be a powerful player that has direct access to the Ethiopian government at senior levels (ministers and above). Meanwhile, because of Fujin's potential influence on China's industrial capacity cooperation with Ethiopia, it was elected as a Board of Director unit firm in the CCCE once it moved to Ethiopia. Fujin is the type of firm that has significant power with regard to government relations amongst Chinese firms.

In addition to firm type, entrepreneurs' backgrounds and *guanxi* networks with government actors offered another layer of differentiation among Chinese firms. The chairman of Fujin Footwear was awarded political titles after his initial investment in Ethiopia in 2011. In China, he was appointed Vice-Chairman of the China–Africa Business Council. This political profile made Fujin a frequent stop for visiting delegations and officials and increased the density of its connections with Ethiopian agencies. Unlike many SMEs that relied on associations (such as the CCPPNR) to speak collectively, Fujin could approach senior Ethiopian officials more directly. Because political influence formed part of Fujin's accumulation strategy in Ethiopia, its investment reflects SBRs and aspirations while most other firms avoid such a political spotlight.

Overall, Chinese business associations provide mechanisms for collective voice, including regular briefings, translation and circulation of regulations, joint reporting of incidents, and—at times—direct escalation through embassy-linked channels. Their bargaining power was uneven: larger or more politically connected firms could use these platforms to amplify influence, while many SMEs remained outside them. Where associations worked, they turned dispersed firm complaints into shared agendas and created recognised interlocutors for Ethiopian agencies; where they did not, firms often shifted to more informal (or more personalised) bargaining mechanisms through tacit networks.

The Role of Tacit Networks Among Chinese Private Firms

In addition to formal business associations, many Chinese private firms relied heavily on tacit networks—personal ties and informal channels—to access information, coordinate responses and approach officials. These networks were especially important when formal complaint mechanisms were slow, fragmented, or difficult to navigate. For many managers, relationship-based problem-solving also drew on familiar repertoires from

China, where local officials had historically played a decisive role in facilitating investment.

In the Ethiopian setting, however, tacit networks did not operate as a single, predictable channel. Their effectiveness depended on who could mobilise them, at what level of government, and for what issue. Rather than taking the form of uniform extraction, many interactions were framed by managers as reciprocal exchanges of access, information, favours, and occasional sponsorship—an approach that resembled the "transactional" side of state–business relations described in Chap. 2 (see also Ang, 2020).

Interviewees repeatedly pointed to politically connected intermediaries as important brokers. For instance, one firm described establishing a business group with a number of influential Ethiopians (including some children of government officials) to strengthen what managers called "government relations." Several firms also hired well-connected local staff for similar purposes. Others offered training opportunities in China, sponsorship or other forms of support in the hope of easing day-to-day frictions with local offices. These practices were contested and did not guarantee outcomes, but they formed part of how many firms sought to manage uncertainty in the pre-2020 period.

However, some firms, especially family-owned SMEs who neither play dominant roles in business associations nor have ties to political elites, are unable to secure patronage. Despite not able to effectively bargain through a formal channel, they would use their tacit networks to approach the government. They either seek to cooperate in groups to strengthen their collective bargaining power or find an intermediate agent to facilitate dealing with key political elites. Social media (such as Wechat and QQ) has constituted a new platform to consolidate the tacit networks for Chinese investment in Ethiopia. People can easily approach each other through a common friend's recommendation. It is less formal than face-to-face meetings. For instance, any individual firm can add each other's Wechat (or QQ) if they find any common interest and problem that they want to discuss. This is particularly useful for firms in the industrial parks to deal with local politics, changes in government policies and operational constraints (see Section "Labour Conflicts" for more details).

Summary

This section shows that Chinese business bargaining mechanisms in Ethiopia are diverse and uneven. Formal associations differed in remit and in whose interests they served, while tacit networks offered flexible but unequal channels to information and negotiation. In practice, actors often combined these mechanisms: associations were used to raise cross-cutting issues, while tacit ties were mobilised to pursue firm-specific deals or to work around day-to-day bottlenecks. The diversity of mechanisms mattered for outcomes, because firms' ability to make themselves heard depended not only on formal membership but also on their resources, connections, and position within Ethiopian and Chinese institutional hierarchies.

Chinese Business Institutional Bargaining Mechanisms in the EIP

The EIP is a microcosm for different Chinese private firms in Ethiopia. Communication and dialogue with relevant government agencies are conducted through three main bargaining mechanisms: the CCCE, the Eastern Industrial Park Management Committee (EIPMC) and the Eastern Industrial Zone Investors Association (EIZIA) (see Table 4.1).

The first mechanism is a formal one, as explained in the previous section. The EIP has become one of the Vice President unit firms in the CCCE since 2015 (CBA-1). The EIPMC arose as a semi-formal committee established by the EIP. In 2018, the EIP and firms within the EIP registered a formalised association (i.e., the EIZIA) at the EIC in a process that is explained in the sections below.

Eastern Industrial Park Management Committee

The EIPMC was established in January 2017. It was a semi-formal committee initiated by the EIP, with member firms as the core decision-makers, but it was not registered as a formal investors' association with the EIC, unlike some other investor associations in Addis Ababa. In the pre-2020 period, it became a key bargaining mechanism for coordinating firm concerns inside the park.

For many firms, the EIPMC was helpful because it provided an organised channel to raise concerns and coordinate responses, especially for firms that lacked individual access to officials. However, the asymmetrical power relations between the EIP and the Ethiopian government impeded the ability of the EIPMC to bargain effectively. The committee's influence

Table 4.1 Chinese Business Institutional bargaining mechanism in the EIP, and main activities between the EIP, firms, and governments

Association	*Type*	*Ethiopian government*		*Chinese Government*	*Chinese Firms*	*Year that the EIP joined the association and its position*
		Federal Government Agencies	*Local Government Agencies*			
CCCE	Formal, legitimate (under the supervision of MOFCOM) (registered under the EIC in 2017)	N/A	N/A	Weekly meeting (co-chaired by the MOFCOM)	N/A	2012 2015 (became VP)
EIPMC	Semi-formal (EIP's internal management committee did not officially register)	Quarterly meeting with high officials Monthly report to the EIC and the PMO Monthly report to the EIC and the PMO EIP (OSS)	N/A	Quarterly report to MOFCOM (Ethiopia)	Monthly meeting with all Chinese firms	2008 President Unit firm
EIZIA	Formal, legitimate (registered under the EIC in 2017)	EIP (OSS)	N/A	N/A	Monthly meeting with all Chinese firms	2017 President Unit firm

Source: Author's own illustration

depended heavily on relationships and on the willingness of Ethiopian agencies to respond. In China, the management committee of SEZs is set up by the Chinese government. For example, the management committee of Suzhou Industrial Park is run by the Vice Mayor of Suzhou Municipal City (CCM2-2-b). In Ethiopia, the EIP was developed and operated by a private Chinese firm. This happened before the IPDC[5] was established, before the strong drive to build industrial parks in the country. It was a pioneer in many ways, so that meant the EIP had to develop its own organisational bargaining mechanisms.

Instruments in use through the EIPMC included regular meetings, collective issue aggregation, and written reporting to the Chinese Embassy and relevant Ethiopian agencies. As a bargaining mechanism, the committee translated individual firm complaints into a shared agenda and provided a routine channel for negotiation from within the park. At the same time, because it lacked formal legal status, its leverage remained contingent on personal relations and on the park's strategic value within Ethiopia's industrial policy.

Eastern Industrial Zone Investors Association

The EIP established a new association—the Eastern Industrial Zone Investors Association (EIZIA)—with the EIC in September 2017. This was created in part in response to the EIC's demand for a clearer, formal interlocutor. The objectives of setting up the EIZIA were to work collectively to ensure that the EIP and firms within the industrial park met Ethiopian "standards for safety, environmental compliance, employee rights and business needs" (EIZIA Protocol, 2017, p. 4). This followed a long conversation between the EIP and the EIC. Park managers recognised the need to strengthen their bargaining framework so that they could engage the host country government through a more formal channel. Many firms supported the association because it provided a clearer and potentially more effective mechanism for expressing a collective voice.

The EIZIA officially represented investors' interests in engagement with Ethiopian agencies and sought to participate in discussions over policies affecting park operations. It was a legitimate association in Ethiopia

[5] The IPDC was established in 2014 to oversee the development of industrial parks and to function as an industrial land bank, responsible for leasing, transferring, and selling land to developers.

with defined protocols and an institutional framework, marking a shift in the park's institutional setting from semi-formal to formalised representation.

The association was governed by its Articles of Association and operated within Ethiopia's legal framework for investment, incentives, and business registration, including the Investment Proclamation No. 769/2012 (as amended), the Council of Ministers Regulation No. 270/2012 on investment incentives, and the Commercial Registration and Licensing Proclamation No. 980/2016, among other relevant regulations (EIZIA Protocol, 2017, p. 3).

Instruments in use through the EIZIA included formal representation protocols, collective compliance commitments, and a recognised channel for communication with the EIC and other agencies. As a bargaining mechanism, the association strengthened collective voice within the park and clarified who could speak for investors in formal engagements with the state. The move from semi-formal coordination (EIPMC) to a registered association (EIZIA) also shifted bargaining from ad hoc problem-solving towards more institutionalised negotiation over standards, responsibilities, and enforcement.

Ethiopian Government Agencies

At the early stage of the EIP's construction and operation, the park received personalised support from the Ethiopian government at the level of the Office of the Prime Minister (PMO). For instance, a temporary committee—the Eastern Industrial Zone Committee of Guidance—was formed by key Ethiopian government agencies and held quarterly meetings to review the EIP's problems and to seek solutions (CCM2-2-b).[6] Over time, decision-making shifted from this personalised PMO-led support to more institutionalised arrangements centred on the EIC and, to a lesser extent, agencies such as the MoI, the IPDC and the Prime Minister's senior advisers. These hierarchies and divisions of labour were not fixed; they evolved gradually through the 2010s.

During the GTP II (2016–2020) period, the Ethiopian government adopted a cluster-based approach and provided targeted support to

[6] This privilege was also given in an informal manner, based on a verbal agreement between the PMO and the EIP. This arrangement was terminated once the development of the EIP reached a more mature stage (CCM2-2-b).

developers, park management and tenant firms within industrial parks. In practice, these "tailored" support services often depended on a small number of powerful officials and agencies (PMO, EIC and IPDC in particular). The roles of other line ministries were often marginalised, while the EIC played a leading and coordinating role, responsible for attracting, promoting and managing FDI (Hauge & Chang, 2019).

Each industrial park in Ethiopia also had an EIC One-Stop Service (OSS) station. These were initiated under GTP II to coordinate developers, tenants, and government agencies at various levels with the aim of removing binding constraints. Each OSS operated within a clear institutional framework, but its day-to-day functioning remained flexible and context-specific.

The key instruments used by Ethiopian agencies in the EIP case included ad hoc high-level interventions (through PMO-linked committees and meetings) and, later, more routinised coordination through the EIC and the OSS stations. As bargaining mechanisms, these arrangements provided firms and park institutions with channels to escalate problems, but access remained uneven and often depended on who could secure the attention of a small number of decision-makers. The gradual shift from personalised support to more institutionalised coordination shaped how disputes were addressed and how responsibilities were allocated among agencies.

Dealing with the Local Government, Labour Conflict, and Export Targets

Fei and Liao (2020, p.637) correctly point out that although the EIP received considerable attention from both the Chinese and Ethiopian governments, this attention did not facilitate institutional and policy support early on in the EIP's development. Instead, Chinese private firms took the initiative to build local connections, secure funding and deal with the Ethiopian government. This section provides empirical evidence, exploring how the EIP and Chinese firms dealt with firstly the local government and their services (in terms of land conflict, service provision and environmental governance); secondly, labour conflict; and thirdly, export targets set by the Ethiopian government.

The causes of the conflicts identified below were highly complex and multifaceted. Some of the problems are historical, and some are structural—due to the specific political system that Ethiopia has. They are interrelated, involving multiple actors (Chinese private firms, host country government agencies at various levels, local communities, and workers) and reflecting multi-layered frictions and contestation. These conflicts were at the heart of the 2017–2018 troubles.

This section will illustrate problems with each set of conflicts and the root causes based on empirical evidence. This section will also explore whether these frictions have been solved and how or, if not, why. Finally, the implications will be discussed to better understand how these different steps and institutional mechanisms, with the EIC as a major driver, led to solutions to problems identified in this part. This reveals dynamic SBRs and offers valuable lessons to Ethiopian policymakers. Findings from this section come from qualitative interviews, management-level surveys, and my 25-week participant observation in the EIP (see Appendix A for more details).

The Local Government

Problem 1: Land Conflict

Land conflict was a particularly sensitive issue in Ethiopian politics, reflecting constitutional provisions on land and the tensions embedded in Ethiopia's political system of ethnic federalism. It has affected the EIP and many firms within the park because land allocation required negotiation beyond federal approval.[7] Although the investment proposal was endorsed by the federal government, firms had to deal with regional and local governments regarding land acquisition (Adem, 2019; Fiseha & Gebresilassie, 2019). In 2007, some high officials advised the EIP developer to seek land in regions such as Mekelle, Southern State and Amhara rather than Oromia, given tense relations between the federal government and the Oromia regional state at the time. One official even suggested it would be impossible to obtain land in Oromia (CCM2-1-a). Despite these warnings, the developer chose Oromia because of its resources, labour supply, arable land and favourable geographical location (CCM2-1-a).[8]

[7] As of December 2025, the land issue relating to the second phase of the Eastern Industrial Park (EIP) had not yet been resolved.

[8] The EIP is located approximately 30 kilometres from Addis Ababa and Bole International Airport. It is directly connected to the national highway and railway linking Addis Ababa to Djibouti and lies approximately 850 kilometres from the Port of Djibouti.

Drawing from Chap. 2, in China, local states are the leading agents or direct regulators of capital accumulation (Ang, 2018). Local improvisation (in China) largely depends on the relations between businesses and local government agencies. The developer of the EIP drew confidence from China's experience with SEZs—especially in Jiangsu province, where he was from—and he expected that regional and local authorities in Ethiopia would support the park once it was established as an industrial investment. He therefore focused on bargaining directly with regional and local government actors (CCM2-1-a). As he recalled, "during that time, they (i.e. the Oromia state authority) were happy as the land was issued by the regional government" (CCM2-1-a), but "lots of problems occurred afterwards."

In 2008, the EIP developer signed the land agreement with the Oromia land authority (and Dukem city administration) (CCM2-1a; PO1). The local authority agreed to an extremely low price (1 ETB/m^2/year, valid for 99 years of the lease). Within two years, however, the value of land in and around the park increased sharply. By 2010, land in the EIP area had increased to 74 ETB/m^2/year. The development fee the EIP charged tenants was around 850.5–1064 ETB/m^2. When local officials compared what they received with what the EIP charged tenants, they felt they had underestimated the economic effects of the park (CCM2-1-a). They (i.e., the local authority) later described the first-phase land price as a costly lesson, but this admission fuelled friction with local communities, especially as many residents had been forced to move when land was appropriated for the park.

Thus, for the second phase, the local authority asked the EIP to pay 77.84 ETB/m^2/year (CCM2-3-c). The EIP paid the full amount (130 million ETB) to the local authority on May 31, 2017 (CCM2-3-c). However, as of February 2020, this land had still not been transferred to the developer, and the EIP could not tell investors when the second phase of the development would become available. This inevitably resulted in delays for the second phase of development for the EIP.

Between October 2017 and February 2018, protests took place around the EIP over land compensation and resettlement. "They [i.e. the local community] thought those lands belonged to themselves while the local authority claimed the land belongs to the [local] state," one EIP middle-level manager said. Some residents were retired soldiers and had guns, and they threatened to shoot anyone who came close to their communities (CCM2-3-c).

Despite these tensions, the EIP management knew little about how local residents had been compensated by local authorities or how resettlement had been handled. According to a senior manager, the park treated land enclosure and compensation as the responsibility of the local authority (CCM2-1a). This distance reduced the park's ability to anticipate and manage disputes that emerged outside the factory gates but directly affected firms' operations and security.

Problem 2: Service Provision

Given the set-up of the EIP, it became highly dependent on the local government. Increasingly, the EIP went to the local authorities with problems, and the local authority did not provide the expected services to resolve them.

Lack of Legitimacy

The EIP has encountered enormous legal constraints. Since the EIP was the first industrial park in Ethiopia, there was no corresponding legal support for it at the early stages of planning, construction, and implementation. In 2007, there was no law to support land services (such as leasing and sub-leasing) for the EIP. Consequently, the EIP could not sub-lease land to investors. Firms within the park could not apply to sub-lease land, and this resulted in the EIP losing potential investors (CCM2-3-a) (also see Fei & Liao, 2020). The EIPMC reported this problem to the then Prime Minister Meles Zenawi. After a prolonged negotiation (lasting two years), the PM eventually helped firms obtain land through executive orders. Since then (2013), more firms, including Fujin, Dongsheng Dyeing, and Haicheng Garment (all pseudonymised, see Appendix B Interview code for more details), have moved in (CCM2-1-a).

Although the problems of land acquisition and sub-leasing have been solved, the processing of land services (e.g., granting contracts and permits), which has to be done by the local authority rather than the federal government, creates many additional problems. The EIP was kicked back and forth between local authorities—the Oromia regional land agency and Dukem city administration, which refused to provide services because of the EIP's registered name ("industrial zone"). This happened most frequently between November 2017 and February 2018 (before the second state of emergency).

The EIP senior manager admitted that it had been a mistake to register with the title "industrial zone" rather than "industrial park" (CCM2-3-b).

According to the manager, the EIP consulted a local lawyer at the initial phase, who advised them that the name "industrial zone" would not be a problem. This name only became a problem in 2017 (and escalated in 2018; CCM2-3-b), when the EIP asked to be managed by the federal government and enjoy treatment according to the Industrial Park Proclamation (IPP).

Fractious Relations Between the EIP and Local Authorities

In addition to the lack of legitimacy, time lags and discrepancies in the services delivered resulted in mistrust between the EIP and local authorities, reflecting the fractious relations between them. One example of problems with service provision was the request to donate housing units for displaced Oromo people from Ethiopia's Somali state in December 2017. Almost all firms in the EIP received request letters from the Dukem city administration (author's participant observation; see Request for Support in Appendix F for more details). But when the EIPMC calculated the total number of units the firms were required to donate, it was equal to the figure that the entire region was required to donate (more than 1,000 units), which meant that firms had to bargain with the local authority to get them to agree to a reasonable number of units to donate.

Application to the Industrial Park Proclamation

In April 2015, Ethiopia issued *Proclamation no. 886/2015 A Proclamation on Industrial Parks*. As the very first industrial park in Ethiopia, the EIP provided an important reference and support to the enactment of the IPP. However, the EIP itself was not included in the IPP, partly because the establishment of the EIP (n.d.) predated that of the IPDC (2014) and the IPP (2015). Moreover, the EIC claimed that it had limited capability to govern the EIP as it was a Chinese private industrial park that was not owned by the Ethiopian government (i.e., IPDC). However, the fundamental reason is that the EIP's land was initially granted by the Oromia regional state.

As a result, the EIP could not enjoy the same treatment (such as tax holidays and duty-free privileges) that other state-owned IPs have. The operations of the EIP had to be subjected to the Oromia regional state's regulations.[9] As a result, every year, the local authority charged building (construction) taxes from (all) investors in Oromia, while state-owned IPs

[9] In Ethiopia, each region has its own specific regulations.

did not need to pay this fee, as stated in the IPP. As of August 2018, the EIC OSS was still not fully functional in the EIP as it only had the EIC and customs offices, while in the Hawassa Industrial Park (HIP) and other state-owned IPs, there were management committees, banks, police and customs offices, and other facilities, which provided a whole ecosystem of services.

Problem 3: Environmental Governance

Environmental governance was another critical issue that created enormous social conflict between the EIP, the local community, and local authorities. Some firms in the EIP used coal boilers that did not have proper pollution mitigation facilities. Occasionally, I saw black smoke coming from factory chimneys. Since my dormitory was near a heavily polluting factory, I had to shut my dormitory windows to prevent yellow dust from flying in. The pungent smell that accompanied the pollution was, however, unavoidable (author's observation, Dec 18, 2017).

In early 2018, responding to the complaints made by the local community, the local environmental bureau started investigating environmental issues in the EIP. Although the EIP was equipped with a sewage treatment facility that handled 3,000 tonnes per day, the investigation found that this capacity was far from sufficient. The local environmental bureau, therefore, required the EIP to improve its waste treatment and also to insist that heavily polluting firms resolve their environmental problems. The local administration threatened that if the EIPMC could not reduce the park's environmental pollution, it would stop all services to the EIP.

Seeking Resolutions

All three problems were highly complex and interlinked. The EIP used various channels to lobby host country government agencies about the problems. However, lobbying through the CCCE over IP-related issues was ineffective for two reasons. First, the CCCE had limits to its remit, as discussed in the previous section. Thus, it might not be interested in dealing with local-level disputes or the issues of a particular company or group. Second, it was not clear whom the EIP might trust to lobby on its behalf. As a result, the EIP mainly relied on its internal mechanisms (EIPMC (before 2018) and EIZIA (after 2018)) to approach the Ethiopian government.

Due to the asymmetrical power relations between the EIP and the host government, lobbying for policy changes and institutional support for land-related issues was extremely difficult. Although the EIP asked the federal government for assistance through the EIPMC, its problems remained unsolved for a long time. The EIPMC had tried to arrange a meeting between the federal government and the regional (Oromia) and local (Dukem) governments to discuss these issues, but, as of June 29, 2018, the two sides have yet to meet (author's participant observation; PO1).

Through the EIZIA, the EIP established an institutionalised bargaining mechanism with the EIC. The first activity that the EIZIA organised was to pay a group visit to the HIP. A delegation of 63 people, including representatives of firms, Dukem city administration (e.g., the Mayor of Dukem), the police office, the labour office, and the EIC OSS, visited the HIP in June 2018. The main objective of the visit was to learn about best practices in industrial park governance, advanced management skills, and environmental treatment from the HIP.[10] The EIC head office facilitated this trip and afterwards called a meeting to collect feedback and see what kinds of service and support the EIC could provide.[11]

Accordingly, the EIZIA asked the EIC to intervene and coordinate three main actions. First, the EIP hoped the EIC could play a facilitating role and bridge key stakeholders (especially the local authorities) to further discuss the land transfer issue. The second request was full-service provision and the full application of the IPP within the EIP, which wanted to be treated more like other state-run IPs (such as the HIP) and have the same rights provided by the IPP. The third issue is related to sewage treatment and environmental governance in the park. The EIP manager accepted that the zero-discharge technology that the HIP had adopted was a valuable example for the EIP to learn from; however, this had resulted from a demand by high buyers (such as the US lead buyer in HIP), which the IPDC and the Ethiopian government then enforced in the HIP to attract investors. The EIP nevertheless promised to expand the sewage treatment capacity from 3,000 to 13,000 tonnes/day.[12] Given the

[10] Approximately 40 firm representatives and 10 local government officials participated in a visit in April 2018.

[11] A meeting between the EIP and the EIC was observed by the author in July 2018. Three senior managers attended on behalf of the EIZIA, and an investigator represented the EIC (PO1).

[12] See Appendix C, PO5.

difficulty of governing so many firms in different industries, however, the EIP hoped that the local government agencies would provide standards on environmental governance (author's participant observation; PO1).

Although the problems mentioned above had been raised several times by the EIP (mainly through the EIPMC), the intervention of the EIZIA was the first time that the EIP had used a formalised, institutionalised bargaining mechanism to conduct a dialogue with the Ethiopian government. On the one hand, it shows that this new institutionalised mechanism within the EIC enabled effective communication and fosters active learning and adaptation. Evidence shows that some issues that the EIZIA raised were based on an investigation and ongoing learning, while other issues they could have learned about outside Ethiopia. Moreover, a variety of actors participated in this learning process. It was striking to see that the two conflicting parties (i.e., the EIP and local authorities) participated in this process together. Based on the author's observations, perhaps it was partially thanks to the personnel connections in local authorities after Dr Abiy became PM (in early 2018). The new mayor of Dukem and officials had just taken office, and the EIP saw this as a good opportunity to rebuild relations with the local authorities. With the promise of donations (1,000 units of housing) in exchange for good service, the Dukem local agencies were incentivised to support the EIP.

On the other hand, the EIC had the incentive and the means to guide the EIP to be more like other IPs. Since the Eastern Industrial Park registered the association at the EIC in 2017, through the EIZIA, the EIC has gained a certain level of legitimacy to govern the EIP.

Owing to the fractious relations between the EIP and the Ethiopian government (at the federal and local levels), between federal and local government agencies, and even within the federal government agencies, the EIC had to carefully intervene in some conflictual areas that involved different institutions at various levels. Two main issues that the EIC were seeking to resolve: environmental and land issues. In order to have a comprehensive understanding of the situation on the ground, the EIC conducted a thorough investigation (EG1-1-b) with various actors, including the EIP, the EIC OSS, local government agencies, and representatives of the local community. It was found that distorted fiscal incentives were one of the main factors that make the local administration reluctant to provide services. One problem was tax revenue distribution. For example, it was found that the location written on the investment and business licence was different from the location of actual operations. Although investment and business licences are both issued by the EIC, some firms have different registered locations (for instance, "Addis Ababa" according to the investment licence but "Oromia region" on the business licence). As one senior manager of the EIP stated during a meeting:

> Firms do not mind revising addresses on their licences to Oromia state as we understand that the actual employment, manufacturing activities happen in Oromia rather than Addis Ababa. However, this couldn't be amended by firms themselves. Instead, it requires the Oromia regional government to coordinate with the federal government agencies for the approval of amendments. (author's participant observation; see Appendix C, PO-3)

Such legitimacy problems, which might indirectly affect investors in ways they do not anticipate, bring to light the lack of coordination and coherence among licensing procedures at the time these firms started investing and suggest that the EIP had become a "battlefield" in local conflicts of interest and multiple competing demands, in a context of weak state legitimacy. They also showcased the weak organisational capabilities of firms and their unfamiliarity with context, which underscored the importance for firms to understand the local political context and nuances of territorial administration.

The local community is not an amorphous entity but a collective with contrasting interests, and very often, its voices are only partially heard if not completely neglected. According to Fujin Footwear (pseudonymised), the largest employer in the EIP, the majority of its workforce consisted of migrants from other regions (CCM1-6). This points to potential tensions within the surrounding community, particularly among groups that did not benefit directly from employment opportunities generated by the park. These tensions were evident in a meeting between the EIP and the Dukem city administration observed by the author (participant observation; see Appendix C, PO-8), where unemployed young men from the area were among the most vocal critics of the EIP. Protests were organised outside the city administration building and at the entrance to the park. As the author's accommodation was located near the EIP perimeter, between November and December 2018 disturbances were frequently audible in the evenings, including gunshots and shouting. On one occasion, trucks were set alight on the road outside the park (author's observation).

Perhaps there were some groups with louder voices or driven by a political agenda and using the environmental effects as ammunition. However, since I did not interview local communities in this case, all data are based mainly on qualitative interviews of Chinese management and participant observation of meetings between Chinese firms and Ethiopian government agencies (both federal and local). Further investigation is required to prove this assumption.

This friction reflects the mismatched expectations between Chinese firms, local governments, and the surrounding community. According to the investigation conducted by the EIC, the local community saw the EIP as a foreign entity that did not take the environment seriously. The EIP, for its part, took it for granted that local people would not show any resentment for its behaviour because it contributed significantly to the community by creating jobs, donating goods, and constructing infrastructure. But, according to the investigator of the EIC:

> In fact, the local community is not pushing too much on municipal services (e.g. such as water and electricity) that the EIP could provide or already provides. They are angry about what has happened to the local environment. (EG 1-1-b)

No matter how many roads the EIP asphalted, it did not address this problem directly. Furthermore, the EIP did not appreciate the differentiation of "locals" and their divergent interests and perceptions. A lack of communication and asymmetrical information between the local community and the EIP triggered conflicts by mismatching expectations.

The local community also had issues with the local administration, which, according to the EIC investigator, lacked commitment to the local community (EG1-1-b). How tax revenue was spent was the main bone of contention. Arguably, the EIP had become a battleground for groups in the local community to combat a local administration perceived as being too lenient with "outsiders." In other words, the EIP could not insulate itself from the complicated dynamics of centre–periphery tensions in Ethiopia's political structure, which were exacerbated by the protests that began in 2016 (Clapham, 2018; Hardy & Hauge, 2019).[13]

After the investigation, the EIC started coordinating with the EIP and local authorities over these issues. The environmental issues became the

[13] To understand Ethiopia's political dynamics, it is essential to examine the uneasy relationship between the central and peripheral levels of government, which extends beyond unitary or purely ethnic explanations (Adeto, 2014; Clapham, 2018).

entry point for the EIC to intervene, as these were regarded as the main cause of resentment among the local community. The EIC advised the local administration to provide full services to operators in the EIP. In return, the EIC helped to coordinate with the EIP to improve their environmental treatment so that resentments from the local community could be mitigated.

In this case, the EIC played an intermediate role between the EIP and local authorities. It required the EIP to find a solution to the current waste treatment problem. Moreover, the EIP was to provide a detailed environmental impact assessment for its future expansion (CCM2-2-b; author's participant observation, PO3). The EIC accordingly required each firm to draft environmental protocols to reduce industrial pollution and meet at least the minimum standard (EG1-1-b). All tenants in the EIP were to have shared responsibility for controlling pollution levels and protecting the environment. The EIZIA was to monitor whether each firm's operation matched Ethiopian standards by checking each firm's evidence (certificate). This proposed solution was agreed upon by both the EIP and the local authorities during the meeting.

Regarding the terms "industrial park" and "industrial zone," the EIC suggested that the EIP change its name to "industrial park" and, from a legal perspective, both the EIC and the local government agencies suggested establishing a new proclamation or regulation for the EIP's case. This issue needed to be raised with the Oromia regional state authorities, who agreed to process it after a meeting. In order for it to function in the same way as the HIP, the EIC suggested that the EIP provide a space where all services would be grouped together (e.g., customs, bank, labour unit, and immigration) (EG1-1-b). The EIC agreed to provide full services according to the IPP, but not until the EIP had met its environmental responsibilities.

As the key institution governing FDI, the EIC showed its vision and commitment to providing streamlined services for firms within the park and tried to bring together the corresponding government agencies and the EIP management to discuss solutions to the three main problems. However, the EIC was still not sufficiently powerful in relation to local politics and local demands due to the peculiarity of Ethiopia's ethnic federalist system. Because of the prevailing legal and land administration system in Ethiopia, the second phase of the development was still subject to the Oromia regional state.

Lessons Learned

The three sets of conflicts discussed above highlighted several weaknesses in the political and institutional setting in Ethiopia during the pre-2020 period. First, as the EIP was the first Chinese Overseas Economic and Trade Cooperation Zone (OETCZ) in Ethiopia, there was no dedicated institution, policy, or law to support its development at the outset. In its initial stage, the EIP "was treated as an ordinary industrial zone in Ethiopia" (Brautigam & Tang, 2011: 38). Although the EIP was officially recognised, the federal government did not provide the necessary institutional support and policy coordination during the earliest stage of development. This lack of support later contributed to friction once local politics became more contested.

Second, EIP management severely underestimated the complexity of local politics. The EIP is an industrial park owned by a private foreign entity and, as such, initially chose to deal with the local/regional government, while maintaining only an informal line of communication with the Ethiopian government. The reason for this might be that they thought it would be easier to "manage" a weak local government—to "buy" them and get benefits in return. The EIP may had thought that local politics was simple and that, given the Park's supposed positive impact on the "community," the local administration would be on their side. However, simply replicating the Chinese model did not work in a foreign territory with a completely different historical background and political economy conditions. While relations between businesses and the Chinese local government are "transactional" (Ang, 2020), the evidence presented in this chapter shows that relations between the Ethiopian local government agencies and the EIP were more likely to be "extractive." This reflects a miscalculation of the advantages and disadvantages of dealing with local government.

Third, land conflict also reflected the contradictory nature of ethnic federalism and Ethiopia's Constitution in relation to entitlement to and use of land. As one of the major ethno-national groups in Ethiopia, Oromia established its own regional state with a constitution and mandates that "allow the group to control the regional and local political institutions" (Fiseha & Gebresilassie, 2019, p. 85). Ethiopia's Constitution "separates the legislative and administrative aspects of the use of land" (ibid., p. 59), which implied that the federal government set norms related to land utilisation and conservation, while the Oromia regional state implemented these norms and laws (ibid.).

Whether the local government compensated local residents for their loss of land during the first phase of the development remains unknown. However, given the price the EIP paid (1 ETB/m^2/year), it is unlikely that any compensation was sufficient. Taking land without properly compensating local residents caused more resentment against foreign investors and the local government.

Fourth, the incentives of local authorities mattered. "Asymmetrical centre–periphery relations entrenched in the state-building processes of the imperial and military regimes continued under the present regime, rendering" the Oromia state subject to repression and exploitation (Adeto, 2014, p. ii). Local authorities were naturally unwilling to transfer the EIP to federal management, as this would have affected local economic benefits such as taxes, fees, and informal contributions (including donations and sponsorship). This suggested that aligning incentives for local government from the beginning of industrial park planning was important for securing active engagement and reducing conflict.

The fifth weakness that has been highlighted is the lack of professionalism at the middle-management level, which generated or exacerbated other problems. Interviews and surveys show that managers of the EIP and the firms therein were inadequately prepared, made assumptions about how things work based on limited overseas experience, lacked information about the requirements of global buyers, did not know the "standards" but learned them from the HIP, as discussed in Chap. 3, some firms (early investors in particular) were relocating to flee more onerous regulations in China. This implies that some would have known what the higher standards were but did not want to (or did not have the incentive to) enforce them in Ethiopia and were then surprised when local communities protested. Managers also assumed that local authorities would not pose obstacles, as they would welcome foreign investors with open arms. This reflects a failure of the EIP and certain investors to understand and anticipate the local impact of their actions, to build alliances to facilitate their operations, and to find ways of engaging local communities and obtaining a "buy-in" for their operations in the area—in short, a lack of understanding of context and of the "organizational capabilities" that are critical for success in manufacturing investments overseas.

Fifth, limited professionalism at the middle-management level generated or exacerbated other problems. Interviews and surveys suggested that some park managers and firm managers were inadequately prepared for operating in Ethiopia's regulatory and social environment and lacked familiarity with requirements associated with global buyers. Several firms learned "standards" reactively through the HIP and, as discussed in Chap. 3, some early investors relocated partly to avoid more onerous regulations in China. This implies that some would had known what the higher standards were but did not want to (or did not have the incentive to) enforce them in Ethiopia and were then surprised when local communities protested. Managers also assumed that local authorities would not pose obstacles, as they would welcome foreign investors with open arms. This reflects a failure of the EIP and certain investors to understand and anticipate the local impact of their actions, to build alliances to facilitate their operations, and to find ways of engaging local communities and obtaining a "buy-in" for their operations in the area—in short, a lack of understanding of context and of the "organizational capabilities" that are critical for success in manufacturing investments overseas.

Across these disputes, governance was mediated through a set of tools and arrangements, including land leases, compensation and resettlement agreements, provisions for local services, environmental inspections, and a range of formal and informal payments and contributions. Firms and park managers bargained through a mix of direct negotiation with regional and local authorities and collective escalation through park institutions and federal agencies. The weakness of formal coordination at the outset—and misaligned incentives across federal and regional levels—shaped both the frequency of conflict and the uneven ability of firms to secure workable solutions.

Labour Conflicts

Employment Preference vs Reality

The EIP often encountered labour shortages as new firms entered and existing factories expanded. In my 2018 survey, all interviewed firms (14/14) claimed that, although hiring local labour was not difficult, recruiting workers with the required skills and qualifications was extremely difficult, despite firms providing training opportunities (mainly through learning by doing). Comparatively large-scale, labour-intensive LM firms (such as Fujin Footwear, Dongshen Dyeing and Linyu Apparel) and CM firms (such as Xinhua Cement, Zhenxing Steel and Dongxin Steel) (all firm names are pseudonymised) reported particular difficulty in finding "required" labour. Employers' preferences often mismatched the available labour supply. In the survey, 80% of firms (12/15) reported that a lack of technically trained staff was one of the top constraints impeding normal operations.

Based on interviews and observation, I found that language difficulty and communication were key problems for Chinese expatriate supervisors and local staff (also see Schaefer & Oya, 2019). Most Chinese expatriates and supervisors could not speak English, and they needed time to adapt to local workplaces and to develop a good way to communicate with local workers. The EIP and firms had previously relied on local intermediaries and on hiring at the park gates, but since 2017 the local labour bureau had become the main source, partly because of rising security concerns (after the 2016 state of emergency) and labour conflicts within the park. Firms increasingly preferred to recruit through formal channels. As a result, the local labour bureau acted as the main conduit for labour recruitment for the EIP. However, with the bureau acting as a "broker," worker selection could also be influenced by the EIP's and individual firms' connections.

In the 2018 survey, all firms (15/15) complained that the local labour bureau often supplied workers who did not match their requirements. This issue was frequently raised during EIP monthly meetings (author's observation). In response, the EIPMC coordinated a collective approach to recruitment and labour issues. An investigation conducted by the EIPMC at the end of 2017 found that, in the previous months, most workers who participated in strikes were male. Firms therefore reached a consensus during a monthly meeting and decided not to hire male workers (author's participant observation; see Appendix C, PO5-4). When firms submitted this request, however, the Dukem labour bureau argued that it faced political pressure because of high unemployment among local young men, and that excluding men could worsen social instability. The bureau therefore asked firms to recruit equal numbers of men and women (CCM6-1-a; CCM3-2-a). In the end, the EIP and tenant firms remained subject to local political and social pressures.

Workplace Tension and Labour Disputes

Terminating workers, strikes, and forms of "negative resistance" (such as absenteeism, turnover, and theft) were the three main types of labour conflict reported in the EIP. The limited presence of effective worker organisation in the park further exacerbated these conflicts.

Terminating Workers

In the 2018 management-level survey, all interviewed firms (14/14) described Ethiopian labour laws as “too protective” of workers. This was a management perception, and it reflected frustrations with dispute resolution and enforcement rather than an objective assessment of the legal framework. One example concerned a textile factory that terminated several workers after issuing three warning letters. According to the factory manager, the workers refused to sign the reprimands and brought the issue to court; the firm was eventually required to pay a penalty for the termination (CCM3-2-a).

In response, some firms began to document incidents more systematically and to collect witness statements and other evidence before pursuing terminations. For example, one firm obtained video evidence and dismissed workers for misconduct. Despite this, the local labour bureau required the firm to rehire them (CCM2-3-b). Whether the dismissals complied with the labour law was not always clear, as these accounts were drawn primarily from management interviews. Managers’ complaints could partly reflect limited understanding of local labour regulations and the contrast with labour enforcement practices they were familiar with in China.

Strikes and Disputes

The EIP manager argued that, even though the EIP paid higher wages than the Hawassa Industrial Park, the park still experienced frequent labour conflicts (author’s participant observation; see PO3). This comparison was not analytically robust, however, because the HIP operated in a different location with lower average wages. IDCEA[14] findings showed that wages depended on multiple factors, including productivity, workers’ negotiation capacity and individual characteristics, and that location and whether firms were in an industrial park also mattered (Schaefer & Oya, 2019, pp. 46–51). IDCEA findings also showed lower wages on average in IPs. Although EIP wages were higher than HIP wages, they were still lower than wages in many areas outside industrial parks.

Based on qualitative interviews and observation (October 2017–March 2018), I found that strikes and disputes in the EIP were not solely driven by low wages. Larger firms—including medium-large manufacturers such

[14] IDCEA project overview and outputs are available at https://idcea.org/overview/(accessed December 24, 2025).

as Fujin Footwear, Yuande Ceramic and Dongxin Steel—experienced frequent protests and labour conflicts even though they tended to pay higher wages than most SMEs in the park. Wage grievances formed part of the picture, but managers and officials also pointed to other factors, including workplace communication, supervisory practices, and local political dynamics. The relationship between wage levels and labour conflict was therefore not straightforward and often reflected the visibility of flagship firms as well as broader contestation in the surrounding area.

An investigation conducted by the EIPMC and the EIC attributed strikes to three main factors: misconduct by a small number of Chinese supervisors; ineffective communication between firms and workers; and political dynamics (author's participant observation; see Appendix C, PO5-4). Between October and November 2017, frequent strikes occurred in the EIP, mainly at medium- to large-scale factories. According to the EIC OSS manager, some strikes found were political as anti-government pictures and messages were found in workers' phones (ibid). Firms acknowledged that the first two factors were linked to internal management weaknesses and stated that they would improve their management to mitigate disputes. Political unrest, however, lay beyond the capacity of individual firms. Hardy and Hauge (2019, p. 24) similarly argued that the Ethiopian government needed to take the socio-economic and political dimensions of its development plans more seriously, in light of ethnic-based protests and political change.

Worker Representation and Collective Bargaining Power

Schaefer and Oya (2019, p. 58) noted that labour market institutions and labour relations were shaped by both sectoral characteristics and country context. In the EIP, many investors resisted trade union formation, and enforcement by the Ethiopian state remained limited (Fei & Liao, 2020). Without effective unions, workers had few institutional channels for collective bargaining with management. Strikes nonetheless remained widespread: during fieldwork in 2017–2018, recent strikes in the EIP were predominantly wildcat strikes, which firms found difficult to anticipate and manage. This pattern reflected an investor preference for direct, management-led engagement rather than collective representation, which in turn contributed to abrupt work stoppages.

In the 2018 survey, 80% of Chinese firms (12/15) either declined to respond or were very conservative in their responses to the statement: "All workers are free to exercise their right to form and/or join trade unions or to refrain from doing so and to bargain collectively." The remaining firms (3/15) that focused on exporting to Western markets had established worker-representation arrangements (often referred to by managers as "unions") to meet buyer requirements. One firm had previously established such an arrangement and, according to managers, it was frequently sued by workers and fined by the court system (CCM8-1-a). This account circulated widely in the EIP and shaped how other firms interpreted the risks of formal representation.

Over time, many Chinese firms reached a consensus that they should not allow formal unions inside their factories. Some interviewees argued that it was not the right time to establish a union in Ethiopia, citing low average education levels and fears that workers could be mobilised by political actors. They worried that a poorly governed union would not mitigate conflicts between workers and enterprises, but could instead become another arena of contestation (also see Schaefer & Oya, 2019, p. 59).

After verification, I found that the "unions" established by the three firms were not strictly trade unions but worker committees. Chinese private firms generally had limited knowledge about Ethiopian unions and often drew on their experience with unions in China. Anner (2015, p. 292) argued that China represented an extreme case of a state labour control regime, in which "labour is controlled by a system of legal and extra-legal mechanisms designed to prevent or curtail independent worker organisation and collective action." For many managers, the objective of worker representation was therefore framed as conflict mitigation rather than collective bargaining.

However, interviewees increasingly recognised the necessity and potential benefits of worker representation for two reasons. First, for export firms, worker representation was a requirement from buyers (especially those linked to brand firms and retailers from the Global North). To secure orders, manufacturers often had to establish a worker-representation arrangement at the factory level. Most firms (13/15) claimed that they would prefer a neutral third party to help mitigate labour conflict and protect both enterprise and worker rights. Many interviewees stated that they welcomed third parties such as the International Labour Organisation (ILO) or the International Trade Centre (ITC) to help create a platform linking worker representatives, the EIZIA and the local labour bureau. Firms expected such organisations to provide systematic training and to build monitoring and evaluation systems so that representation could function in a more transparent way.

Second, as part of the EIZIA Protocol, the EIP was expected to establish worker representation together with the local labour bureau. Learning from the Hawassa Industrial Park, the EIP also introduced worker committees, with each firm selecting two worker representatives. It is important to distinguish between two types of worker representation. The first was to establish a branch of an existing trade union, which would be an official, recognised union connected to a sector federation. The second was for management to set up a worker committee that operated alongside the management team, often initiated by human resources staff.

However, the relevant proclamation stated only that workers had the right to representation; it did not specify who should represent them. Representation therefore did not have to take the form of a union. Establishing the first type required workers to organise themselves to form a basic union and connect to a trade union, which was legally permitted but often discouraged by corporate management. Many firms instead established the second type, which was more likely to be influenced by senior management. Interviews and observation suggested that the EIC and local authorities often encouraged investors to adopt this second approach (PO3). Although this resembled aspects of China's state-led union model, Ethiopia's union system differed from the ACFTU-style arrangement and could not be assumed to operate in the same way.

Problem-Solving Mechanism for Labour Management

Multiple bargaining mechanisms operated simultaneously in relation to labour conflict. For issues that were suspected to have a political dimension—such as frequent strikes between October 2017 and February 2018—the EIP sometimes raised concerns through the CCCE, which then approached Ethiopian government agencies to discuss the problems.

Labour management in the EIP relied more heavily on the park's internal bargaining mechanisms. The EIPMC acted as a broker to help firms deal with recruitment and labour disputes, and it increasingly played a coordinating role. Because of frequent strikes and conflicts from October 2017 onwards, firms were expected to channel employment-related issues through Mr A (pseudonymised), the manager of the EIPMC, who served as the focal person liaising with the Dukem labour bureau. For instance, if a firm wanted to hire 100 workers, it could send a request to Mr A, who would handle communication with the bureau. In this way, firms reduced direct confrontation and procedures became more standardised.

If workers were unqualified or displayed misconduct, firms were expected to inform Mr A before pursuing termination. He collected the relevant information and reported it to the labour bureau. Functioning as a third party, the EIPMC helped with communication and coordination. This arrangement also reflected underlying communication problems between Chinese middle managers and Ethiopian workers, which could exacerbate conflict. Having a local broker became an ad hoc way to "translate" solutions for the local context and reduced the frequency of some disputes (author's participant observation; see Appendix C, PO5-3).

As noted earlier, some workers moved between factories in search of better wages, contributing to high labour turnover. The EIP established its own system to deal with turnover. In September 2018, it introduced a card system: employees' physical features and ID information were recorded in the system. According to an EIP manager, once an employee was terminated due to serious misconduct, he or she could be denied re-entry to the park (author's participant observation; see Appendix C, PO5-3). In addition, the EIZIA functioned as a formal, institutionalised bargaining mechanism that lobbied key government agencies. By establishing worker committees, the EIP attempted to deal with labour issues in a more systematic and formalised way.

Firms usually used multiple channels to voice problems and intensify lobbying impact. Beyond park-level coordination, individual firms could also approach Ethiopian government agencies directly, depending on their influence and networks. Large-scale firms such as Fujin Footwear and Sicheng Pharmaceuticals (all firms are pseudonymised) were more able to do this. SMEs that encountered similar labour-related problems sometimes undertook collective action to lobby the local labour bureau. In the EIP, a WeChat group was set up among Chinese managers and expatriates from different factories to communicate labour-related issues. Through frequent communication, firms—especially SMEs—could coordinate messages on issues such as termination procedures and dispute handling. Some managers also described these tactics as ways to push back against labour bureau decisions they perceived as unfavourable (based on interviews and observation).

Across these labour disputes, the instruments in use included recruitment brokering through the local labour bureau, evidence collection and documentation for terminations, factory-level worker committees, and park-level systems (such as the EIPMC's brokerage role and the card system). Bargaining mechanisms ranged from firm-level negotiation with workers to collective coordination through the EIPMC and EIZIA, with occasional escalation via the CCCE to federal agencies when disputes were framed as security or political issues. These mechanisms reduced some day-to-day frictions but also reinforced a preference for management-led representation, leaving worker collective voice weak and contributing to the prevalence of wildcat strikes. The result was a negotiated order in which compliance and dispute resolution depended heavily on brokers and informal coordination rather than on robust labour institutions.

Export Target

Change in Policy and Increase of Export Target

Since 2010, the Ethiopian government pursued a "carrot-and-stick" industrial policy designed to attract, promote, and manage manufacturing-led FDI, with the triple objectives of accelerating industrialisation, generating foreign exchange and creating jobs. As discussed in Chap. 2, Hauge (2019, p. 2083) argued that Ethiopia "implemented the carrot, but no stick" in promoting and governing manufacturing-led FDI. However, the EIP evidence suggested that some "sticks" were introduced, although they were implemented in a targeted way for particular sectors (garment/textile and leather) and categories of firms (Chinese private firms in the EIP in particular).

The EIC issued a new policy for the garment/textile and leather industries in August 2017 and required new investors in light manufacturing to export 100% of output. Before that, although the Textile Industry Development Institute (TIDI) encouraged firms to export, there were few sanctions on firms that did not do so, as the TIDI "was only a supportive and not a regulatory agency and had no enforcement authority" (Whitfield et al., 2020, p. 12). There were several reasons why the Ethiopian government became more active in enforcing export conditions. FDI had been regarded as a strategic engine in Ethiopia's industrial strategy. Ethiopia also faced persistent balance-of-payments (BoP) problems, which increased the imperative to generate more sources of foreign exchange in the medium term (Whitfield et al., 2020).

The policy shift appeared to target less capable foreign-owned SMEs that focused on low-end production for the domestic market. Given foreign-exchange imperatives, the Ethiopian government became less keen on foreign investors—especially SMEs—that aimed primarily to sell domestically. Although domestic production could generate foreign-exchange savings through import substitution, the government increasingly framed the role of FDI as generating foreign exchange and bringing organisational capabilities for competing in global markets. In other words, the government implicitly preferred not to attract firms that produced goods that domestic firms could potentially supply.

The increasingly rigorous export targets set by the Ethiopian government became a major challenge for some early investors in the EIP. According to interviewed firms (CCM3-2-a; CCM5-1-a; CCM-6-1-a), before 2017 there was no strict enforcement of export targets. Most LM firms in the EIP focused on the domestic market, driven by the motivations discussed in Chap. 3 (lucrative profit, increasing demand and less competition in Ethiopia's domestic market). After the launch of the new policy in 2017, firms had to increase their export contribution (relative to total production) in order to qualify for key incentives and permissions, including duty-free imports (e.g., duty-free tariffs for a share of spare parts), extensions of tax holidays, permission to sell in the domestic market, access to foreign exchange, and renewal of a business licence or approval of a new investment licence.

A key determinant of viability for manufacturers in Ethiopia was access to foreign currency because factories could not operate without intermediate and capital imports. Ethiopia still had weak supply chains, and manufacturing investors depended on global markets for a significant range of raw materials and inputs. For garment and textile firms, the privilege of selling in the protected (or increasingly protected) domestic market was made conditional on the fulfilment of export targets. For existing investors that focused only on the domestic market, firms could obtain only a US$150,000 foreign-currency limit if they did not export, which was insufficient to import the materials needed for production. Under pressure to access foreign currency, some firms exported small volumes to surrounding countries such as Djibouti, South Africa and Saudi Arabia in order to earn the minimum foreign exchange needed to import raw materials (CCM6-1-a). With increasing pressure from the EIC, some early garment investors were also forced to export (CCM3-2-a). One factory general manager claimed that Haicheng Garment initially lost money on exports but had no option if it wanted to access foreign exchange (CCM3-2-a).

Negotiation of a Deal

Some firms claimed that they would not have considered exporting if they had the option, arguing that exports were not competitive in terms of price. In practice, many firms made more profits by selling domestically and therefore viewed exporting as reducing relative profitability (CCM9-1; see Chap. 3 for details). A common claim was that there were few incentives (such as preferential policies or supportive bilateral trade arrangements) to export to other African markets. Moreover, the logistical costs of regional trade were high. Although the Ethiopia–Djibouti Railway began operating in January 2018, it mainly reduced transportation time and provided an alternative route. Interviewed firms argued that logistics costs and taxation reduced incentives to export to the surrounding African countries (CCM2-3-b).

The preference for the domestic market was also shaped by difficulties in selling to regional markets and by limited global competitiveness for exporting to European or US markets (CCM2-3-b). For most firms in the EIP, the profitability of the domestic market was higher than that of regional exports, unless firms secured large, stable orders from major clients in the US and/or European markets—something that was difficult given barriers to entry and intense competition in global production networks. Some firms also lacked the organisational capabilities to export. In such cases, the constraint was not primarily the absence of government incentives; firms did not know how to export and therefore struggled even when incentives existed. Producing for the local market was much easier.

Nevertheless, it became clear that the export requirement was negotiable and that the percentage of exports varied among existing firms (often between 15% and 40% in the first year of exporting). Firms' bargaining power varied depending on their connections with political elites and their ability to mobilise bargaining mechanisms (tacit networks in particular). The variation in enforcement created room for different bargains and deals. Some firms approached Ethiopian agencies to negotiate enforcement conditions. Others used connections to bargain for additional "carrots" (for instance, extensions of tax holidays) in return for agreeing to higher export targets, in order to compensate for potential losses. Some firms persuaded agencies to allow gradual increases in export shares for existing factories while establishing new factories that focused solely on exports.

At times, the enforcement of new requirements also contributed to the collapse of foreign investors. For instance, one firm that manufactured military uniforms for Ethiopia initially faced little pressure to export, presumably because of connections with powerful wings of the Ethiopian government. However, as policy priorities and personnel in key decision-making roles changed, the firm was required to export beginning in late 2018. Difficulties with this requirement, combined with internal management problems, eventually contributed to its closure in early 2019 (CCM2-3-c).

By pushing firms in certain sectors to export, the pressure also indirectly increased demands for environmental and labour compliance. Compared with Ethiopia's domestic market, export markets generally imposed more stringent requirements not only for product quality and delivery timeliness but also for environmental and human-rights standards, often transmitted through buyers. At the same time as the EIP attempted to improve environmental governance, export pressure added constraints on less capable and more highly polluting firms. In this way, linked requirements on export targets and compliance helped the Ethiopian government to pressure some less competitive firms to exit and to favour firms with higher organisational capabilities.

Between 2017 and 2019, a number of SMEs in the EIP exited under increasingly rigorous requirements imposed by the Ethiopian government. Among eight light manufacturing firms surveyed, six either focused on exporting or agreed to increase exports year by year, while the remaining two shut down. Among the six exporting firms, four also established five new factories in the EIP that focused solely on exporting (author's fieldwork data). Given that more firms increased exports and met targets, the government's strategy of linking incentives to performance appeared to have been effective in shifting firm behaviour.

Concurrently, exiting firms were replaced by more capable, more technology-intensive and/or more labour-intensive firms moving into the EIP (e.g., Sicheng Pharma (CCM10) and Jintai Textiles (CCM13), pseudonym). Until August 31, 2019, the total number of firms in the EIP increased from 86 to 103, with a higher proportion of firms able to compete in global markets than previously.

Taken together, the export-target episode showed how the Ethiopian state used a concrete policy tool—conditional incentives linked to export performance—to shift firm behaviour. Firms bargained over the interpretation and sequencing of this instrument, using meetings with the EIC OSS, park associations (EIPMC and EIZIA), and tacit networks to negotiate percentages, timelines, and compensating incentives. The resulting deals produced differentiated compliance: some firms upgraded and expanded, while others exited. In this sense, bargaining mechanisms shaped not only conflict resolution but also industrial selection within the park.

Ways Forward

A Process of Formalisation and Institutionalisation

Although Chinese private firms reacted and adapted to political and economic changes in the host country at the firm level, they often remained fragile and reactive in bargaining with host-country authorities because of asymmetrical power relations. As private investors, when the EIP negotiated with Ethiopian agencies and lobbied on policy issues, it typically occupied a weaker position. This limited its ability to resolve major problems in the park's development—especially land acquisition and local service provision—without support from higher-level institutions.

Over time, the EIP sought multiple channels to strengthen collective bargaining power with Ethiopian agencies. It moved from a self-organised, semi-formal mechanism (the EIPMC), which was not officially registered, to a formal, institutionalised association (the EIZIA), legitimised by the EIC. This shift illustrated a broader process of formalisation and institutionalisation in state–business relations and how institutional form shaped outcomes for both firms and the Ethiopian state. Evidence in this chapter also showed that the EIP adapted to local realities under political and social pressure. As developer, manager, and operator, it also had strong incentives to sustain operations over the long run.

An Evolving Role for the EIC

This chapter also traced the evolving role of the EIC and how, step by step, it sought to overcome capacity constraints and mandate limitations. In the EIP case, the EIC effectively represented the IPDC for many services. Because of controversy over land in Oromia and the private (Chinese) ownership of the EIP, the EIC did not always regulate the park consistently. Nevertheless, it used a range of measures to discipline the EIP and incentivise it to operate more like state-run industrial parks, while arguing that the EIP should receive similar treatment to other industrial parks (for instance, regarding tax incentives).

The institutional bargaining mechanism created with the EIC—the EIZIA—proved important for addressing issues such as environmental pollution, but it was less effective in resolving land disputes, which remained politically difficult. Although the EIC had limited ability to intervene directly in land transfer for the second phase of development, it played an intermediary role in convening stakeholders. It also coordinated local agencies to provide services to the EIP. In return, the EIC pushed firms to meet environmental targets, which local communities identified as a major grievance.

On labour management, the EIC guided the EIP towards the government's preferred direction. With respect to worker representation, the EIC encouraged the EIZIA to establish worker committees to reduce labour disputes. However, during the period covered by this chapter, it remained too early to judge whether these forms of representation would address the structural drivers of labour conflict in the EIP.

On export targets, the EIC played a powerful role in regulating and pressuring certain firms to enhance performance. Actual outcomes nevertheless depended on individual firms' deals with agencies and on firms' ability to mobilise bargaining mechanisms, including tacit networks.

Complex and Multifaceted Causes of Conflicts

As Ethiopia's first industrial park, the EIP and its tenant firms faced multiple tensions in state–business relations. The causes of conflict identified in this chapter were complex and multifaceted. Some problems were internal to the EIP—such as limited middle-management professionalism, weak context knowledge, inadequate preparation, and assumptions about how "things worked" based on limited overseas experience—while others were rooted in Ethiopia's political system and decentralised governance structure. A third set of factors related to external discipline: the absence (or late arrival) of strong requirements from global buyers reduced pressure for early compliance upgrading. Together, these factors pointed to the importance of organisational capabilities for successful manufacturing investment abroad.

In addition, the EIP became entangled in political contestation at national, regional, and local levels. It could not insulate itself from centre–periphery tensions in Ethiopian politics, which were exacerbated by protests that began in 2016 (Clapham, 2018; Hardy & Hauge, 2019). Land conflict, in particular, was politically sensitive and reflected how Ethiopia's ethnic federalism and constitutional arrangements shaped authority over land. Understanding these dynamics required attention to the uneasy relationship between the centre and periphery, and not only to unitary ethno-national explanations (see Clapham, 2018; Adeto, 2014).

Finally, at the early stage of industrialisation, limited legitimacy, institutional support and policy clarity for industrial park issues created another layer of complication (Fei & Liao, 2020). Newer industrial parks were more clearly under federal control and therefore faced simpler accountability structures. By contrast, EIP managers often found themselves mediating between different layers of government for day-to-day management, while also dealing with limited federal leverage over certain local issues. This institutional "in-between" position affected EIP operations, especially on land, labour, and environmental governance.

Overall, the EIP case suggested that strengthening bargaining mechanisms required both formalisation (from EIPMC to EIZIA) and clearer state instruments (OSS coordination, compliance enforcement and performance-linked incentives). Where instruments were clear and enforceable (export conditionality and environmental standards), bargaining produced adjustments; where instruments were politically contested (land), bargaining remained unstable. Aligning incentives across levels of government and building organisational capabilities within park management and firms therefore mattered for reducing conflict and sustaining manufacturing investment.

Conclusion

Despite the Ethiopian government's commitment to attracting FDI for its emerging manufacturing sector and the shared interests between the Ethiopian state and Chinese private businesses in building profitable firms, relations between Chinese private businesses and Ethiopian government agencies were not always amicable. "Win–win" narratives tended to oversimplify the realities of Chinese investment in Ethiopia's manufacturing sector, even where interests overlapped.

This chapter first outlined the institutional bargaining mechanisms between the Ethiopian government and Chinese firms and highlighted the role of tacit networks. The analysis clarified how these mechanisms worked in practice, for which kinds of firms, and with what limits. The chapter then used the EIP as a case study to examine the dynamics of state–business relations between host-country government agencies and Chinese private businesses during the pre-2020 period.

According to Khan's typologies, Ethiopia's political settlement was "relatively politically weak and lacking in productive capabilities" (Khan, 2010, p. 75), though arguably this was changing (Oqubay, 2015). Goodfellow (2017, p. 215) similarly emphasised that Ethiopia's governing regime was clientelist, relying substantially on patronage and the inconsistent application of laws and rules, and that the way institutions were used to maintain political settlement varied.

In line with this view, the EIP case showed that different deals were agreed between Chinese private businesses and a range of Ethiopian political actors at different levels. The three sets of conflicts analysed above manifested different configurations of formal and informal institutions and shifting power relations. Consistent with Kar et al.'s (2019) argument (see Chap. 2), the evidence suggested that outcomes depended only minimally on formal rules. Instead, informal institutions (*guanxi* networks in particular) and informal instruments (such as donations, sponsorship, and lobbying) were central to how firms sought to secure solutions. As this discussion illustrated, relations between Chinese private businesses and host-country governments did not fit simple "win–win" narratives; they were complex, context-specific, diverse, and fluid.

"Rapid economic growth always brings with it unintended consequences" (Fiseha & Gebresilassie, 2019, p. 87). In the EIP case, contestation over land, services, labour, and environmental standards reflected protective responses from local communities and workers as industrial expansion intensified. These dynamics underscored the embeddedness of capital in local political and social relations and the fact that industrialisation generated both opportunities and resistance.

Overall, this chapter offers a deeper understanding of how state–business relations around Chinese manufacturing investment are organised in practice, and how Ethiopian agency shapes investor behaviour. It challenges the tendency to homogenise "China in Africa" by showing that outcomes depend on firm diversity, on the instruments states deploy, and on how those instruments are enforced and renegotiated. In terms of Chap. 2's framework, the EIP case provides concrete evidence for P3 and P4—policy tools as shapes, and bargaining as the mechanism through which instruments take effect—while also linking back to P1 and P2 through differences in how MEFs and GPN-IFs navigated these channels.

Chapter 5 turns to the post-2020 period and foregrounds P5 by examining how bargaining mechanisms and policy tools adjusted amid shocks, political settlement shifts, and heightened instability. It contrasts the pre-2020 configuration documented here with the evolving post-2020 landscape, drawing on follow-up interviews conducted up to mid-2025.

References

Adem, T. (2019). Land tenure and land policy in Ethiopia (1950–2000). In F. Cheru, C. Cramer, & A. Oqubay (Eds.), *The Oxford handbook of the Ethiopian economy* (pp. 48–65). Oxford University Press.

Adeto, Y. A. (2014). *Conflict complexity in Ethiopia: Case study of Gambella Regional State* (PhD thesis). University of Bradford. Retrieved December 10, 2025, from https://bradscholars.brad.ac.uk/bitstream/handle/10454/8860/Final2%20and%20Revised%20Thesis%20Y%20A%20Adeto.pdf?sequence=1&isAllowed=y

Anner, M. (2015). 'Labour control regimes and workers' resistance in global supply chains'. *Labour History, 56*(3), 292–307.

Ang, Y. Y. (2018). Decentralization and development in China. *Studies in Comparative International Development, 53*(4), 449–471.

Ang, Y. Y. (2020). *China's gilded age*. Cambridge University Press.

Brautigam, D., & Tang, X. (2011). African Shenzhen? *The Journal of Modern African Studies, 49*(1), 27–54.

CCPIT Zhejiang Sub-Council. (2018). Ethiopia Trade and Investment Fair held in Addis Ababa. Retrieved August 19, 2019, from http://www.ccpitzj.gov.cn/article/10566.html

Clapham, C. (2018). The Ethiopian developmental state. *Third World Quarterly, 39*(6), 1151–1165.

Deller, R. (2018, January 9). Book review: *Deals and Development: The Political Dynamics of Growth Episodes*, edited by Lant Pritchett, Kunal Sen and Eric Werker. *LSE Review of Books*. Retrieved December 9, 2019, from https://blogs.lse.ac.uk/lsereviewofbooks/2018/01/09/book-review-deals-and-development-the-political-dynamics-of-growth-episodes-edited-by-lant-pritchett-kunal-sen-and-eric-werker/

Eastern Industrial Park (EIP). (n.d.). 'About Eastern Industrial Park'. Available at: http://www.e-eiz.com/about.php.

EIZIA Protocol. (2017). *Articles of Association for Eastern Industry Zone Investors Association*. Internal document collected from the EIP Committee, September 2017.

Federal Democratic Republic of Ethiopia (FDRE) (2014) Industrial Parks Development Corporation Establishment Council of Ministers Regulation No. 326/2014. Addis Ababa: Federal Negarit Gazette.

Federal Democratic Republic of Ethiopia (FDRE) (2015) Industrial Parks Proclamation No. 886/2015. Addis Ababa: Federal Negarit Gazette.

Fei, D., & Liao, C. (2020). Chinese Eastern industrial zone in Ethiopia: Unpacking the enclave. *Third World Quarterly, 41*(4), 623–644. https://doi.org/10.1080/01436597.2019.1694844

Fiseha, A., & Gebresilassie, F. (2019). The interface between federalism and development in Ethiopia. In F. Cheru, C. Cramer, & A. Oqubay (Eds.), *The Oxford handbook of the Ethiopian economy* (pp. 80–94). Oxford University Press.

Goodfellow, T. (2017). 'Seeing political settlements through the city: A framework for comparative analysis of urban transformation. *Development and Change, 49*(1), 199–222. https://doi.org/10.1111/dech.12361

Hardy, V., & Hauge, J. (2019). Labour challenges in Ethiopia's textile and leather industries: No voice, no loyalty, no exit? *African Affairs, 118*(473), 712–736.

Hauge, J. (2019) 'Should the African lion learn from the Asian tigers? A comparative-historical study of FDI-oriented industrial policy in Ethiopia, South Korea and Taiwan'. *Third World Quarterly, 40*(11), 2071–2091.

Hauge, J., & Chang, H.-J. (2019). The developmental state in Ethiopia. In C. Cramer, J. Sender, & A. Oqubay (Eds.), *African economic development: Evidence, theory, policy.* Oxford University Press.

Khan, M. (2010). *Political settlements and the governance of growth-enhancing institutions* (SOAS Working Paper). SOAS, University of London.

Kar, S., Pritchett, L., Raihan, S., & Sen, K. (2019). Political settlements and growth episodes. In A. Noman & J. Stiglitz (Eds.), *Efficiency, finance and varieties of industrial policy.* Columbia University Press.

Lee, C. K. (2017). *The specter of global China: Politics, labour, and foreign investment in Africa.* University of Chicago Press.

Oqubay, A. (2015). *Made in Africa: Industrial policy in Ethiopia.* Oxford University Press.

Pritchett, L., Sen, K., & Werker, E. (2013). *Deals and development: The political dynamics of growth episodes.* Oxford University Press.

Schaefer, F., & Oya, C. (2019). Labour regimes and global production. *World Development, 113*, 1–12.

Whitfield, L., Staritz, C., & Morris, M. (2020). Global value chains, industrial policy and economic upgrading in Ethiopia's apparel sector. *Development and Change, 51*(4), 1018–1043.

CHAPTER 5

Adaptation and Resilience: Firm Strategies and Institutional Recalibrations (Post-2020)

Introduction

By 2019, Ethiopia had emerged as a leading late industrialiser in Africa. Manufacturing inflows were rising; factory employment exceeded 200,000 across 13 state-led industrial parks and 7 privately developed parks; and Chinese private investors—concentrated in apparel, footwear, and basic metals—occupied most available sheds (NBE, 2020; EIC, 2020; IPDC, 2024).[1] Expansion rested on a hybrid governance structure. Formal institutions and policy tools—the EIC, the IPDC, the OSS regime, and the IPP—operated alongside informal institutions to solve problems between firms and states. This combination enabled rapid entry in the late 2010s, even as performance diverged across parks and regions. For example, the EIP faced repeated friction over land, services, labour management, and environmental enforcement, in contrast to more standardised service provision and compliance arrangements in several state-led industrial parks (see Chap. 4).

Between January 2020 and December 2024, overlapping shocks reset trajectories. COVID-19 reduced operating days, depressed external demand, and pushed freight rates on Ethiopia–China corridors to roughly

[1] IPs counts vary across agencies and over time. The figures reported here combine state-led parks developed by IPDC and privately developed parks licensed under the IPP; they draw on NBE (2020), EIC (2020), and IPDC (2024).

W. Chen, *Chinese Manufacturing Firms in Ethiopia*, Palgrave Studies in African and Development Economics,
https://doi.org/10.1007/978-3-032-24322-5_5

four times pre-pandemic levels, squeezing margins and distorting delivery schedules (UNCTAD, 2022; EG4-1-a, 2025). In January 2022, the US revoked Ethiopia's eligibility under the AGOA, restoring tariffs of roughly 16–32% on garments, textiles, and footwear and triggering cancellations (EG3-1-a, 2025; EG4-1-a, 2025). A US Lead buyer's exit from Hawassa Industrial Park (HIP) amplified the shock, with immediate spillovers to suppliers and park employment (EG4-1-a, 2025). Government estimates indicate more than 45,000 jobs were lost in export-oriented parks during 2022–2023 (EIC, 2022; Ethiopian Policy Centre, 2025; EG3-1-a; EG4-1-a). Meanwhile, armed conflict in Tigray, Amhara, and Oromia damaged park infrastructure, disrupted trunk roads, and delayed raw-material shipments. Mekelle and Kombolcha experienced looting of machinery, spares, and inventory; Dire Dawa, near the main corridor, faced intermittent stoppages and bottlenecks (IPDC, 2024; EG4-1-a). These meso-level shocks interacted with macro and geopolitical headwinds—sharp Birr depreciation relative to early 2020, persistent FX scarcity, intensifying US–China frictions, and spillovers from the Russia–Ukraine war—to weaken demand and raise working-capital needs (UNCTAD, 2022; EG1-1-c; EG4-1-a).

The divergence in outcomes after 2020 highlights the limits of Chap. 3's typologies of GPN-IFs and MEFs, which were developed under the 2010–2020's political settlement. Under sustained shocks, boundaries blurred. Survival hinged less on firms' ownership categories than on how quickly they reweighted markets, protected shop-floor operations, and managed relations with state actors as policy tools and enforcement practices shifted`

The post-2020 divergence in outcomes reinforces the need for the relational-institutional framework developed in Chap. 2. The typologies of GPN-IFs and market-embedded firms remain useful for identifying typical production network positions and institutional interfaces, but the crisis years show that these categories are not static: firms switched commercial logics, and the ways in which policies were implemented and enforced also changed. Survival—and, in some cases, upgrading—depended on how quickly firms shifted their market orientations, consolidated daily production, and worked through evolving policy tools and bargaining channels, rather than on the types or nationality of firm.

Export-oriented GPN-IFs tended to adjust early. Several reoriented buyer relationships towards Europe and Asia, switched destinations, and redeployed capacity into domestic and regional markets (e.g., COMESA and the Gulf). Some firms moved from export to mixed strategies or import substitution as AGOA preferences vanished, freight costs spiked, and FX scarcity lengthened purchase cycles. Birr depreciation made domestic sales comparatively more attractive, while public procurement and HGER-related measures[2] generated demand for standardised items, including uniforms (e.g., military and aviation) (EG4-1-a; CCM5-1-e). Some market-embedded firms expanded opportunistically, deepened local supply chains, and relied on self-provision of power and water when public supply proved unreliable. Firms depended on a small number of buyers, high FX intensity, or weak or unstable relations with regional or local authorities, and contracted or suspended operations. Importantly, most Chinese manufacturers remained in Ethiopia and adjusted how they operated rather than exiting: they renegotiated contracts, shared tariff costs with long-standing buyers, diversified into HGER-linked import-substituting production lines, relocated production away from the most conflict-affected parks, and stabilised cash flow through standardised garment and kit orders during peak conflict months (EG4-1-a; CCM5-1-e).

To situate firm experience, I first map the macro-institutional environment after 2020. Ethiopia's fiscal and political capacity was being reconfigured. At the federal level, reform measures adopted in early 2020 prioritised continuity of production and export revenues but also tightened tax enforcement and introduced temporary levies as the state sought to finance wartime expenditure and manage growing fiscal pressure. Regional authorities—most visibly in Oromia—exercised greater latitude; revenue extraction became more decentralised and, for investors, less predictable. By 2025, recurrent conflict and fiscal stress had produced more discretionary and fragmented governance: enforcement varied by jurisdiction, and federal regulators prioritised macro stability and FX management. Firms, therefore, faced different "rules of the game" in 2019, 2021, and 2024. The same policy tools and institutional arrangements—industrial park administration and OSS coordination, customs routines, and FX administration—worked differently across time and place, narrowing or expanding the room for negotiated solutions (see Chap. 4).

The analytical framing is relational-institutional. Production is embedded in relations among firms, buyers, and state organisations, where shocks are shaped through firms' market relationships and their engagement with

[2] HGER (Homegrown Economic Reform) combines foreign exchange generation with a deliberate push towards import substitution, in contrast to the export-centric logic of GTP II.

state institutions (Coe & Yeung, 2019; Mohan & Tan-Mullins, 2013; Lavers & Terrefe, 2021). Following Chap. 2, I treat policy tools as institutional practices: extending beyond formal policy and institutional context that includes the administrative routines, discretionary decisions, and enforcement patterns through which firms encounter the state in everyday operations. This chapter, therefore, examines how crisis reconfigured these practices and how firms responded by moving across markets and renegotiating with public actors.

Two framing choices guide the analysis. First, the GPN-IF/MEF distinction is retained as a heuristic for anticipating typical institutional interfaces, but it is not treated as fate: under shocks, firms switched commercial logics as relative prices and risks shifted, including export-oriented producers moving into import substitution. Second, the chapter emphasises mechanisms over labels. It traces how firms (i) shifted markets (buyer/destination reweighting; domestic and regional pivots), (ii) protected operations (workforce continuity, process upgrades, utilities backstops, logistics rerouting), and (iii) navigated state–business relations across federal, regional, local, and park layers. The analysis identifies which combinations generated resilience, why similarly situated firms diverged, and how these interactions reshaped the scale, sectoral composition, and organisational forms of Chinese manufacturing investment over time.

The analysis draws on a decade of research on Chinese manufacturing investment, combined with additional fieldwork conducted between 2020 and 2025. The evidence base comprises 54 semi-structured interviews with Chinese and Ethiopian managers, industrial park administrators, officials from the EIC, IPDC, and MoI, as well as donor representatives; 12 participant observations in industrial parks; and systematic document analysis. Interviews were conducted in Mandarin and English, transcribed by myself, and coded using a structured coding framework. Quantitative data are cross-checked against data collected from the EIC, National Bank of Ethiopia (NBE), MoI, UNCTAD, and MOFCOM, and triangulated with firm- and park-level evidence. Field diaries document day-to-day bargaining, improvisation, and shifts in policy implementation (see Appendix A for details).

The empirical evidence covers not only firms operating in the EIP but also more export-oriented manufacturers in other state-led industrial parks, and post-2020 entrants in EV assembly operating under knock-down (KD) regimes. All firms in this chapter are pseudonymised (see Appendix B Interview Code for more details).

Differentiated Firm Strategies and Adaptations

Overview of Chinese Manufacturing Investment in Ethiopia (post-2020)

Official EIC records point to a reconfiguration rather than an exit of Chinese manufacturing investment after 2020. Between 2015 and early 2025, the EIC registered 1549 Chinese manufacturing projects: 1302 (84%) are wholly owned by a single Chinese parent, while 247 (16%) involve hybrid ownership (China–Ethiopia joint ventures (JVs) or third-country partnerships). Six hundred eighty-two (44%) are recorded as operational, with realised investment of roughly ETB 227 billion (author's calculations from EIC records, 2015–2025). Approvals continued, but the near-term pipeline has narrowed: 169 projects are classified as "implementation" compared with 597 at "pre-implementation." Annual approvals fell from 182 (2019) to 78 (2020) and 66 (2021), rebounded in 2023 (222; ETB 205.5 bn) and 2024 (219; ETB 106.7 bn), and then declined again in the first half of 2025 (123; ETB 78.2 bn).

The post-2021 approval waves also differ in composition: they skew towards fewer, larger, and more technology-intensive projects, often backed by listed parent companies or provincial-level investment consortia, and more frequently paired with Ethiopian equity participation (author's calculations from EIC records, 2015–2025).

Relative to the pre-2020 baseline, the change is structural as well as numerical. By the late 2010s, China ranked first by number of licensed investment projects and by projects in operation, and manufacturing dominated recorded Chinese FDI stock. Since 2020, EIC data point to a recomposition of manufacturing investment: less volume at the margin, but a greater share of larger projects and more complex ownership structures—consistent with a move from rapid entry and park clustering to more selective scaling and localisation.

Two measurement issues matter for how these figures are interpreted. First, apparent gaps between "approved" investment totals (often reported at regional or project-stage level) and aggregate realised investment reflect a straightforward distinction: approved investment records announced commitments across project stages, whereas realised investment records funds actually invested in operating factories. Second, interviews indicate that approval figures can overstate effective FX inflows, given asset-valuation practices and the widespread use of franco valuta to import inputs. Frequent leadership turnover and shifting mandates have also made it harder for the EIC to maintain fully consistent time series across units (CCM27-1-; EG1-1-).

Sectoral distribution shifted after AGOA's suspension. Licences in apparel and footwear largely stalled, while new commitments moved towards more capital- and skill-intensive, import-substituting sectors. The strongest growth is in pharmaceuticals, construction materials (e.g., steel, cement, PVC pipes), and automotive KD assembly.

Ownership structures shifted alongside sectoral change. Of the 1549 projects approved between 2015 and 2025, about 16% include an Ethiopian equity stake; joint ventures are the fastest-growing category (EIC, 2015–2025). After 2021, a larger share of approvals is linked to listed parents in China or provincial consortia in new energy, new materials, pharmaceuticals, and digital equipment. This aligns China's outbound investment guidance with Addis Ababa's incentives for equity participation and technology transfer (EIC, 2015–2025; CCM10-4-1-a; CCM21-1-a). Approvals dropped from 182 (2019) to 78 (2020) and 66 (2021), rebounded to 222 (2023) with macro stabilisation and HGER incentives, and then moderated in the first half of 2025 (123). The approval waves are smaller, but heavier: fewer projects, higher capital intensity, and stronger local anchoring—consistent with consolidation rather than breakneck expansion.

Chinese manufacturing investment remains concentrated in Addis Ababa and Oromia, with gradual movement into second-tier corridors. Before 2019, more than 70% of projects were clustered in Addis Ababa and in parks within Oromia. Since 2020, new approvals more often reference Dire Dawa, Jimma, and the Hawassa–Shone belt, alongside private parks in Amhara and Somali. Firms pointed to three practical reasons: lower wage pressure, improved road connections on the Addis Ababa–Adama–Dire Dawa–Djibouti and Addis Ababa–Debre Birhan–Dessie corridors, and more proactive regional investment bureaus seeking post-conflict job creation (EG1-1-c; EG4-1-a). Even so, operations remain anchored where sunk capital and administrative reach are deepest. Addis Ababa hosts about 710 licensed projects, while Oromia carries the greatest capital weight (around ETB 286 bn across 648 projects). Amhara's share has risen (around ETB 76.8 bn), and emerging locations such as Dire Dawa (around ETB 2.8 bn) and Southern Nations, Nationalities, and

Peoples' Region (SNNP) (around ETB 2.0 bn) are growing from a low base. The share of operational projects outside Addis Ababa fell from 68% pre-2020 to about 60% by early 2025. This points to some decentralisation in approvals, but continued concentration of production in established hubs (author's calculations from EIC data, 2015–2025).

Within the EIP, tenant numbers shifted as some firms relocated to state-led industrial parks in Addis Ababa or exited after heavy fiscal actions, while others consolidated and reinvested on site. By mid-2025, interviews and on-site observation indicated substantial turnover beneath apparently stable occupancy: about 137 tenants in late-2023 (128 out of 13 are Chinese-owned) fell to fewer than 110 by mid-2025, with most exits among Chinese firms (CCM2-6-c; CCM26-1-a; CCM24-1-a; author's observation, June 2025).

The HGER agenda (late 2019) signalled a shift away from the single focus on labour-intensive export manufacturing under GTP II towards a dual mandate: earning FX and deepening strategic import substitution. By 2025, licensing and monitoring data show a clear swing away from low-wage apparel towards more capital- and technology-intensive projects (e.g., pharmaceuticals, metals, cement, PVC, and EV-related assembly). Sections "Light Manufacturing Firms: Strategic Adaptation and Resilience under Compounded Crises" and "Heavy and Strategic Import-Substitution Manufacturing Firms: Negotiating Rules, Inputs and Procurement" illustrate how firms translated this shift into concrete expansion strategies. Pharmaceutical producers scaled operations through public tenders and framework contracts while managing skills and FX constraints; automotive KD assemblers raised local value added to clear rebate thresholds; and steel rebar producers assembled cost and supply evidence to support tariff adjustments that redirected scarce FX towards billets (CCM10-4-1-a; CCM21-1-a; CCM8-1-d; EIC, 2015–2025).

Across interviews with managers and policymakers, triangulated with official data, the picture is consistent: Chinese manufacturing capital reconfigured rather than retreated. The trend is towards fewer, larger, and more technologically advanced projects, paired with deeper local partnerships—through JV, supplier localisation, and targeted procurement. Under the 2020–2025 shocks, industrial resilience depended on predictable rules, predictable access to FX, and managerial capacity to adjust products, inputs, and markets (EG3-1-a; EG4-1-a; IO1-a).

Light Manufacturing Firms: Strategic Adaptation and Resilience Under Compounded Crises

As Section "Introduction" shows, light manufacturers entered 2020 with different exposure profiles. The loss of AGOA preferences, together with pandemic-related logistics breakdowns and park-level disruptions intensified by domestic conflict, exposed the fragility of single-market reliance and increased the value of diversified buyers and dense local ties. Firms heavily concentrated on the US market paused or contracted. By contrast, multi-market exporters redirected orders towards Europe and Asia, shared tariff costs with long-term buyers, tightened process control to offset higher freight costs, and stabilised output by recruiting experienced supervisors from South Asia. A third group—domestically embedded, regionally active MEFs—reoriented product lines towards Ethiopia and COMESA, temporarily accommodated workers on site to protect delivery schedules, and later drew on public procurement as private orders weakened (CCM1-15-a; CCM22-1-a; CCM3-3-a; CCM4-3-a; CCM5-1-e; IO1-a). This aligns with a GPN interpretation: diversified buyers and embedded local ties expand switching options that single-market firms do not have.

The firm-level evidence below focuses on the mechanisms behind divergence—switching capacity, buyer relations, and local embeddedness. Three recurring strategic profiles emerge (Table 5.1). First, single-market-dependent firms—tied almost entirely to either US exports or Ethiopia's domestic market—were the most exposed: once preferences were removed or domestic routes became insecure, revenue concentration quickly became a viability risk. Second, multi-market, network-integrated firms (GPN-IFs) reallocated orders across regions and used relational contracting to absorb tariff shocks and logistics frictions. Third, hybrid domestic–regional firms (often MEFs) relied on local embeddedness and diaspora links to reorient product lines for Ethiopia and COMESA, protected delivery through on-site accommodation during lockdowns, and accessed public procurement when private orders weakened.

Single-Market Dependence: High Exposure, Slow Recovery

The most fragile configuration was firms with more than 90% of sales tied to a single destination—either US-bound export or Ethiopia's domestic market. In such cases, a sudden loss of market access or disruption to transport and security translated quickly into cash-flow stress because

Table 5.1 Strategic profiles and light manufacturing firms' responses to major crises (2020–2025)

Profile	*Representative cases (pseudonym)*	*Market orientation*	*COVID-19 impact and response*	*AGOA suspension*	*Conflict and instability*	*Geopolitics*	*Core adaptation*	*2025 status*
Single-market focus	Fujin Footwear; Haixing Textiles	>90% sales in one market	Fujin: complete three-year halt; >100 expatriates COVID-positive; erosion of trained line staff; Haixing: pre-conflict cost-saving relocation to Mekelle; later looted	Fujin: catastrophic loss of US orders; margins erased; Haixing: no direct export exposure	Fujin: operations paralysed by demand collapse; Haixing: plant looted, workforce dispersed	Buyer withdrawal; loans re-priced; no alternative routes	Fujin: deferred diversification; Haixing: explores Gulf relocation	Fujin: restarting at reduced capacity; Haixing: viability stressed by debt service
Multi-market (GPN-integrated)	Shenglong; Garments; Rongxin Garment	US/EU/Asia mix	Partial operations; delays offset by auto-spreaders/auto-cutting; imported supervisors to stabilise lines	Orders reallocated to EU/JP; tariff-cost sharing with anchor buyers	Alternative routing via Mombasa; FX hedging preserved production	Sourcing via Hong Kong/ASEAN avoided direct tariff hit	Contract renegotiation; buyer diversification; cross-border redundancy	Near pre-crisis output; workforce stabilised; diversified client base

(*continued*)

Table 5.1 (continued)

Profile	*Representative cases (pseudonym)*	*Market orientation*	*COVID-19 impact and response*	*AGOA suspension*	*Conflict and instability*	*Geopolitics*	*Core adaptation*	*2025 status*
Hybrid local–regional	Haicheng Garment Linyu Apparel; Yichen Textiles & Auto; Dongsheng Dyeing	30–70% domestic/ COMESA	Haicheng: dormitory conversion (~RMB 10 m); Dongsheng: closed-loop quarantine; ~ETB 2 m for testing/ provisioning; Yichen: mask line later disapproved	Limited direct effect; regional sales maintained; domestic-first product pivots	Dongsheng: >3 m uniforms via public procurement; Yichen: EV assembly (federal park) and denim (Uganda)	Lower US exposure; regional markets partly insulated	Rapid product pivots; diaspora networks; state procurement; selective relocation	Sustained/ expanded operations; stronger regional footprint; diversified lines

Source: Author's elaboration based on interviews (2020–2025; e.g., CCM1-15-a; CCM3-3-a; CCM4-3-a; CCM5-1-e; CCM6-1-e; CCM12-2-b; CCM22-1-a; IO1-a), EIC data (2020- 2025), and field diaries

there was no alternative channel to absorb demand swings or price shocks. Two pseudonymised cases—Fujin Footwear (Type 2, CCM1) and Haixing Textiles (Type 1, CCM12)—illustrate how the same concentration risk played out differently across export- and domestic-facing configurations.

Fujin Footwear was heavily dependent on US orders (over 90%). In late 2019, it relocated from the EIP to its own estate on the Addis Ababa–Oromia boundary—"against explicit advice," as a mid-level manager put it—disrupting a workforce built over several years (PO-16). COVID-19 then triggered a full shutdown after more than 100 Chinese expatriates tested positive. "All the production lines stopped. Almost everyone went back to China; around 30 Chinese staff remained," a senior production manager recalled in 2021 (CCM1-13-c). Production restarted only in 2023. The senior manager described "a three to four year gap in training and hiring," which broke the continuity of skilled labour (CCM1-15-a; PO-17). Even by late 2022, the situation remained stagnant: "we have no orders and aren't exporting... orders from Europe and the US have completely stopped" (CCM1-13-d).

AGOA's suspension then removed the firm's core commercial advantage. "Ethiopia's primary advantage—tariff benefits—was gone," the senior manager said, and orders collapsed (CCM1-15-a). With no prepared compliance route for European or other alternative buyers, the firm could not pivot quickly. Managers were still asking basic tariff questions—"is this an additional 10% on top, or just a flat 10%?"—underscoring how little market preparation had been done beyond the US channel (PO-17, 2025). A GIZ advisor who had brought buyers to Ethiopia made the same point: Fujin "focused too heavily on the US market... We suggest firms, including Fujin, diversify... but they said, 'Then we'll react tomorrow'" (IO1-a, 2025). Market concentration, limited redundancy in buyer relations, and the move away from park-based support services combined to prolong the firm's standstill.

Haixing Textiles represents the domestic-only configuration of the same exposure logic. Seeking lower operating costs and a more workable bureaucracy than in Oromia, the firm relocated from the EIP to Mekelle Industrial Park before the war. In 2021, management described the local business ecosystem as "better than Dukem," citing the presence of federal staff in the park (CCM12-2-a). The conflict reversed that assessment. The factory was looted, the workforce dispersed, and by early 2024, interest on outstanding bank loans exceeded monthly turnover. With internal trade routes disrupted and buyers' liquidity tightening, management began exploring relocation to Gulf markets in 2023, where access to foreign currency is less constrained (CCM12-2-b). Although Haixing was not exposed to AGOA, its domestic-only revenue model left no external outlet when the home market seized up. The same single-channel concentration that insulated the firm from US tariff volatility now magnified local security and fiscal shocks into a threat to solvency.

Taken together, the two trajectories show how concentration risk travels through different channels but converges on similar outcomes. For export-exclusive firms like Fujin, the loss of preferences and long-haul logistics frictions removed the margin and reliability needed to keep lines running. For domestic-exclusive firms like Haixing, localised security shocks and a domestic cash-flow drought generated equivalent distress. In both cases, switching capacity—not firm size—was essential. Firms without secondary buyers, credible compliance routes into alternative markets, or resilient local–regional trade corridors converted shocks into existential threats, consistent with expectations from GPN and varieties of capital perspectives (CCM1-15-a, 2025; CCM12-2-b, 2025; IO1-a, 2025; PO-16/17, 2025).

Multi-market Exporters: Switching Capacity and Relational Contracting

By contrast, firms embedded in multiple buyer networks across regions showed stronger adaptive capacity. Shengdong Garment (Type 3, CCM22, pseudonymised) entered the crisis with a diversified order mix across the US, EU, and Japan. After AGOA preferences were withdrawn, management redirected over half of its US-bound orders to EU buyers within two production seasons and invested in auto-spreaders and automated cutting to reduce fabric waste and buffer freight spikes. To stabilise lines amid turnover, the firm recruited supervisors from Bangladesh and India (CCM22-1-a). Lead buyers agreed to share incremental tariff costs; shipments were rerouted via Mombasa when congestion on the Djibouti corridor intensified; and offshore accounts helped smooth FX rationing (EG4-1-a, 2025). The firm also drilled wells and arranged private power in Bole Lemi to reduce exposure to grid instability, protecting delivery schedules despite service volatility inside the industrial-park system (CCM22-1-a).

External intermediaries reinforced these shifts. Rongxin Garment (Type 3, CCM14, pseudonymised) participated in a GIZ buyer-development programme that brought 22 largely European buyers to Ethiopia; visitors "were all impressed with the quality at Rongxin," which accelerated EU orders (IO1-a). IPDC similarly reported that lead suppliers renegotiated cost-sharing on new US tariffs with buyers and redistributed volume across plants in several countries, reducing margin pressure on Ethiopian operations (EG4-1-a). The evidence suggests these were not opportunistic switches but the use of relational contracting and multi-site compliance to move orders while maintaining quality and audit compliance standards.

Friction nonetheless persisted. Shengdong faced customs disputes—including retroactive challenges to duty-exemption eligibility worth ETB 40 million—alongside high turnover that kept workforce size below the 4000–6000 target and rising costs in Addis Ababa. Yet process upgrades backed by buyer commitments, together with off-park solutions for utilities, meant that the COVID-era logistics shock and the AGOA suspension—devastating for single-market peers—were managed through order rebalancing rather than firm-level retrenchment. In GPN terms, redundancy and relational depth expanded switching options that single-market firms did not possess (CCM22-1-a; EG4-1-a; IO1-a).

Hybrid Domestic–Regional Firms: Embedded Ties and Rapid Pivots

A third set of firms enjoy long relevant experience (with an average of ten years or above in terms of time of entry) in Ethiopia and have good business and social networks across COMESA and the Gulf to get through the shocks.

Haicheng Garment (Type 1, CCM3, pseudonymised) moved fast when the pandemic hit. "We converted two auxiliary warehouses... into temporary dormitories," installing welded bunk beds and bedding for about 1000 workers at a cost of roughly RMB 10 million; production stopped for around three months, then resumed (CCM3-3-a). By 2025, Haicheng was selling skirts and jeans mainly into Congo, with warehouses in Dubai and sales offices in Kenya. It tried to protect its "***" brand[3] but faced local and Chinese copycats in Merkato. Managers complained about stepped-up individual income tax enforcement and higher electricity and fees inside EIP, which pushed several firms to move out or explore Uganda and Kenya (CCM3-3-a). On the shop floor, Haicheng built a deeper local bench—"long-term employees... seven years or more, account for 70%"—and hired assistants from Bangladesh and India where English and cost profiles fit (CCM3-4-a).

[3] The brand is named after the owner. For confidentiality, the name is concealed as "***".

Linyu Apparel (Type 3, CCM4, pseudonymised) showed a similar reconfiguration of product lines in response to market disruption. The firm had made trousers for a large US (wholesale) buyer that "didn't prioritise quality very much but was particular about quantity and punctuality" (CCM4-3-a). After the AGOA was suspended, its US buyers first covered tariffs, then asked the factory to absorb part of the cost. Management walked away from those orders and "shifted to jackets because the Ethiopian market favours items like jackets more." Prior trading experience with Ethiopian merchants made the switch easier. Dollar shortages that once forced a two-to-three-month wait to pay wages eased after an IMF deal, but managers stressed this relief came from outside, not from fixes in local banking (CCM4-3-a).

Yichen Textiles & Auto (Type 1, CCM6, pseudonymised) moved from textiles to face masks during COVID-19, importing equipment and non-wovens from China. The Ministry of Health (Ethiopia) disapproved the N95 valve design, leaving an RMB 600,000-700,000 (equivalent to approximately USD 92,000-108,000) loss for Yichen. The firm kept going by placing workers in container-built accommodations near the factory during quarantine. Yichen shut its textile factory due to the escalating, worsening business ecosystem in that region, and later shifted out of EIP to Bole Lemi IP to assemble EV while investing in denim production in a Chinese-led park in Uganda. Managers described a steady rise in fines and back payments in Ethiopia, particularly in the past two years (i.e., 2023–2025)—work-permit issues, ID fees, and individual tax penalties that started small but "became increasingly severe," sometimes reaching hundreds of millions of Birrs irrespective of firm size (CCM6-1-e).

Dongsheng Dyeing (Type 3, CCM5, pseudonymised) maintained a strict closed-loop production regime during the first waves of the Covid-19 pandemic, spending nearly ETB 2 million on testing and basic bedding, paying wages through stoppages, and keeping 300-400 workers on site (CCM5-1-e). The war years brought both risk and temporary demand: Dongsheng supplied more than three million uniforms as the national defence forces expanded. At the same time, seven EIP firms—Dongsheng among them—were hit with heavy tax penalties. Firms tried a collective lawsuit; negotiations with federal and regional offices dragged on, and penalties often stuck. Managers also pointed to customs valuations above actual costs—"our procurement cost is around $1.20/kg, but the customs system insists on a valuation above $2/kg"—which tightened already scarce dollar flows (CCM5-1-d; CCM5-1-e). An account from the owner's family recalled an early export-policy swing: an initial agreement with no export quota was later changed to a 70% export requirement; the firm focused on the local market in practice (CCM5-3-a).

Across these cases, managers kept orders moving by accommodating workers on site to meet delivery schedules; reorienting product lines when buyer requirements or regulatory constraints rendered existing lines unviable; and using nearby regional sales and public procurement to backfill when US orders or local retail demand fell. None of this removed pressure from taxes, customs, or FX, but it kept factories open and bought time to adjust (CCM3-3-a; CCM3-4-a; CCM4-3-a; CCM5-1-d; CCM5-1-e; CCM5-3-a; CCM6-1-).

Heavy and Strategic Import-Substitution Manufacturing Firms: Negotiating Rules, Inputs, and Procurement

Heavy, largely import-substituting lines—steel, cement, pharmaceuticals, packaging, and automotive KD assembly—sat at the centre of HGER's second phase and behaved differently from light manufacturing. Their trajectories turned less on buyer diversification and more on three execution constraints: (i) whether firms could reduce FX requirements for inputs by localising fuel, raw materials, or sub-components; (ii) whether they could contest or negotiate down retroactive tax and customs-valuation claims; and (iii) whether they could stabilise demand through protected public procurement. For these sectors, AGOA's suspension was marginal. The same shocks—COVID-19, domestic conflict, and geopolitical frictions—travelled instead through fuel and quarry access, customs valuation practices, FX queues, and tender eligibility. Plants maintained output where managers reduced import dependence, secured predictable access to FX, and kept disputes from escalating into account freezes. Capacity idled where firms waited for bank LCs or relied on formal procedures alone. In short, day-to-day state–business relations around inputs, valuation, FX allocation, and procurement—not portfolio shifts across buyers—were the key resilience lever (CCM8-1-d; CCM2-4-g; CCM10-4-1-a; CCM21-1-a; CCM23-1-a; CCM26-1-a; CCM27-1-a).

Three recurring profiles structure the evidence (Table 5.2). First are energy-intensive localisers that reduced FX requirements by substituting imported fuel and shortening raw-material logistics, while brokering quotas, access, and tax exposure with regional authorities. Second are regulated health and food producers that stabilised cash flow through

Table 5.2 Strategic profiles and heavy/import-substitution firms' responses to major crises (2020–2025)

Profile / Logic	*Representative cases (pseudonymised)*	*Pre-2020 import exposure*	*Core shock(s)*	*Adaptive levers (2020–2025)*	*2025 status*
Energy-intensive localisers	Dongxin Steel. Zhongxuan Steel. Xinhua Cement.	>70% imported fuel/spares	Freight quadrupling; Birr depreciation; corridor insecurity; ad hoc price controls	Switch from imported coal to eucalyptus; barter fuel-wood quotas with regional government; open satellite quarry to cut haulage; multi-level mediation to reduce back-tax	Plants running ~85% of 2019 capacity; margins restored by 2023. Xinhua cut an ETB 80m claim to ~ETB 10m; Dongxin's rebar share up after tariff action.
Regulated health and food	Sicheng Pharma. Huaren Pharma.	Sterile-grade inputs imported from CN/IN/ Dubai; FX-rationed	Dollar scarcity; volatile logistics; surges in public demand	Split POs across Shanghai/ Hyderabad/Dubai; duty-free raw materials; multi-year MoH frame contract	Output +42 % vs 2019; workforce doubled
Asset-heavy compliance burners	Puxing Packaging. Bei KD	Large fixed assets; virgin inputs; high audit visibility	Retroactive tax/ valuation claims; KD tariff changes; FX rationing	Dual track: formal appeals plus back-channel negotiation; partial localisation of sub-components to meet rebate thresholds; on-site accommodation to reduce stoppages	Puxing survived >ETB 100m retroactive fines amid freezes; Bei KD held employment by lifting LVA to ~33% while sales flat

Source: Author's elaboration based on interviews (2020–2025; e.g., CCM8-1-d; CCM23-1-a; CCM2-4-g; CCM10-4-1-a; CCM21-1-a; CCM26-1-a; CCM27-1-a), EIC data (June 2025), and field diaries.

multi-node sourcing and longer-horizon public procurement. Third are capital-intensive compliance firms—highly visible investors exposed to retroactive assessments and shifting KD rules—who survived by combining formal appeals with targeted localisation and relational advocacy. Across all profiles, resilience was mediated through routine bargaining and coordination over customs valuation, FX allocation, and tendering, not through reweighting buyers across export markets (CCM8-1-d; CCM2-4-g; CCM10-4-1-a; CCM21-1-a; CCM23-1-a; CCM24-1-a; CCM26-1-a; CCM27-1-a).

Energy-Intensive Localisers—Fuel Substitution and Negotiated Access

Energy-intensive domestic producers reset their cost base by substituting imported coal and long-haul limestone with domestic biomass and nearer quarrying, while negotiating fuel quotas, road access, and tax exposure with multiple authorities. The operating logic was straightforward: reduce FX requirements for inputs, secure supply through negotiated local arrangements, and draw on firm-level cost evidence to argue with the GoE for trade and pricing rules that protect domestic throughput when corridors were insecure, and FX queues lengthened.

Dongxin Steel (Type 3, CCM8, pseudonymised) switched kilns from imported coal (South Africa) to locally sourced eucalyptus at roughly 45–50% of the delivered cost of imported coal, while absorbing an estimated 30% increase in refractory wear. Management commissioned an analysis of FX leakage from finished rebar imports, which supported a 15% surcharge on rebar. This expanded domestic share and freed FX for billet imports (CCM8-1-d). The general manager described Ethiopia as "good for business," but noted more discretionary enforcement under fiscal stress in 2023: an initial ETB 80 million assessment was negotiated down to just over ETB 10 million, with officials insisting the relief be recorded as a fine (CCM8-1-d).

Zhongxuan Steel (Type 3, CCM23, pseudonymised) embedded fuel substitution in a barter compact with the regional government: billets to public works in exchange for eucalyptus quotas, easing corridor frictions. This insulated the mill from seasonal wood shortages and reduced checkpoint delays on a corridor with intermittent insecurity (CCM23-1-a). Managers also pointed to a rise in extra-statutory levies—road "maintenance" fees and recurring personal-income-tax fines on expatriate staff with no clear legal basis. Firms rarely litigated; they negotiated to cap exposure. Zhongxuan viewed its Amhara location near the Oromia border as comparatively stable and close to Addis Ababa, but park-level checks on vehicles and containers still slowed the movement of raw materials and semi-finished goods (CCM23-1-a).

Xinhua Cement (Type 3, CCM2, pseudonymised) localised logistics by opening a satellite quarry in 2021 to reduce haulage from limestone faces. In 2023, auditors issued an ETB 80 million retroactive assessment after re-pricing intra-group clinker transfers and revising price-cap enforcement. A multi-tier negotiation team—local elders, youth-league liaisons, and a retired revenue official—reduced liability to roughly ETB 10 million (CCM2-4-g). The case shows that competitiveness depended as much on bargaining capacity as on cost control once price ceilings, corridor insecurity, and aggressive multi-agency enforcement converged (CCM2-4-g). Sectoral dynamics also mattered: a temporary cement shortage explains the brief period of elevated margins; as entrants ramped up, prices and volumes normalised, while a leading multinational retained structural cost advantages (CCM2-5-1-a). Security risks along the A3 corridor further complicated dispatch planning and encouraged redundant routing and local political mediation channels (CCM2-4-g).

Regulated Health Producers—Procurement-Led Stabilisation

Sicheng Pharma (DBG, CCM10, pseudonymised) faced a classic constraint: pharmaceutical inputs sit under Ethiopia's strictest import-licensing rules, making dollar scarcity the largest production risk. Management reduced risk by splitting purchase orders across Shanghai, Hyderabad, and Dubai free zones, and using offshore escrow seeded with export earnings for the latter two routes. This multi-node sourcing sustained line utilisation above 90% when peer factories averaged near 60% during the 2022–2023 FX crunch (CCM10-4-1-a).

Demand volatility also favoured Sicheng. Due to the escalating domestic war in recent years, it urged the Ministry of Health to front-load central procurement. Consequently, Sicheng secured a two-year frame contract for essential antibiotics with exchange-rate pass-through protections. By late 2024, monthly output stood roughly 42% above the 2019 baseline.

Demand volatility also worked in the firm's favour. As domestic conflict escalated, management urged the Ministry of Health to front-load central procurement. Sicheng secured a two-year framework contract for essential antibiotics with exchange-rate pass-through protections. By late 2024, monthly output stood roughly 42% above the 2019 baseline. Locating in

EIP brought stable electricity at the official tariff and in-zone wastewater treatment, reducing stoppages. Duty-free raw-material access and resumed monthly FX allocations in 2024 (about USD 200,000 per approval, often syndicated across banks) restored profitability, though treasury remained tight because domestic payments required fortnightly advances. Staffing constraints persisted: despite training since 2018, managers estimated only about 10% of the initial trainee cohort remained. Packaging still relied on manual processes, revealing a bottleneck in local automation and upstream supplier development (CCM10-4-1-a). Although the firm held WHO certification and expressed regional ambitions, it continued to sell mainly into domestic tenders—illustrating how protected procurement can substitute for fragile private demand in crisis periods (CCM10-4-1-a).

Asset-Heavy Compliance Firms—When Formal Compliance Offers Limited Protection

Puxing Packaging (DBGs, CCM26, pseudonymised) illustrates the costs of visibility under tightening FX and fiscal enforcement. The firm is a joint venture backed by two listed parents and, by its account, displaced imports of plastic bottles—"we were a benchmark among import-substitution enterprises," a senior manager recalled (CCM26-1-a). Up to 2021 it relied on bank LCs—"we never used the black market"—with banks opening USD 8–12 million in letters of credit annually (CCM26-1-a). When dollar allocation collapsed in 2022, the firm refused off-book FX due to listed-company rules. Capacity fell to around 20%, leaving equipment idle and losses mounting by 2024 (CCM26-1-a).

Fiscal enforcement tightened. Retroactive audits and reclassifications generated assessed liabilities exceeding ETB 100 million. The senior manager recalled that "each of our bottles weighs 18 grams, yet officials recorded them as 16 grams," then layered VAT, income, and dividend taxes, applying new standards "as if they had been in force since 2018" (CCM26-1-a). When FX dried up, and the firm bought resin locally, gross margin slipped to about 9%, but auditors still assessed on an assumed 18% margin (CCM26-1-a). Appeals required large deposits and triggered account freezes; cases then stalled, with only partial remission after prolonged negotiation (CCM26-1-a). Management's assessment was direct: strict compliance offered little protection where enforcement was discretionary; legal channels were available but slow (CCM26-1-a). Cost competition compounded these frictions: competitors blended recycled feedstock and undercut prices, while Puxing maintained food-grade inputs and "zero" additives (CCM26-1-a). Fixed costs were high; employment levels contracted sharply (from over 50 Chinese staff and 96 local workers to 24 and 11, respectively) (CCM26-1-a). The firm sought exit—"we'd sell at half our book value, but there are no buyers"—and reported limited support in customs and tax disputes (CCM26-1-a). In short, an asset-heavy import substituter absorbed the brunt of FX scarcity and retroactive enforcement while smaller, more flexible peers adjusted informally (CCM26-1-a).

Bei KD (Type 1, CCM21, pseudonymised) operated under shifting rules. Under FX scarcity, import rules and tariff classifications changed, rebate thresholds were revised, and enforcement tightened unevenly. Management described spending substantial time tracking policy changes, renegotiating documentation requirements, and re-sequencing procurement and production. The firm pursued incremental localisation where feasible, but its dependence on imported components meant survival hinged on continuous regulatory negotiation and on maintaining compliance channels with customs, standard bodies, and tax authorities (CCM21-1-a).

Across heavy and import-substituting lines, resilience rested on getting inputs, taxes, and tenders to align. Fuel and quarry localisation bought time but created new local risks—from eucalyptus quotas to price ceilings and environmental checks. Procurement of essential goods could stabilise cash flow where framework contracts were in place, but staffing and certification still constrained output. Highly compliant, asset-heavy firms were often the most exposed to retroactive enforcement. Across all three profiles, managers who maintained active working relationships with offices controlling fuel, customs valuation, FX allocation, and public orders kept production going; those who relied on formal process alone saw capacity idle (CCM8-1-d; CCM2-4-g; CCM10-4-1-a; CCM21-1-a; CCM23-1-a; CCM26-1-a; CCM27-1-a).

Summary

Evidence from export-oriented light manufacturing and strategic import-substitution activities during Ethiopia's 2020–2025 polycrisis points to a shared mechanism of survival: firms sustained throughput when they could reconfigure market channels and input systems quickly, and do so through the bargaining interface that governs key policy tools in practice (FX allocation, customs valuation, tax enforcement, procurement); firms without switching options, or those exposed to discretionary enforcement without workable bargaining channels, stalled.

In apparel and footwear, outcomes differentiated most clearly by switching capacity and buyer relations. Multi-market exporters such as Shengdong Garment and Rongxin Garment redirected volume away from the US towards Europe and Japan within two seasons, shared incremental tariff costs with core buyers, installed process equipment to reduce fabric waste and offset freight spikes, and stabilised lines by recruiting experienced supervisors from South Asia (CCM22-1-a; IO1-a; EG4-1-a). By contrast, single-market-dependent firms concentrated either on the US market or on Ethiopia alone—exemplified by Fujin Footwear and Haixing Textiles—faced prolonged stoppages, erosion of trained workforces, and (in Mekelle's case) debt-service strain following looting (CCM1-15-a; CCM12-2-b). Hybrid domestic–regional firms (often MEFs) were buffered less by export switching than by local embeddedness: they reoriented product lines towards Ethiopia and COMESA, protected delivery schedules through on-site accommodation during lockdowns, and later relied on regional sales and public procurement as private orders weakened (CCM3-3-a; CCM4-3-a; CCM5-1-e; CCM6-1-e).

In heavier and regulated lines, resilience moved primarily through input localisation and procurement, rather than buyer switching. Dongxin Steel reduced kiln fuel costs by substituting imported coal with eucalyptus and drew on firm-level cost evidence to support a 15% surcharge on finished rebar imports, redirecting scarce FX towards billet purchases (CCM8-1-d). Xinhua Cement reduced haulage by opening a satellite quarry and negotiated an ETB 80 million retroactive assessment down to roughly ETB 10 million (CCM2-4-g). In pharmaceuticals, Sicheng split purchase orders across Shanghai, Hyderabad, and Dubai and secured a two-year framework contract with exchange-rate pass-through protections, lifting monthly output to around 42% above the 2019 baseline (CCM10-4-1-a). Where compliance visibility was highest and FX allocation thinned—as at Puxing Packaging—retroactive audits generated assessed liabilities exceeding ETB 100 million and account freezes; capacity fell to around 20% despite strict adherence to formal rules (CCM26-1-a).

Two overarching findings follow. First, concentration risk remained the main transmission channel from external shocks to cash-flow stress: without secondary buyers, credible EU/Asia compliance routes, or regional domestic hedges, firms could not switch fast enough to keep production lines running (CCM1-15-a; CCM12-2-b; IO1-a). Second, localisation is a workable response to dollar scarcity, but it introduces new political and administrative exposures—fuel quotas, corridor permissions, and valuation disputes—that require continuous negotiation and local political mediation channels, not formal compliance alone (CCM8-1-d; CCM2-4-g; EG4-1-a). The next section examines how policy recalibration, regional asymmetries, and fiscal extraction widened or narrowed the space for these firm-level adjustments.

Institutional Responses: Flexibility, Fragmentation, and Fiscal Extraction

Although Chinese manufacturing FDI did not fall sharply after 2020, what remained and how it operated changed. Firms that stayed kept production going by relying more on local sourcing, domestic and regional markets, and day-to-day engagement with Ethiopian agencies, often investing in practical fixes such as warehousing, back-up generators, and basic compliance systems to cope with uncertainty. A tighter macro-financial environment also pushed some sectors towards greater involvement of local partners and JVs, especially where access to public procurement and administrative approvals mattered most. As one long-term Chinese trader in Ethiopia put it, the firms that stayed were those that could "move quickly" and work through local channels as rules shifted (PO6).

Policy Recalibration and Production Continuity

In early 2020, several government measures aimed to prevent production breakdowns. The EIC suspended export-ratio requirements and approved franco valuta waivers, allowing manufacturers to import essential inputs when bank LCs stalled. IPDC complemented these steps with rent rebates and temporarily permitted higher domestic-sales shares for export-oriented industrial parks. ILO wage support reduced the risk of large-scale layoffs at the trough (EG1-1-c; EG4-1-a). Evidence from two non-Chinese foreign firms illustrates how this window was operationalised: one export manufacturer agreed with a major US buyer to split post-AGOA tariff costs roughly 15/15 and maintained output, while another reallocated volume from US programmes to Korea and several European markets by drawing on production and compliance capacity across several countries (EG4-1-a).

On the import-substitution side, HGER's designation of pharmaceuticals, metals, cement, and KD assembly as "strategic" eased some input frictions and opened tender pipelines. In pharmaceuticals, Sicheng Pharma combined a two-year framework contract with multi-node sourcing to lift monthly output to around 42% above its 2019 baseline despite persistent FX constraints (EG3-1-a; CCM10-4-1-a).

These measures helped firms get through the shock, rather than changing the underlying model. Multi-market apparel exporters used the added flexibility to redirect orders towards Europe and Asia and to share tariff shocks with core buyers. Park-level permissions for domestic sales helped hybrid firms maintain employment levels during the demand trough (EG4-1-a; CCM22-1-a). In heavy industry, the same mix of waivers and permissive domestic sales reduced the penalty for input reconfiguration (fuel substitution, quarry localisation), while public procurement helped anchor orders (CCM8-1-d; CCM2-4-g; CCM10-4-1-a).

Uneven Implementation and Slow Translation from Policy to Practice

Policy announcements often moved faster than delivery. Although the MoI endorsed domestic-market sales for export factories after AGOA's suspension, detailed implementing guidance lagged by months. Managers reported sustained losses while waiting for routine approvals to sell locally; Fujin Footwear was repeatedly cited as a "victim" of these delays (EG3-1-a, 2025). FX administration was also unstable: interviewees counted 13 National Bank circulars between 2020 and 2024, often without grandfathering for live orders, which complicated treasury planning and supplier commitments (EG1-1-c). Customs practice introduced further uncertainty as exemptions previously granted were re-priced or retroactively questioned—either at clearance or months later—creating unbudgeted liabilities and tightening working capital (CCM22-1-a).

Overall, the post-2020 period did not produce a uniform "exit" of Chinese manufacturing firms. Instead, it sharpened differences between firms with switching options and those without. Exporters with network resources and compliance capability were better able to reroute markets and logistics. Import-substituting producers with localisation options and procurement access were better placed to operate under FX scarcity. The development effects of Chinese manufacturing investment—employment, wages, exports, and learning—will therefore increasingly depend on which sectors and organisational forms remain viable under stress, not simply on aggregate investment figures.

Fragmentation and Regional Asymmetries

Institutional fragmentation after 2020 made policy delivery less predictable and widened differences across regions. Interviewees noted that the EIC cycled through "six to seven" leaders in recent years, which weakened coordination across agencies and reduced confidence in investor services. At the same time, core functions—such as ID processing and parts of incentive administration—shifted to other ministries, further dispersing responsibility (EG1-1-c). Frequent circulars from the National Bank and ad hoc changes in customs valuation added to the instability, creating a moving target for procurement and treasury planning. Shenglong Garments, for example, described post-clearance reclassifications that imposed large, unbudgeted costs on already thin margins (CCM22-1-a).

Regional differences then amplified that uncertainty. One Chinese manufacturing manager reported informal container fees at Oromia checkpoints; by contrast, selective fee waivers in parts of Amhara were used to retain key investors and discourage relocation (CCM23-1-a). Security risks along key routes—especially the A3 corridor—raised exposure for cement and steel dispatches and encouraged firms to develop corridor-level relationships and alternative routing to keep deliveries moving (CCM2-4-g). Labour governance also differed across parks. In and around Hawassa, recruitment rules tied to local districts and politicised contestation over "local jobs" increased turnover and limited the movement of experienced workers across districts, weakening park-wide learning effects (EG1-1-c). These differences encouraged jurisdiction shopping: between 2022 and 2024, several firms moved warehouses or production lines to districts where enforcement was more predictable and informal burdens were lighter (EG1-1-c).

A parallel shift in policy emphasis towards SEZs added another layer of uncertainty. Overlaps between the SEZ framework and the industrial parks regime remained unresolved, while the EIC's reduced convening role left questions about who would administer incentives and arbitrate disputes across agencies (EG1-1-c).

Fiscal Pressure and Retroactive Enforcement

Tight fiscal conditions translated into more aggressive revenue collection, often through retroactive audits and reclassifications. Puxing Packaging (pseudonymised), an asset-heavy joint venture backed by listed parents, faced assessed liabilities exceeding ETB 100 million. Managers described disputes triggered by technical re-measurement (PET bottles recorded at 16 g rather than 18 g) and the application of new standards as if they had been in force since 2018. Appeals required large deposits and could trigger account freezes, while cases then stalled (CCM26-1-a). Similar practices appeared elsewhere: personal-income-tax fines for expatriates—often on uncertain legal grounds—and recurring "road maintenance" charges were reported across multiple districts. Firms rarely litigated, relying instead on case-by-case negotiation to cap exposure (CCM23-1-a).

Heavy-industry cases show both the reach and the limits of formal process. Xinhua Cement reduced an ETB 80 million assessment to roughly ETB 10 million through multi-tier local mediation after auditors re-priced intra-group transfers under price caps (CCM2-4-g). Dongxin Steel reported an initial assessment reduced to just over ETB 10 million, alongside a successful push for a 15% surcharge on finished rebar that redirected scarce FX from imports towards billet purchases and expanded domestic share (CCM8-1-d). The broader pattern is clear: under directive churn and fiscal urgency, outcomes were frequently determined through bargaining and negotiated settlements, rather than formal compliance alone.

A wider FX reality underpinned these dynamics. One manufacturing manager described routine reliance on franco valuta for inputs and widespread under-invoicing across the investor base, as bank LCs were scarce, slow, or informally priced through side payments. Several interviewees argued that official FDI tallies can overstate net FX inflows because of asset revaluation and equipment-pricing practices (CCM27-1-a). The distributional result was uneven: visible, compliant investors became attractive targets for extraction, while lower-profile operators navigated grey zones at the cost of uneven quality and occasional shutdowns (CCM26-1-a).

Relational Governance as a Compensatory Mechanism

In this setting, informal and relational channels became key to how policy was interpreted and delivered. Energy-intensive localisers embedded fuel substitution in political barter—for example, exchanging billets for eucalyptus quotas—which reduced checkpoint friction and stabilised kiln fuel (CCM23-1-a). Cement managers mobilised local elders, youth-league liaisons, and a retired revenue official to settle retroactive liabilities when statutory routes stalled (CCM2-4-g). Large mills also shaped market rules by financing technical analysis on the FX leakage associated with finished rebar imports, feeding directly into tariff decisions (CCM8-1-d).

Donor-led channels attempted to formalise parts of this brokerage but faced political limits. GIZ's public–private dialogue convened Chinese, European, and Indian firms; when Chinese managers raised corruption concerns, government representatives closed the discussion in plenary, after which Chinese participants continued separately (IO1-a). Targeted programmes nonetheless had bounded effects: ILO wage support preserved park jobs in 2020–2021, and buyer-matching visits (22 buyers in one round) helped selected exporters secure EU orders (IO1-a; EG4-1-a). These interventions helped individual firms, but they could not substitute for coherent inter-agency delivery or predictable enforcement.

Park-level associations faced similar constraints. At the EIP, external partners reported that institutional bargaining mechanisms such as EIZIA (Chap. 4) had weakened by 2025, limiting collective problem-solving capacity with customs, utilities, and local administrations (IO1-a). As collective channels eroded, bilateral firm-specific ties became more important, and the returns to formal platforms diminished.

Summary

Evidence across light and heavy sectors points to a consistent pattern. Short-term measures—allowing franco valuta imports for key inputs, reducing park rents, and temporarily relaxing domestic-sales limits for export-oriented parks—helped many firms stay open during the peak shocks. But delays in implementation, frequent rule changes, bottlenecks between parks and ports, and uneven practice across regions reduced predictability. Retroactive customs valuation and ad hoc fines became more common as revenue pressures intensified.

Firms that sustained output combined formal permissions with workable access through relationships: they secured FX beyond the main bank queues, kept corridors and fuel supplies functioning, and dealt directly with ministries and agencies that shape procurement and tariff decisions. Where such channels were weak or absent, formal compliance alone often left capacity idle or pulled firms into prolonged disputes, with knock-on effects for employment and reinvestment (EG1-1-c; EG3-1-a; EG4-1-a; IO1-a; CCM2-4-g; CCM8-1-d; CCM10-4-1-a; CCM23-1-a; CCM26-1-a).

Conclusion

This chapter has shown how the post-2020 shocks reworked the terms under which Chinese private manufacturers could keep producing in Ethiopia. Across both light manufacturing and construction materials, divergence widened not because firms faced different crises, but because they entered the crisis with different market positions, organisational capabilities, and exposure to external discipline. For GPN-IFs, buyer requirements and delivery schedules amplified pressure for rapid adjustment; for MEFs, FX ceilings, procurement cycles, and day-to-day enforcement became decisive constraints.

The evidence also clarifies what the relational-institutional framework adds. Policy tools did not operate as a stable "package." Their effects depended on how they were delivered in practice—through routines, discretion, enforcement, and cross-agency coordination—and on the bargaining mechanisms available when rules did not fit operational realities. Crisis therefore becomes a revealing moment for both firm strategies and institutional governance: it serves as a pressure test that shows which strategies and governance routines hold, which break down, and why.

The next chapter draws these mechanisms together across the book. It revisits the five propositions (P1–P5), consolidates the policy implications, and sets out the main limits of the evidence and priorities for future research.

References

Coe, N. M., & Yeung, H. W.-C. (2019). Global production networks: Mapping recent conceptual developments. *Journal of Economic Geography, 19*(4), 775–801. https://doi.org/10.1093/jeg/lbz018

Ethiopian Investment Commission (EIC). (2020). *Manufacturing investment bulletin 2019/20*. Addis Ababa.

Ethiopian Investment Commission (EIC). (2022). *Policy brief on the suspension of AGOA and its implications for Ethiopian manufacturing*. Addis Ababa. Internal document.

Ethiopian Policy Centre. (2025, July 11). *Ethiopia after AGOA: Industrial policy options for a post-preference era*. Retrieved December 10, 2025, from https://ethiopianpolicy.com/2025/07/11/ethiopia-africa-agoa/

Industrial Parks Development Corporation (IPDC). (2024). *Security and logistics report* (January). Addis Ababa. Internal document.

Lavers, T., & Terrefe, B. (2021). Industrial parks and Ethiopia's developmental state. In T. Lavers & B. Terrefe (Eds.), *Ethiopia's "developmental state"* (pp. xx–xx). Cambridge University Press.

Mohan, G., & Tan-Mullins, M. (2013). Negotiating China: Reinserting African agency into China–Africa relations. *African Affairs, 112*(446), 92–110. https://doi.org/10.1093/afraf/ads065

National Bank of Ethiopia (NBE). (2020). Annual report 2019/20. Addis Ababa.

United Nations Conference on Trade and Development (UNCTAD). (2022). *World investment report 2022: International tax reforms and sustainable investment*. United Nations.

CHAPTER 6

Conclusion: Firm Diversity, Policy Tools, and African Industrial Futures

Introduction

This book has examined Chinese private manufacturing investment in Africa through a grounded, firm-centred study centred on Ethiopia. It follows investors and managers from the initial decision to locate production, through installation and early operation, to adaptation under a series of overlapping shocks between the early 2010s and the mid-2020s. The period covered has been unusually turbulent: rising costs and tighter environmental regulation in China; accelerated but contested industrial policy experimentation in Ethiopia; and, from 2020, the combined effects of COVID-19, maritime bottlenecks, FX scarcity, conflict-related disruption, logistics insecurity, and the suspension of AGOA trade preferences.

Returning to the puzzle posed in Chap. 1, this concluding chapter synthesises how a decade of evidence from the factory floor upward resolves the book's core questions about firm heterogeneity and the practical forms of implementation capacity through which industrial policy operates.

In aggregate terms, Chinese FDI in Africa remains modest and does not match the more expansive rhetoric of a deep strategic partnership. Available figures are also distorted by structural data problems. Some flows are overstated when announcements or approvals are treated as materialised capital, while other flows are understated because of offshore routing, intra-group transactions, and the under-reporting of smaller

W. Chen, *Chinese Manufacturing Firms in Ethiopia*, Palgrave Studies in African and Development Economics,
https://doi.org/10.1007/978-3-032-24322-5_6

private firms and diaspora-linked "translocals" (Jerven, 2013; Sharman, 2010; Shen, 2015; Sun et al., 2017). For these reasons, the "rise" discussed in this book does not imply a historically unprecedented scale. Instead, it captures a step change from an almost negligible base to a still small but substantively significant flow in the 2010s, alongside its sectoral and geographical diversification into manufacturing and into locations historically bypassed by Western capital (Chen, 2025).

The core move of the book has been to shift the analytical lens away from aggregate investment figures towards the composition of Chinese manufacturing investment—by firm type, sector, and host-country institutional context. Heterogeneity is not invoked to offset small aggregate volumes; rather, it is used to explain why investments of similar scale can generate sharply different outcomes once we examine who is investing, how investment is organised and channelled, and the governing arrangements under which it operates (Shen, 2015; Sun et al., 2017; Lee, 2017; Chen, 2025).

Methodologically, the book adopts a multi-scalar approach, but not in the sense of moving linearly or automatically from "micro" to "macro." It begins at the firm level—on the shop floor, in management offices, in industrial park meetings, and in encounters with customs and revenue officers—and then traces how these everyday practices are shaped by sectoral regimes and by policy tools as they operate in practice. The analysis combines comparative ethnography with process tracing, using within-case reconstruction to link causes to outcomes by identifying the causal mechanisms in between. In practice, this involves tracking how specific industrial policy tools—such as land access, foreign exchange allocation rules, customs administration, and compliance enforcement—are delivered, how firms respond, and how bargaining mechanisms reshape both formal rules and informal routines over time. Industrial park proclamations and state-to-state statements may establish the formal frame, but it is the day-to-day design and delivery of export-linked access to FX, park governance, customs valuation, tax practice, and procurement routines that ultimately determine which firms enter, which survive, and which learn (Oqubay, 2015; Page & Tarp, 2017; Hauge & Chang, 2019; Whitfield et al., 2020).

Two premises set out in Chap. 2 have guided the analysis. First, neither "China" nor "Africa" can be treated as a single actor. Chinese outward investors differ by sector, scale, region of origin, social background, and accumulation trajectory (Peck & Zhang, 2013; Zhang & Peck, 2016; Lee,

2017). African states differ in their political settlements, fiscal structures, administrative capabilities, and industrial strategies (Oqubay, 2015; Cheru & Oqubay, 2019; Page & Tarp, 2017). Second, outcomes are shaped less by abstract national categories than by the interaction between heterogeneous firms and the specific policy tools and institutional mechanisms they encounter in particular locations. This book, therefore, treats policy tools in use—rather than strategy documents—as the key sorting mechanisms shaping investment trajectories, learning process and resilience under crisis.

The remainder of this chapter consolidates the findings and develops their implications. Section "A Firm-Centred Lens That Scales Up" revisits the book's firm-centred, multi-scalar approach. Section "Policy Tools as Sorting Mechanisms" clarifies how policy tools operate as sorting mechanisms. Section "Key Findings and Contributions" summarises the main findings and contributions. Sections "Policy and Practical Implications" draws out policy implications. Section "Limits and Data Gaps" sets out the main limits and data gaps, and Section "Future Research" outlines future research directions. Section "Closing" closes by restating the core claim.

A Firm-Centred Lens That Scales Up

The distinctive move in this book has been to begin with firms and then scale up. At the firm level, the analysis follows everyday workforce organisation: how production lines are arranged; how supervisors and translators mediate control and communication; how wages, allowances, and discipline are managed; how inputs are sourced under FX scarcity; how shipping delays are handled; and how managers interpret and respond to shifts in customs valuation, standards enforcement, tax assessment, and export rules. These are not peripheral "micro details" that can be abstracted away. They are the mechanisms through which policy tools become real for investors and workers, and through which the same shock takes different forms across firms (Burawoy, 1985; Evans, 1995).

The firm-centred lens is also longitudinal. Rather than treating factories as fixed units, the book follows firms through the entire investment trajectories, including entry, installation, early operation, and repeated adaptation. It shows, for example, that initial attraction to Ethiopia was shaped by wage differentials and preference policy, but that realised investment depended on navigating land access, utilities provision, customs clearance, recruitment and training, and the interface between park administrations and external agencies. Following firms through time also makes visible the difference between formal status and effective operation: approvals, renewals, and changes in legal status can coexist with delayed installation, intermittent production, downsizing, or quiet exit (Jerven, 2013; Chen, 2021a, 2025).

At the meso level, the analysis distinguishes sectoral regimes and market orientations. Light manufacturing export lines—garments, footwear, and related activities—are governed by delivery pressure, quality documentation, and repeated audits. These routines shape feasible forms of production organisation and workforce management, and they impose continuous external discipline on managers (Staritz et al., 2019; Whitfield et al., 2020). By contrast, domestically anchored and often more capital-intensive manufacturing—construction materials, pharmaceuticals, packaging, steel, ceramics, and timber processing—depends more heavily on utilities, tariff structures, municipal services, procurement calendars, and the volatility of FX allocation and revenue enforcement (Oqubay, 2015; Hauge & Chang, 2019; Chen, 2021a). In these sectors, the most consequential constraints are often not buyer audits but working capital, input availability, and the credibility of payment and enforcement routines.

At the macro level, the book maps the policy tools and interfaces that structure state–business relations: industrial parks and their one-stop services; export-linked FX allocation and retention rules; customs valuation and standards enforcement; tax administration; utilities provision; and public procurement. These policy tools do not operate in isolation. They are delivered by agencies embedded in Ethiopia's political settlement, including federal investment and park authorities, customs and revenue bodies, regional and municipal administrations, and sectoral regulators. Their operation is affected by leadership churn, mandate overlaps, fiscal pressures, and the politics of Ethiopia's federal system (Clapham, 2018; Hauge & Chang, 2019). The book, therefore, treats the state not as a unitary actor but as a set of interacting organisations whose routines and incentives shape how rules are applied and contested.

Across the empirical chapters, two recurring embedding configurations help organise the analysis without flattening heterogeneity. GPN-IFs are firms whose core business is organised through GPNs and buyer-driven chains. In Ethiopia, these are typically light manufacturing exporters operating in or through industrial parks. Their revenues, discipline, and survival are anchored in external buyers, delivery schedules, and compliance routines, and their access to key incentives and FX windows is linked to export performance and documentation. MEFs are firms rooted primarily in domestic and regional markets. They include construction materials producers and other manufacturers whose growth depends on local demand structures, procurement and payment cycles, tariff regimes, utilities provision, and the practices of agencies controlling FX, customs, taxation, licensing, and procurement.

The typology is relational rather than classificatory. It is not a proxy for ownership, nor is it meant to assign firms a fixed identity. A private garment exporter and a state-owned garment producer can both be GPN-IFs if they are governed by buyer discipline and export-linked state policy tools. Likewise, a private cement plant and a state-affiliated construction materials producer can both be MEFs if their main constraints and bargaining channels run through domestic demand, utilities, procurement, and revenue administration. A single corporate group may occupy both positions at the same time or across time, operating an export line to secure FX access while running domestically anchored manufacturing or logistics to stabilise cash flow. Firms may also move between positions when shocks hit or when policy tools change. The analytic purpose is therefore to capture relational location—where a firm's core routines, discipline, and problem-solving are anchored—rather than to replace one essentialist label with another (Lee, 2017; Chen, 2021a).

Empirical chapters in this book show that, when crises hit, firms typically adjusted along three interlinked aspects. They sought to switch markets, shifting between buyers and destinations and, where permitted, between export, domestic, and regional sales. They reconfigured inputs and processes, localising inputs where possible, reworking production lines, changing shift patterns, switching fuels and routes, and re-timing procurement to cope with input uncertainty and logistics disruption. They also renegotiated with state actors—through formal and informal channels—over FX allocation, customs valuation and classification, tax assessment, licensing, and procurement. The point is not that managerial skill can neutralise structural constraint. It is that resilience is produced through relational work: the capacity to translate policy tools into workable routines, and to sustain bargaining channels under stress, is central to survival and to the protection of learned capabilities.

Chapter 3 mapped the range of Chinese manufacturing firms in Ethiopia and showed how different motives and sectoral conditions shaped entry and early performance. It explained why a park-based export strategy encouraged some light manufacturing exporters, while domestically oriented producers faced a different set of constraints.

Chapter 4 then examined the EIP in the pre-2020 period and documented how bargaining worked in practice: over land and services, environmental requirements, labour disputes, and export targets. It showed that the most important institutions were not only ministries and proclamations, but also the park management company, one-stop services, and collective platforms such as CCCE and EIZIA through which firms raised problems and sought remedies.

Chapter 5 carried the analysis into the post-2020 period and traced how firms and state agencies responded to overlapping disruptions. The next section consolidates what these chapters show about how policy tools, enforcement practices, and bargaining channels shaped divergence within "Chinese investment."

Policy Tools as Sorting Mechanisms

Across the book, a consistent finding was that policy mattered most through the tools that firms encountered in everyday operation. Industrial parks and their one-stop services, export incentives, and access to foreign exchange, customs valuation and standards enforcement, tax practice, utilities provision, and procurement routines did not merely "support" investment. They shaped which firms could operate on reasonable terms, which could scale, and which were pushed towards short horizons.

In the pre-2020 period, Ethiopia's park-based export push created a clearer runway for export-oriented GPN-IFs in light manufacturing. Export requirements and buyer discipline encouraged investment in production routines, documentation, and workforce organisation. For MEFs, especially in construction materials and other domestic sectors, the binding constraints were different: reliable power and water, the tariff and tax treatment of inputs, access to foreign exchange for machinery and spares, and the credibility of procurement and payment cycles.

Chapter 4 showed how these policy tools were negotiated in practice. In the Eastern Industrial Park, firms did not interact with a single state actor: they navigated a web of park management, regional and federal authorities, and external agencies. Collective platforms such as CCCE and EIZIA, as well as the park's own committees and meetings, became the practical channels through which firms bargained over services, compliance, and disputes. These mechanisms sometimes solved problems and reduced uncertainty, but they also revealed how uneven enforcement and mandate overlaps could raise costs.

Predictability emerged as a decisive issue. When customs valuation, classification, or tax assessments changed abruptly—or when foreign exchange directives shifted without clear transition rules—firms faced higher working-capital requirements and could not plan production. This was most damaging for firms that were already operating on thin margins or investing in more formal compliance.

One implication was a simple "compliance paradox." Firms that tried hardest to comply—keeping complete documentation, meeting export reporting rules, and maintaining transparent accounts—were often the most exposed to sudden reclassification, retroactive claims, or shifting procedures, because they were visible and had fewer options to evade. By contrast, firms that moved into short-term trading, informal brokerage, or evasive practices could sometimes reduce immediate exposure, but at the cost of weaker production learning and a thinner contribution to industrial upgrading.

The post-2020 disruptions amplified these dynamics. Chapter 5 traced how firms responded to COVID-19, the suspension of AGOA, tightened foreign exchange, and rising insecurity. Many exporters searched for new buyers and products, adjusted production lines, localised some inputs where possible, and reworked logistics and shipping strategies. Some sought temporary domestic sales to keep lines running. MEFs relied more on managing input shortages, price volatility, and arrears in procurement and construction cycles.

State responses also mattered. Where agencies provided time-bound flexibility—such as clearer rules for temporary switching or practical support in customs and logistics—some firms retained production and labour. Where the response was dominated by abrupt rule changes, inconsistent enforcement across offices, or delayed problem-solving, firms were more likely to downsize, switch into trading, or exit. These patterns differed systematically across MEFs and GPN-IFs because their constraints and bargaining channels were different.

Across both periods, the book showed that the ability of institutions to coordinate, apply rules consistently, and resolve disputes was as important as the design of incentives. "Implementation capacity" in this sense was not abstract: it was visible in whether one-stop services worked, whether park-level coordination held, whether appeals could be resolved, and whether agencies could manage shocks without turning crisis management into moving targets.

The conclusion is therefore straightforward. Divergent firm trajectories were not random and were not explained by broad claims about "Chinese investment." They reflected firm diversity, sectoral conditions, and the way Ethiopia's policy tools and bargaining mechanisms operated in practice—sometimes productively, sometimes unevenly.

Key Findings and Contributions

This book manuscript builds on my PhD thesis (Chen, 2021a), an UNU-WIDER working paper (Chen, 2021b), and related published work (Chen, 2025), but the relevant material has been substantially rewritten and updated with new fieldwork and evidence—especially for the post-2020 period—and with the relational-institutional framework developed in Chap. 2.

The chapters are designed to address the three research questions in a progressive and integrated manner. Chapter 3 explains why firms invested and maps the diversity of Chinese private manufacturers, developing the MEF/GPN-IF typology. Chapter 4 then shows how Ethiopia's policy tools worked in practice before 2020, and how bargaining mechanisms shaped delivery and enforcement. Chapter 5 carries the analysis into the post-2020 period, explaining how firms consolidated, adapted, or exited as shocks accumulated, and how institutions recalibrated under stress.

Revisiting the propositions (P1–P5) sharpens the book's central claim. P1 is supported by evidence that firm diversity is not statistical "noise": ownership structures, financing, managerial organisation, and operating models shaped how firms could absorb disruption and sustain production. P2 is reinforced by the contrast between GPN-IFs, disciplined by buyers and delivery schedules, and MEFs, exposed more directly to FX ceilings, procurement cycles, and day-to-day enforcement.

P3 and P4 explain why similar firms diverged under the same formal rules. Ethiopia's policy tools—industrial parks, one-stop services, export discipline, customs and standards routines, and FX allocation rules—worked as sorting mechanisms. Their effects depended on how they were delivered in practice, and on the bargaining mechanisms through which firms sought exceptions, negotiated compliance, or solved operational bottlenecks.

P5 is most visible after 2020. Shocks did not simply "hit" firms; they reconfigured the operating environment and exposed the gap between policy design and workable delivery. Outcomes depended on the organisational capabilities built before crisis and on whether state agencies could adapt routines without undermining predictability. Methodologically, the combination of comparative ethnography and process tracing makes these mechanisms legible by reconstructing sequences of policy delivery, enforcement, and bargaining over time.

Policy and Practical Implications

The policy implications of this book follow from a simple point: industrial policy is implemented through concrete policy tools, and those tools shape the investment ecology by sorting firms, activities, and time horizons. Design matters, but delivery in practice—through routines, discretion, enforcement, and cross-agency coordination—determines whether investment becomes sustained production.

First, predictability is itself a form of industrial policy. Under FX scarcity and corridor risk, firms can plan only if customs clearance, FX allocation routines, and compliance enforcement are stable and rule-based. Where discretion is unavoidable, it is most productive when it is transparent, time-bound, and channelled through clear bargaining forums rather than ad hoc personal negotiation.

Second, industrial parks should be treated as governance institutions, not only as infrastructure platforms. One-stop services, aftercare capacity, and credible dispute-resolution routines can lower transaction costs and keep production running when shocks disrupt logistics, inputs, or inspections. Without these capabilities, parks can relocate constraints rather than resolve them.

Third, FX allocation rules and public procurement are not neutral macro tools. They are industrial policy levers that decide which firms can access inputs, maintain machinery, and meet delivery schedules. Treating FX ceilings and procurement timing as part of industrial strategy—rather than as residual controls—reduces uncertainty and limits the space for informal rents.

Fourth, compliance and labour governance need to be built into the investment model from the start. Buyer compliance requirements, workforce turnover, and regulatory inspections are not "externalities"; they structure day-to-day production discipline. Credible enforcement works best when it is consistent over time and paired with problem-solving support, rather than retroactive fiscal extraction that raises exit risk.

Limits and Data Gaps

The evidence in this book is grounded in extensive fieldwork and repeated firm-level engagement, but it also has limits. These limits are substantive because they mirror how manufacturing investment is governed and recorded in practice.

First, official registries track approvals and formal status changes, but realised capital and operational activity often diverge from administrative categories. Layered ownership structures, the use of offshore jurisdictions, and frequent re-registration make headline figures difficult to interpret without triangulation.

Second, access constraints are uneven across firms, sites, and time. Conflict, pandemic restrictions, and political sensitivity limited observation in some periods and locations, and some types of firms—especially smaller or more informal operations—remain harder to document systematically.

Third, firm-level reporting on finance, profits, and intra-group transactions is necessarily partial. For these reasons, the book relies on process tracing and comparative ethnography to weigh competing explanations against diagnostic evidence, rather than claiming comprehensive measurement of all outcomes.

Future Research

The book points towards a future research agenda that is empirical and comparative and that takes firm diversity and policy implementation seriously. It also raises questions about how research on Global China is produced: who gains access, which kinds of evidence can be assembled, and how political sensitivities shape what is recorded.

Future work could build on this study by: (i) tracing how firms manage risk and uncertainty through everyday negotiation with state agencies, buyers, and intermediaries; (ii) developing stronger firm-level datasets—ideally linking registries, customs, taxation, and labour records—to track entry, reinvestment, exit, and upgrading; (iii) following firms across multiple African sites to compare how the same firms respond to different policy environments; (iv) examining the politics of access and representation in Global China research; and (v) extending worker-centred research, especially on women workers' employment trajectories, skills, and longer-term outcomes.

Closing

This book has argued that the outcomes of Chinese manufacturing investment in Africa are shaped less by broad narratives about "China" and more by firm diversity and by how host-country policy tools operate in practice. In Ethiopia, industrial parks and export incentives enabled some firms to build export routines and industrial jobs, but uneven enforcement and abrupt shifts in foreign exchange, customs, and tax practice could just as quickly erode those gains—often hitting the most compliant firms hardest. The practical lesson is therefore to focus on the everyday policy tools that firms and workers actually encounter: stabilising key rules, coordinating across agencies, and keeping problem-solving channels open, especially during periods of shock. Where these conditions hold, manufacturing investment is more likely to support employment, learning, and industrial upgrading; where they do not, short-term trading, exit, and limited capability building become more likely.

The book advances a deliberately focused argument. Under tight structural constraints, it is policy tools in use—not slogans, strategies, or partnership rhetoric—that determine which fractions of Chinese manufacturing capital arrive, how they embed, and what kinds of learning and resilience they can sustain. In Ethiopia, industrial parks, export-linked access to foreign exchange, and buyer-driven standards selected for firms capable of building and maintaining export routines; after 2020, these same tools were recalibrated—sometimes unevenly—to permit temporary shifts in product mix and market orientation while attempting to protect accumulated capabilities. Resilience travelled through factory-level discipline, supervisory systems, and the ability to sustain quality and delivery under external audit, even as firms negotiated new constraints around logistics, policy change, and security.

For wider debates on globalisation, South–South cooperation, and late industrialisation in an era of polycrisis, the implication is straightforward: outcomes hinge less on headline partnership narratives than on whether states can deliver predictable, contestable, and learning-oriented policy tools at the points where firms, workers, and bureaucracies meet.

References

Burawoy, M. (1985). *The politics of production: Factory regimes under capitalism and socialism*. Verso.

Chen, W. (2021a). *The dynamics of Chinese private outward foreign direct investment in Ethiopia: A comparison of the light manufacturing industry and the construction materials industry*. PhD thesis, SOAS University of London. https://doi.org/10.25501/SOAS.00035764

Chen, W. (2021b). The dynamics of state–business relations between the Ethiopian state and Chinese private firms: A case study of the Eastern Industry Park, WIDER Working Paper No. 2021/122. Helsinki: UNU-WIDER. https://doi.org/10.35188/UNU-WIDER/2021/890-0.

Chen, W. (2025). Heterogeneity and drivers of Chinese manufacturing FDI in Africa: Evidence from Angola and Ethiopia. *Journal of International Development*. https://doi.org/10.1002/jid.70038

Cheru, F., & Oqubay, A. (Eds.). (2019). *The Oxford handbook of the Ethiopian economy*. Oxford University Press.

Clapham, C. (2018). The Ethiopian developmental state. *Third World Quarterly, 39*(6), 1151–1165.

Evans, P. (1995). *Embedded autonomy: states and industrial transformation*. Princeton University Press.

Hauge, J., & Chang, H.-J. (2019). The role of manufacturing in Africa's future. In C. Cramer, J. Sender, & A. Oqubay (Eds.), *African economic development: Evidence, theory and policy* (pp. xx–xx). Oxford University Press.

Jerven, M. (2013). *Poor numbers: How we are misled by African development statistics and what to do about it*. Cornell University Press.

Lee, C. K. (2017). *The specter of global China: Politics, labour, and foreign investment in Africa*. University of Chicago Press.

Oqubay, A. (2015). *Made in Africa: Industrial policy in Ethiopia*. Oxford University Press.

Page, J., & Tarp, F. (Eds.). (2017). *The practice of industrial policy: Government–business coordination in Africa and East Asia*. Oxford University Press.

Peck, J., & Zhang, J. (2013). A variety of capitalism… with Chinese characteristics? *Journal of Economic Geography, 13*(3), 357–396.

Sharman, J. C. (2010). Shopping for anonymous shell companies: An audit study of anonymity and crime in the international financial system. *Journal of Economic Perspectives, 24*(4), 127–140.

Shen, X. (2015). *Private Chinese investment in Africa: Myths and realities* (World Bank Policy Research Working Paper No. 7318). World Bank.

Staritz, C., Whitfield, L., & Morris, M. (2019). Local content and upgrading in global value chains: The case of apparel in Sub-Saharan Africa. *Oxford Development Studies, 47*(2), 1–23.

Sun, I. Y., Jayaram, K., & Kassiri, O. (2017). *Dance of the lions and dragons: How are Africa and China engaging, and how will the partnership evolve?* McKinsey Global Institute.

Whitfield, L., Staritz, C., & Morris, M. (2020). *The politics of African industrial policy: A comparative perspective.* Cambridge University Press.

Zhang, J., & Peck, J. (2016). Variegated capitalism, Chinese style: Regional models, multi-scalar constructions. *Regional Studies, 50*(1), 52–78.

Appendix A. Data Collection, Analysis, and Ethical Considerations

1.1 Data Collection

This appendix documents the empirical basis of the book. The analysis draws on longitudinal, multi-sited fieldwork conducted between 2015 and 2025 in Ethiopia. Evidence is triangulated across sources, time periods, and respondent categories. The research combines structured management-level surveys, semi-structured interviews, life/work histories, participant observation, site visits, and documentary sources (including meeting notes, internal memos, official letters, and administrative records shared by participants where appropriate).

Field access was developed iteratively through sustained stakeholder engagement. Beginning with participation in the ESRC–DFID-funded *Industrial Development, Construction and Employment in Africa* (IDCEA) project (2015–2019), I travelled frequently to Ethiopia from 2015 onwards and built and maintained *guanxi* with Chinese firms, industrial park actors, and relevant government agencies. These relationships enabled repeated site access, follow-up verification, and long-horizon tracking of firm trajectories.

Prior to the main doctoral fieldwork (2017–2018), I completed a three-week scoping visit (July–August 2017). This visit introduced the research to relevant stakeholders, explained how the research would be undertaken (including confidentiality arrangements), and helped identify

W. Chen, *Chinese Manufacturing Firms in Ethiopia*, Palgrave Studies in African and Development Economics,
https://doi.org/10.1007/978-3-032-24322-5

potential firms for later surveys, interviews, and observation. A small number of pilot firms were selected during this trip to test semi-structured interview guides. The scoping visit was also helpful for understanding the possible limitations and constraints for fieldwork (e.g., difficulties of access, sensitivities around recording, and factory schedules), so that the fieldwork plan could be adjusted for feasibility.

The first dataset draws selectively on the IDCEA project, which examined comparative employment dynamics in Chinese and non-Chinese firms in manufacturing and infrastructure construction. The dataset includes a workers' survey ($n = 1521$), a firm-management survey ($n = 74$), 56 life/work histories, 215 semi-structured interviews, and a follow-up phone survey ($n = 281$). Firms were selected to capture leading firms in key sub-sectors—building materials in both countries and textiles/apparel in Ethiopia—while ensuring variation in firm size, market orientation (export versus domestic), and ownership structure (state-owned versus private, with variation within each group) (see Table A1.1).

The second dataset draws from my doctoral research on Chinese manufacturing FDI in Ethiopia (2016–2021), complemented by remote updates during the COVID-19 period (2020–2024) and follow-up fieldwork in 2025. The doctoral project comprises 16 firm surveys across 4 industrial parks and participant observation in 2 Chinese-owned industrial parks. Interview material was collected in multiple rounds. In total, 105 in-depth interviews were conducted face-to-face (2017–2019), 9 interviews were conducted remotely (2020–2024) via WeChat, and 36 interviews were added in June 2025.

A structured management survey of 16 firms was undertaken between January and April 2018. Fourteen firms were surveyed in the EIP, one in the HIP, and one in the AIP (see Appendix D survey/interview guide for

Table A1.1 Overview of IDCEA data collection instruments and samples

Data collection instrument	*Ethiopia*	*Period*
Workers' survey	839	Ethiopia: Mar–Sep 2017
Firm-management survey	40	Ethiopia: Jan–Aug 2018
Life/work histories	33	Ethiopia: Oct–Dec 2017
Qualitative semi-structured interviews	117	Ethiopia: Nov 2015–Aug 2018
Follow-up phone survey	155	Ethiopia: Sep–Nov 2018

Source: Author's compilation based on IDCEA fieldwork data cited in Chen (2025, pp. 7–8)

more details). In addition, during the same fieldwork period (2017–2018), I conducted a further survey of 15 Chinese manufacturing firms on behalf of the International Trade Centre (ITC). This project helped me gain further opportunities to engage with interviewees and explore critical questions in more depth during the doctoral fieldwork.

Participant observation was an important part of the dataset because tacit networking and informal bargaining mechanisms are difficult to observe through surveys or early interviews. I undertook approximately 32 weeks of participant observation across two Chinese-owned industrial parks and related sites. This included 25 weeks living in the EIP alongside Chinese expatriates (i.e., supervisors and technicians) in the same dormitories, as well as seven weeks in another private Chinese industrial park, where interviews across departments and further observation of internal coordination and external interactions were conducted. These periods of immersion enabled observation of day-to-day operational routines and the handling of labour disputes, land and environmental issues, and security incidents, as well as attendance at regular meetings hosted by the industrial park committee with Chinese firms.

Access was facilitated by my multi-positionality in the field, including partnership work with Ethiopian counterparts. During the fieldwork period, I worked informally with the EIC as a Chinese investment adviser. This was not a paid role, and I did not receive any monetary return or commercial benefit. My main responsibilities included receiving delegations in selected industrial parks, observing the EIC OSS station, collecting constraints and feedback from Chinese firms, and contributing to monthly reports within the EIC. Separately, I obtained permission to engage with industrial park developers and a few flagship firms for interviews and observation, and in some cases supported routine communication (e.g., translation of internal materials and meeting support), which helped build trust and access.

Regarding investment-related data, I used various sources (both institutional and firm level), with particular emphasis on records obtained through the EIC. The rationale for using EIC data is that it is relatively up-to-date and remains the most reliable source of official statistics for selected indicators related to FDI in Ethiopia. While Chinese OFDI statistics may be incomplete because some firms do not register through Chinese administrative channels when investing overseas, all investors in Ethiopia must register with the EIC to apply for investment and business licences. The EIC collects relevant information during the registration process. After registration, an EIC department (i.e., After Care) follows up on investor activity and updates the investor's status as it changes over time. Therefore, for indicators such as investment and reinvestment, licence status, and operational continuity, EIC records provide a more up-to-date and accurate reference point that can be cross-checked against firm accounts and other documentation.

Evidence from the two datasets was triangulated and cross-checked for accuracy and consistency. While the analysis is predominantly qualitative, it is complemented by quantitative evidence from surveys and structured interview materials with workers, officials, and other relevant stakeholders.

1.2 Data Analysis

Qualitative interviews, life/work histories, and participant observation generated detailed, context-specific insights into firm behaviour, investment trajectories, labour-management practices, and interactions with host- and home-country institutions. All interviews were written up by myself, predominantly in Mandarin, and subsequently translated into English. In line with interviewees' preferences and the political sensitivity of the research context, interviews were generally not audio-recorded. Instead, detailed notes were taken during interviews and expanded immediately afterwards to preserve accuracy and contextual detail. Where recording was explicitly consented to, recordings were securely stored and transcribed by myself.

Qualitative analysis proceeded through coding and narrative analysis. Coding was conducted using NVivo. First, open coding was used to identify themes emerging from interviews, observation notes, and life histories. Second, axial coding was used to group these themes into broader categories aligned with the book's main themes, including firm diversity, investment motives, SBRs, and firms' strategies of adaptation. Interview guides operated as flexible frameworks rather than fixed templates, allowing comparable information to be collected across different respondents while leaving space for probing and follow-up depending on the interviewee's position.

In addition to coding analysis, narrative analysis was employed for life histories and ethnographic materials. This approach focused on how respondents structured their accounts, including turning points, justifications, and moral framings, and how these narrative forms related to firms' strategic choices and institutional constraints. Narrative analysis was particularly useful for interpreting long-term investment trajectories and understanding how entrepreneurs made sense of risk, crisis, adaptation, and changes over time.

To enhance analytical reliability, a sample of coded materials was independently reviewed by a second researcher. Discrepancies were discussed and resolved through negotiated agreement, and the refined coding decisions were incorporated into the final codebook. Initial coding and interpretation were also cross-checked with an IDCEA project colleague to ensure consistency in the treatment of shared instruments and overlapping empirical material.

Although the analysis is primarily qualitative, quantitative evidence was used to complement and contextualise qualitative findings. Survey data from workers and firm managers provided baseline descriptive information and helped corroborate interview-based claims. In selected chapters, survey results were visualised using figures and tables to illustrate the relative weight of different determinants shaping firms' investment decisions and relational strategies (see Chaps. 3, 4, and 5 for details).

Throughout the analysis, triangulation was treated as an integral part of the research process. Evidence was cross-checked across various data sources (e.g., surveys, interviews, participant observations, fieldwork diaries, and documentary materials), respondent categories (e.g., owners, managers, supervisors, workers, and government officials), and various research sites (e.g., factories, offices, conferences, and dormitories), and time periods (2015–2025). Where discrepancies emerged, these were treated analytically rather than eliminated, often revealing tensions between official narratives, managerial accounts, and observed practices. Claims were retained only when supported by multiple sources or clearly framed as contested interpretations grounded in the field.

1.3 Ethical Considerations and Positionality

1.3.1 Research Governance, Consent, and Confidentiality

Ethical standards were maintained throughout the research in line with institutional ethics approval and research governance requirements. Participants were informed of the research objectives, how the data would be used, and the limits of confidentiality. Informed consent was obtained verbally in most cases and in writing where required.

Given the political and commercial sensitivity of the research setting, a conservative approach to confidentiality was adopted. Even where a small number of respondents initially agreed to be named and signed consent forms, I ultimately decided to anonymise all individual respondents in order to reduce potential risks, particularly under conditions where scrutiny can intensify after research dissemination. All identifying information was removed from interview notes and transcripts, and respondents are referred to throughout the book using pseudonyms. An internal anonymisation code system was used to track respondent categories, for example, CG for the Chinese government and CCM for Chinese company management. Participant-observation events were anonymised using a parallel coding system. Appendix B provides the full interview code list, and Appendix C lists the participant-observation codes. A small number of industrial parks remain identifiable due to their public profile and because meaningful anonymisation would undermine analytical clarity.

1.3.1.1 Positionality as an Access Enabler and a Source of Constraint

Access in this research was closely linked to my multi-positionality. As a Chinese researcher affiliated with a Western institution, my multi-positional roles created both advantages and constraints. Shared language and cultural proximity enabled me to build *guanxi* with Chinese participants, while sustained presence in the field since 2015 facilitated trust-building over time. Embedded roles and repeated site visits reduced initial scepticism (e.g., being suspected by some Chinese expatriates as a "spy") and made it possible to observe practices and interactions that are rarely accessible to external researchers. In practice, this positioned myself not only as an "outsider" researching the setting, but also, at times, as an "insider" participating in everyday routines, and somewhere in between as a knowledge broker and gatekeeper who translated field evidence into academic knowledge while protecting participants from unnecessary exposure and keeping the research within ethical boundaries.

Field diaries show that this dual positioning was also recognised by participants. A diary entry from 8 November 2017 reads:

> *Chinese factory supervisor joked that my job was basically to act as a "double agent"—Chinese enough to understand guanxi (relationship ties), but foreign enough to be seen as "serious" by Ethiopian officials. It sounded like friendly banter, but it made me uneasy. Could being seen this way weaken my credibility and independence?*

This entry reflects the daily effort required to balance relationships with Chinese expatriate staff—many of whom expected a sympathetic account—and with Ethiopian officials, who often welcomed what they saw as a relatively neutral perspective. Spending long periods in Chinese accommodations gave me closer access to everyday management practices and informal coordination. But it also brought pressure to become too closely aligned with one side, and it required constant attention to academic boundaries. This became especially clear when senior engineers and managers asked personal questions shaped by gender norms about how a "proper Chinese woman" should behave. These moments influenced not only daily interactions but also my own awareness of how gender, nationality, and institutional ties affected my fieldwork.

My informal work with the EIC also required careful boundary-setting. I did not share confidential interview content with the EIC or any other organisation, and interviewees were informed of my institutional connections and field role where relevant. In addition, I did not receive any monetary return or commercial benefit from the informal work with the EIC, and this work did not change the consent and confidentiality arrangements used for academic research.

At the same time, this positionality also generated constraints. Some Chinese participants framed me as a "foreign [i.e. Western-based] expert" and occasionally attempted to steer narratives towards more reputationally positive accounts. In several cases, interviewees asked to review or approve what I wrote—for example, requesting that I write "90% positive and 10% negative" about the firms I studied. In such situations, I prioritised ethical guidelines and excluded materials where consent conditions conflicted with independent analysis

1.3.1.2 Managing Field Risks and Protecting Participants

The research was conducted in an environment marked by protests and conflicts. I encountered several physical and mental challenges and sometimes threats during fieldwork. During the early stages of the doctoral fieldwork, between October and December 2017, protests and conflicts in and around industrial park sites disrupted the planned sequencing of surveys. In response, the fieldwork strategy was adjusted to prioritise observation and documentation of how firms, industrial park authorities, and government agencies responded to crisis situations, with surveys postponed until operational conditions became more stable.

Risks did not end with field access. Research dissemination itself sometimes heightened sensitivity, particularly when findings were misrepresented by third parties. In one instance, a local media mischaracterisation of IDCEA project findings in Ethiopia created reputational tension and led to requests for disclosure of interviewee identities. These requests were refused by me on ethical grounds, reinforcing the decision to strengthen anonymisation across the entire dataset. This "incidence" also showed that risks can intensify after fieldwork, and that protecting participants may require active responses beyond the field stage, including clarification and careful control of what information can be circulated publicly.

As a woman researcher, I also adopted practical measures to reduce gender-related risks during fieldwork, given the possibility of sexual harassment, particularly as a young Chinese woman working in the field for extended periods. These measures included avoiding one-to-one meetings with male informants in the evening, arranging companions in situations perceived as higher risk (e.g., at Chinese-organised drinking occasions), and maintaining regular check-ins and location-sharing with trusted contacts.

1.3.1.3 Bias and Mitigation

As participation in the research was voluntary, the possibility of selection bias cannot be fully eliminated. This risk was addressed through targeted sampling across different firm types and sub-sectors, cross-checking across multiple data sources, and repeated site visits combined with longitudinal follow-ups, including in-person updates in 2019 and 2025, as well as remote communication through WeChat (2020–2025). Conservative inclusion rules were applied to sensitive or unverifiable claims, and information that posed ethical, legal, or personal safety risks was excluded from the analysis, even where it was analytically relevant, in order to maintain participant protection and research governance integrity.

Appendix B. Interview Code (pseudonym)

Table B1.1 Interview Code (Ethiopia)

Code	*Organisation (pseudonymised)*	*Name of Interviewee*	*Position*	*Location*	*Interview Date*
CG		**Chinese Government 1,2,3 (...)**			
CG1	**Municipal government (China)**	P1	Government official	China	April 23, 2018
CG2	**Government agency (national, China)**	P2	Administrative staff	Ethiopia	July 11, 2018
CG3	**Government agency/ development finance institution (China)**	P3	Manager	Ethiopia	July 11, 2018
CCM		**Chinese Company Management1,2,3 (1,2,3)**			
CCM1	**Fujin Footwear**				

(*continued*)

W. Chen, *Chinese Manufacturing Firms in Ethiopia*, Palgrave Studies in African and Development Economics,
https://doi.org/10.1007/978-3-032-24322-5

Table B1.1 (continued)

Code	*Organisation (pseudonymised)*	*Name of Interviewee*	*Position*	*Location*	*Interview Date*
	CCM1-1	P4	Senior manager	China	May 10, 2018
	CCM1-2	P5	Middle manager	China	May 8, 2018
	CCM1-3	P6	Administrative staff	China	May 11, 2018
	CCM1-3-a			Ethiopia	Aug 4, 2018
	CCM1-4-a	P7	Senior manager	Ethiopia	March 21, 2018
	CCM1-4-b			China	May 10, 2018
	CCM1-5	P8	Administrative staff	Ethiopia	March 23, 2018
	CCM1-6	P9	Middle manager		March 22, 2018
	CCM1-7-a	P10	Senior manager		August 4, 2017
	CCM1-7-b				August 7, 2017
	CCM1-7-c				August 9, 2017
	CCM1-8	P11	Senior manager		August 8, 2017
	CCM1-9	P12	Middle manager	China	May 9, 2018
	CCM1-10-a	P13	Senior manager	Ethiopia	June 7, 2018
	CCM1-10-b				May 21, 2020
	CCM1-10-c				Jan 6, 2022
	CCM1-11	P14	Administrative staff		July 20, 2018
	CCM1-12-a	P15	Administrative staff		
	CCM1-12-b	P16	Middle manager		
	CCM1-12-c	P17	Administrative staff		
	CCM1-13-a	P18	Middle manager		Oct 25, 2017
	CCM1-13-b				Nov 14, 2017
	CCM1-13-c				May 19, 2021
	CCM1-13-d				Nov 04, 2022
	CCM1-14	P19	Middle manager		Nov 30, 2017
	CCM1-15-a	P71	Senior manager		June 12 2025
CCM2	**Industrial park developer**				

(*continued*)

Table B1.1 (continued)

Code	*Organisation (pseudonymised)*	*Name of Interviewee*	*Position*	*Location*	*Interview Date*
	CCM2-1-a	P20	Senior manager	Ethiopia	April 3, 2018
	CCM2-1-b			China	April 23, 2018
	CCM2-2-a	P21	Administrative staff	Ethiopia	July 16, 2018
	CCM2-2-b				Sep17, 2018
	CCM2-3-a	P22	Senior manager		Oct 3, 2017
	CCM2-3-b				March 6, 2018
	CCM2-3-c				Sep 20, 2018
	CCM2-4-a	P23	Senior manager		March 27, 2018
	Xinhua Cement				
	CCM2-4-b				Oct 27, 2017
	CCM2-4-c				Oct 26, 2017
	CCM2-4-d	P24	Senior manager		Feb 5, 2019
	CCM2-4-e				Feb 26, 2019
	CCM2-4-f	P25	Middle manager		May 8, 2019
	CCM2-4-g	P78	Middle manager		June 17, 2025
	CCM2-5-a	P72	Middle manager		June 9, 2025
	Industrial park (head office				
	CCM2-6-a	P73	Senior manager		June 9, 2025
	CCM2-6-b				June 10, 2025
	CCM2-6-c				June 14, 2025
	CCM2-6-d				June 16, 2025
	CCM2-6-e				June 21, 2025
	CCM2-7-a	P74	Administrative staff		June 9, 2025
	CCM2-7-b				June 16, 2025
	CCM2-7-c				June 17, 2025
	CCM2-8-a	P75	Administrative staff		June 12, 2025
CCM3	**Haicheng Garment**				
	CCM3-1-a	P26	Senior manager	Ethiopia	Feb 10, 2018
	CCM3-1-b				Jan 28, 2019
	CCM3-1-c				May 17, 2019
	CCM3-2-a	P27	Middle manager		March 16,
	CCM3-2-b	P28	Administrative staff		2018
	CCM3-3-a	P68	Senior manager		June 9, 2025
	CCM3-4-a	P69	Middle manager		June 17, 2025
CCM4	**Linyu Apparel**				

(*continued*)

Table B1.1 (continued)

Code	*Organisation (pseudonymised)*	*Name of Interviewee*	*Position*	*Location*	*Interview Date*
	CCM4-1-a	P29	Senior manager	Ethiopia	Sep 17, 2018
	CCM4-1-b				Oct 18, 2017
	CCM4-1-c				Dec 15, 2017
	CCM4-2	P30	Senior manager		Nov 23, 2017
	CCM4-3-a	P82	Middle manager		June 17, 2025
CCM5	**Dongsheng Dyeing**				
	CCM5-1-a	P31	Senior manager	Ethiopia	Oct 20, 2017
	CCM5-1-b				Nov 23,2017
	CCM5-1-c				Sep 20, 2018
	CCM5-1-d				April 21, 2023
	CCM5-1-e				June 10, 2025
	CCM5-2-a	P32	Senior manager		Oct 18, 2017
	CCM5-2-b				Nov 24, 2017
	CCM5-3-a	P33	Senior manager	China	April 23, 2023
	CCM5-4--a	P67	Senior manager	Ethiopia	June 9, 2025
CCM6	**Yichen Textiles & Auto**				
	CCM6-1-a	P34	Senior manager	Ethiopia	Oct 18, 2017
	CCM6-1-b				Nov 23, 2017
	CCM6-1-c				Sep 17, 2018
	CCM6-1-d				Dec 10, 2022
	CCM6-1-e				June 10, 2025
CCM7	**Rongtai Textiles**				
	CCM7-1	P35	Senior manager	Ethiopia	Jan 18, 2018
	CCM7-2	P36	Middle manager		Oct 25, 2017
	CCM7-2-a				March 3, 2018
CCM8	**Dongxin Steel**				
	CCM8-1-a	P37	Senior manager	Ethiopia	April 3, 2018
	CCM8-1-b				Oct 17, 2017
	CCM8-1-c				Feb 9 2018
	CCM8-1-d				June 16, 2025
CCM9	**Songlin Timber**				
	CCM9-1	P38	Senior manager	Ethiopia	Oct 17, 2017
	CCM9-1-a				Feb 9, 2018
CCM10	**Sicheng Pharma**				

(*continued*)

Table B1.1 (continued)

Code	*Organisation (pseudonymised)*	*Name of Interviewee*	*Position*	*Location*	*Interview Date*
	CCM10-1-a	P39	Middle manager	Ethiopia	Oct 15, 2017
	CCM10-1-b				Oct 17, 2017
	CCM10-2	P40	Senior manager		Oct 20, 2017
	CCM10-3	P41	Senior manager		Feb 9, 2018
	CCM10-4-1-a	P76	Senior manager		June 16, 2025
CCM11	**Yuande Ceramics**				
	CCM11-1	P42	Middle manager	Ethiopia	Oct 20, 2017
	CCM11-2	P43	Middle manager		Oct 18, 2017
	CCM11-3	P44	Senior manager		Dec 22, 2017
	CCM11-3-a				Feb 9, 2018
CCM12	**Haixing Textiles**				
	CCM12-a	P45	Senior manager	Ethiopia	April 3, 2018
	CCM12-b				June 28, 2021
	CCM12-c				April 21, 2023
CCM13	**Jintai Textiles**				
	CCM13-1-a	P46	Senior manager	Ethiopia	Feb 11 and 12, 2018
	CCM13-1-b	P47	Middle manager	China	April 24, 2018
CCM14	**Rongxin Garment**				
	CCM14-1-a	P48	Senior manager	Ethiopia	March 28, 2018
	CCM14-1-b				July 17, 2018
	CCM14-1-c				July 26, 2018
	CCM14-1-d				Feb 23, 2019
CCM15	**Zhenxing Steel**				
	CCM15-1	P49	Senior manager	Ethiopia	Oct 19, 2017
CCM16	**Hongmu Timber**				
	CCM16-1	P50	Senior manager	Ethiopia	Dec 22, 2017
CCM17	**LS Real Estate**				
	CCM17-1-a	P51	Senior manager	Ethiopia	Oct 13, 2017
	CCM17-1-b				Feb 8, 2019
	CCM17-1-c				June 9, 2025
CCM18	**Xingyu Motors**				

(*continued*)

Table B1.1 (continued)

Code	*Organisation (pseudonymised)*	*Name of Interviewee*	*Position*	*Location*	*Interview Date*
	CCM18-1-a	P52	Senior manager	Ethiopia	March 19, 2018
	CCM18-1-b				Feb 22, 2019
CCM19	**Huarui Metals**				
	CCM19-1	P53	Senior manager	Ethiopia	Oct 18, 2017
CCM20	**Zhonggong Overseas (construction contractor (SOE))**				
	CCM20-1-a	P70	Senior manager	Ethiopia	June 10, 2025
CCM21	**Bei KD**				
	CCM21-1-a	P77	Senior manager	Ethiopia	June 16, 2025
CCM22	**Shengdong Garment (SOE)**				
	CCM22-1-a	P80	Senior manager	Ethiopia	June 23, 2025
CCM23	**Zhongxuan Steel**				
	CCM23-1-a	P81	Senior manager	Ethiopia	June 23, 2025
CCM24	**Lianxin Industries**				
	CCM24-1-a	P83	Senior manager	Ethiopia	June 17, 2025
CCM25	**Zhonghe Cement (SOE)**				
	CCM25-1-a	P84	Middle manager	Ethiopia	June 20, 2025
CCM26	**Puxing Packaging**				
	CCM26-1-a	P85	Senior manager	Ethiopia	June 18, 2025
CCM27	**Jinyu Paper**				
	CCM27-1-a	P86	Senior manager	Ethiopia	July 18, 2025
FCM		**Non-Chinese Foreign Company Management**			
FCM1	**Non-Chinese foreign cement firm**				
	FCM1-1	P54	Middle manager	Ethiopia	April 16, 2018
	FCM1-2-a	P55	Senior manager		April 17, 2018
	FCM1-2-b	P56	Middle manager		
	FCM1-3	P57	Senior manager		March 20, 2018

(*continued*)

Table B1.1 (continued)

Code	*Organisation (pseudonymised)*	*Name of Interviewee*	*Position*	*Location*	*Interview Date*
IO		**International organisation**			
IO1	**GIZ**				
	IO1-a	P87	Special advisor	Ethiopia	June 20, 2025
CBA		**Chinese Business Association**			
	Business association (national)				
	CBA-1	P58	Administrative staff		July,16 2018
	CBA-2	P79	Administrative staff		June 20, 2025
EG		**Ethiopian Government**			
EG1	**EIC**				
	EG1-1-a	P59	Administrative staff	Ethiopia	Sep 26, 2018
	EG1-1-b				Aug 1, 2018
	EG1-1-c				June 20, 2025
	EG1-2	P60	Middle manager		Sep 17, 2018
	EG1-3	P61	Senior official		Sep 26, 2018
	EG1-4	P62	Senior official		Aug 1, 2018
	EG1-5	P63	Administrative staff		Feb 8, 2018
	EG1-6	P88	Administrative staff		June 20, 2025
EG2	**MoF**				
	EG2-1-a	P91	Senior official	Ethiopia	June 25, 2025
EG3	**MoTI**				
	EG3-1-a	P89	Administrative staff	Ethiopia	June 25, 2025
EG4	**IPDC**				
	EG4-1-a	P90	Middle manager	Ethiopia	June 26, 2025
A		**Academia**			
	A1	P64	Academic institution (China)-Senior academic	Ethiopia	April 6, 2018
	A2	P65	Academic institution (US)-Junior academic		July 22, 2018
O		**Others**			
	O1	P66	Ethiopian businessman-Senior manager	Ethiopia	March 22, 2018

Appendix C. Participant Observation Code (pseudonym)

Table C1.1 Participant Observation Code (pseudonym)

Participant Observation Code	*Participant(s)*	*Organisation(s)*	*Date*
PO1	Senior manager; Middle managers; Local government representative	PO-EG1-CCM2	June 29, 2018
PO2	Local government representative; Senior managers; Middle managers	PO-EG1-CG3	June 22, 2018
PO3	Factory representatives (industry park firms); National government representative (China); Local government representatives; Government agency representative (Ethiopia)	PO-EG1,2-CG2-CCM2	March 27, 2018
PO4	Senior manager (industry park); Project representative	PO-CCM2-CCM-PI	Jan 12, 2018
PO5	Senior manager (industry park); Media representative	PO-CCM2-M1	July 9, 2018

(*continued*)

W. Chen, *Chinese Manufacturing Firms in Ethiopia*, Palgrave Studies in African and Development Economics,
https://doi.org/10.1007/978-3-032-24322-5

Table C1.1 (continued)

Participant Observation Code	*Participant(s)*	*Organisation(s)*	*Date*
PO5-1	Industry park monthly meeting—Senior manager and firm representatives	PO-CCM2	Aug 15, 2017
PO5-3	Industry park monthly meeting—Senior manager and firm representatives	PO-CCM2	Oct 15, 2017
PO5-4	Industry park monthly meeting—Senior manager and firm representatives	PO-CCM2	Dec 15, 2017
PO5-5	Industry park monthly meeting—Senior manager and firm representatives	PO-CCM2	Jan 15, 2018
PO5-6	Industry park monthly meeting—Senior manager and firm representatives	PO-CCM2	June 15, 2018
PO5-7	Industry park monthly meeting—Senior manager and firm representatives	PO-CCM2	July 15, 2018
PO-6	Senior manager (industry park); Local police representative	PO-CCM2-EG2	Oct 30, 2017
PO-7	Senior manager (industry park); Local government representative	PO-CCM2-EG1	Jan 8, 2018
PO-8	Senior manager (industry park); Middle manager; Local government representative (Mayor)	PO-CCM2-EG2	Nov 28, 2018
PO-9-1	Senior manager (firm)	PO-CCM1-1	Aug 7–9, 2017
PO-9-2		PO-CCM1-1	Oct 25, 2017
PO-9-3		PO-CCM1-1	Nov 20, 2017
PO-9-4		PO-CCM1-1	Dec 9, 2017
PO-9-5		PO-CCM1-1	Feb 10–11, 2018

(*continued*)

Table C1.1 (continued)

Participant Observation Code	*Participant(s)*	*Organisation(s)*	*Date*
PO-10	Local government representative; Middle manager; Administrative staff	PO-EG1-CG2-CCM20	July 18, 2018
PO-11	Senior manager; Local government representative	PO-EG3-CCM2-4	Oct 27, 2017
PO-12	Local government representative; Middle manager	PO-EG1-CM-PI	Oct 29, 2017
PO-13	Administrative staff (industry park)	PO-CCM2-1	Nov 29, 2017
PO-14	Senior manager (firm); Chinese financial institute	PO-CCM17-1-c	June 6, 2025
PO-15	Senior manager (firm); local manager (firm)	PO-CCM17-1-c	June 6, 2025
PO-16	Senior manager (firm); Chinese expatriates	PO-CCM1-15-a	June 12, 2025
PO-17	Senior manager (firm); Chinese expatriates; local middle managers	PO-CCM-15-a	June 13, 2025
PO-18	Senior managers (firm) of two BM firms	PO-CCM27-1-a-CCM23-1-a	July 22, 2025

Appendix D. Survey and Interview Guide

Table D1.1 Survey and Interview Guide

Item	*Content*	*Available Source(s)*
1. Company Profile		
Ownership and Control	Sole proprietor Partnership Limited company or shared company (PLC)	Survey
Location		Survey
Year of the establishment (in China and/or in Ethiopia)	The year that firm obtained the Investment License and Business License in Ethiopia/Angola, respectively	Survey
Sector	Main business(es)	Survey
Investment amount	Registered investment Actual investment Re-investment (and when)	Host country official data Survey

(*continued*)

W. Chen, *Chinese Manufacturing Firms in Ethiopia*, Palgrave Studies in African and Development Economics,
https://doi.org/10.1007/978-3-032-24322-5

Table D1.1 (continued)

Item	*Content*	*Available Source(s)*
Main source of capital and financing (and its percentage)	Self-financed Chinese commercial bank Chinese policy bank Ethiopia/Angola commercial bank Ethiopia/Angola policy bank other channels (to be specific)	Survey
Main reason(s)to invest in Ethiopia/Angola		Survey Interview
2. History and Origin of the Firm		
The basic development trajectory of the firm in China	Origin of the firm Main business Main markets/clients Main competitors	Firm's official website and/or profile. Interview
3. Entrepreneur's Perspective		
Entrepreneur's background	Educational background Family background Working experience Achieved original accumulation	Interview; Life stories
4. Process of Accumulation		
Accumulation	Obtaining investment opportunities; Decision-making Installation Financing Expansion and re-investment	Interview; Life stories
5. Adaption and Change of Production		
Factory rule		Firm profile; Observation
Main products and their final markets (and market that firm intends to explore in the future)		Survey; Interview
Market competition	Main competitor (s); How did the firm respond to competition?	Survey; Interview

(*continued*)

Table D1.1 (continued)

Item	*Content*	*Available Source(s)*
Types of Production (i.g. Flexibility of production; Continuous Production)	How flexible is the production system? Whether orders are based on the client's demand and a specific standard?	Interview
How is productivity measured?	Productivity rate (by piece, by the hour or a mixed methods); Automation level	Survey; Interview
Working shifts	How many shifts/days?	Interview
Raw material sourcing		Survey; Interview
Main operational constraints and how did the firm overcome these problems?		Survey; Interview; Observation Participant observation
6. Adaption and Change of Managerial Ethos		
Firm's management ethos	If there is no fixed management ethos, why? Because invest overseas or it is already changing on the way before?	Company profile; Interview; Observation Participant observation
7. Relations with the State, Government Policies, and Institutional Context		
Local/provincial government policies (China) in supporting Chinese firms' "going out."	The social history of local/regional development; Changes in government policies and institutional arrangements	Desk review; Interview
Main policy constraints that firm encountered		Survey; Interview
Whether the firm has sufficiently involved in Public-Private Dialogue in Ethiopia/Angola?		Survey; Interview; Participant observation
Main government agencies (both Ethiopia/Angola and China) that firm contacts regularly	Problem-solving mechanism (formal or informal)	Survey; Interview

(*continued*)

Table D1.1 (continued)

Item	*Content*	*Available Source(s)*
How did firm join the business association and what kinds of activities did firm take part in?	What types of business association are present in Ethiopia/Angola? Who dominates association and why? The politics of setting up the association	Survey; Interview; Participant observation

Appendix E. Research Informed Consent (Sample)

Research Informed Consent (Sample—June 2025 follow-up version)

Project Title:

Researcher:

Contact Information:

Email:

Telephone:

Purpose of the Research:

This research examines the diversity, motivations, adaptations, and impacts of Chinese manufacturing firms in Ethiopia, particularly after COVID-19. It aims to understand state–business interactions, policy influences, and firm-level strategic responses in Ethiopia. The findings will be published in an academic monograph titled *Chinese Manufacturing Firms in Ethiopia: Firm Diversity and the Political Economy of Investment* in Palgrave Studies in African and Development Economics, Palgrave Macmillan.

Funding:

This research is self-funded and forms part of a broader academic study.

What will your participation involve?

W. Chen, *Chinese Manufacturing Firms in Ethiopia*, Palgrave Studies in African and Development Economics,
https://doi.org/10.1007/978-3-032-24322-5

- Participation in an interview lasting approximately 35–45 minutes.
- The interview may include a management-level survey and participant observation, subject to your permission.
- The interview may be audio-recorded (with your consent). Recordings will be stored securely and transcribed for academic use only.

Confidentiality and Anonymity:

- All data will be strictly confidential and anonymised in any publications unless you explicitly consent otherwise.
- Your identity and organisational affiliation will not appear in the published monograph or any related outputs unless you explicitly request identification.

Risks and Benefits:

- There are no direct risks or personal benefits from participating. The primary benefit is contributing to scholarly understanding of Chinese firms' activities in Ethiopia.

What happens to the results?

- Results will be published academically. You may request an electronic copy of the final published monograph.

Data Protection:

- Your personal data will be managed according to the UK Data Protection Act and GDPR. All data collected will be securely stored and accessed only by the researcher for the purposes outlined.
- Data archiving and sharing will follow the publisher's (Springer Nature/Palgrave Macmillan) policies, including anonymisation prior to archival if applicable.

Consent Declaration

Before completing this consent form, please ensure that you have read the **Participant Information Sheet.**

By taking part in this study, I understand that:

- The information I provide will be used for scientific reports and publications.
- All information I provide will be held in confidence and anonymised prior to publication, unless I explicitly request otherwise.
- Taking part in the study may include being audio recorded. The audio recordings will be stored securely on encrypted devices and will never be made public. In line with common academic practice and the publisher's (Springer Nature/Palgrave Macmillan) policies, fully anonymised interview transcripts may be archived securely and made available for academic research purpose

Taking part in the study	*Yes*	*No*
I consent voluntarily to participate in this study and understand that I can refuse to answer questions or withdraw from the study at any time up until my data has been anonymised, without having to provide a reason.		
I consent to being audio recorded during interviews for this study.		
I consent to the researcher conducting participant observation at my organisation (if applicable).		
I would like any information I provide to be anonymised. Ticking 'no' means my name, job title, and organisational affiliation may be used in publications.		

I confirm that I have read and understood the study information dated contained in the Participant Information Sheet or it has been read to me. I have been able to ask questions about the study and my questions have been answered to my satisfaction.

____________	____________	____________
Name of participant	Signature	Date

Appendix F. Request of support

Request of support

"*As a result of an invasion of the Oromia region by a special police unit and militia forces belonging to the Somali side, almost half a million Oromo people have been displaced from Ethiopia's Somali region and are camped in different site of eastern Oromia. The Oromia regional state has decided to resettle those displaced from Somali region in different part of Oromia.*"

"*Accordingly, one thousand households are assigned to Dukem city administration to resettle in the city*" .... "*Your company has contributed nothing yet. For this reason, from this total resettlement, the city administration is requesting your organisation to support us by building 100 houses for the displaced from their homes. Please, we are looking forward to your response within a day.*"

Dukem City Administration (Dec 2017)

W. Chen, *Chinese Manufacturing Firms in Ethiopia*, Palgrave Studies in African and Development Economics,
https://doi.org/10.1007/978-3-032-24322-5

Index[1]

[1] Note: Page numbers followed by 'n' refer to notes.

W. Chen, *Chinese Manufacturing Firms in Ethiopia*, Palgrave Studies in African and Development Economics, https://doi.org/10.1007/978-3-032-24322-5

FSC
www.fsc.org
MIX
Papier | Fördert gute Waldnutzung
FSC® C083411

Kolibri 360 GmbH
Ferdinand-Jühlke-Straße 7
99095 Erfurt, Deutschland
produktsicherheit@kolibri360.de